PRENTICE HALL
WORLD STUDIES
EASTERN HEMISPHERE

Reading and Vocabulary Study Guide

PEARSON
Prentice
Hall

Boston, Massachusetts
Upper Saddle River, New Jersey

The maps on pages 3, 11, 60, and 210 are based on maps created by **DK Cartography**.

0-13-204235-5

7 8 9 10 11 V0UD 18 17 16 15 14

Table of Contents

How to Use This Book iv

Foundations of Geography 1

Chapter 1 The World of Geography
Section 1 2
Section 2 5
Chapter 1 Assessment 8

Chapter 2 Earth's Physical Geography
Section 1 9
Section 2 12
Section 3 15
Section 4 18
Chapter 2 Assessment 21

Chapter 3 Earth's Human Geography
Section 1 22
Section 2 25
Section 3 28
Section 4 31
Chapter 3 Assessment 34

Chapter 4 Cultures of the World
Section 1 35
Section 2 38
Section 3 41
Chapter 4 Assessment 44

Chapter 5 Interacting With Our Environment
Section 1 45
Section 2 48
Section 3 51
Chapter 5 Assessment 54

Europe and Russia 55

Chapter 6 Europe and Russia: Physical Geography
Section 1 56
Section 2 59
Section 3 62
Chapter 6 Assessment 65

Chapter 7 Europe and Russia: Shaped by History
Section 1 66
Section 2 69
Section 3 72
Section 4 75
Section 5 78
Chapter 7 Assessment 81

Chapter 8 Cultures of Europe and Russia
Section 1 82
Section 2 85
Section 3 88
Chapter 8 Assessment 91

Chapter 9 Western Europe
Section 1 92
Section 2 95
Section 3 98
Section 4 101
Section 5 104
Chapter 9 Assessment 107

Chapter 10 Eastern Europe and Russia
Section 1 108
Section 2 111
Section 3 114
Section 4 117
Chapter 10 Assessment 120

Africa 121

Chapter 11 Africa: Physical Geography
Section 1 122
Section 2 125
Section 3 128
Chapter 11 Assessment 131

Chapter 12 Africa: Shaped by Its History
Section 1 132
Section 2 135
Section 3 138
Section 4 141

Section 5. 144
Chapter 12 Assessment 147

Chapter 13 Cultures of Africa
Section 1. 148
Section 2. 151
Section 3. 154
Section 4. 157
Chapter 13 Assessment 160

Chapter 14 North Africa
Section 1. 161
Section 2. 164
Chapter 14 Assessment 167

Chapter 15 West Africa
Section 1. 168
Section 2. 171
Section 3. 174
Chapter 15 Assessment 177

Chapter 16 East Africa
Section 1. 178
Section 2. 181
Section 3. 184
Chapter 16 Assessment 187

Chapter 17 Central and Southern Africa
Section 1. 188
Section 2. 191
Chapter 17 Assessment 194

Asia and the Pacific 195

Chapter 18 East Asia: Physical Geography
Section 1. 196
Section 2. 199
Section 3. 202
Chapter 18 Assessment 205

Chapter 19 South, Southwest, and Central Asia: Physical Geography
Section 1. 206
Section 2. 209
Section 3. 212
Chapter 19 Assessment 215

Chapter 20 Southeast Asia and the Pacific Region: Physical Geography
Section 1 216
Section 2 219
Section 3 222
Chapter 20 Assessment 225

Chapter 21 East Asia: Cultures and History
Section 1 226
Section 2 229
Chapter 21 Assessment 232

Chapter 22 South, Southwest, and Central Asia: Cultures and History
Section 1 233
Section 2 236
Section 3 239
Chapter 22 Assessment 242

Chapter 23 Southeast Asia and the Pacific Region: Cultures and History
Section 1 243
Section 2 246
Chapter 23 Assessment 249

Chapter 24 East Asia
Section 1 250
Section 2 253
Section 3 256
Chapter 24 Assessment 259

Chapter 25 South, Southwest, and Central Asia
Section 1 260
Section 2 263
Section 3 266
Section 4 269
Section 5 272
Chapter 25 Assessment 275

Chapter 26 Southeast Asia and the Pacific Region
Section 1 276
Section 2 279
Chapter 26 Assessment 282

How to Use This Book

The Reading and Vocabulary Study Guide was designed to help you understand World Studies content. It will also help you build your reading and vocabulary skills. Please take the time to look at the next few pages to see how it works!

The Prepare to Read page gets you ready to read each section.

Objectives from your textbook help you focus your reading.

With each chapter, you will study a Target Reading Skill. This skill is introduced in your textbook, but explained more here. Later, questions or activities in the margin will help you practice the skill.

You are given a new Vocabulary Strategy with each chapter. Questions or activities in the margin later will help you practice the strategy.

CHAPTER 1

Prepare to Read

Section 2 Climate and Vegetation

Objectives

1. Find out what kinds of climate Latin America has.
2. Learn what factors influence climate in Latin America.
3. Understand how climate and vegetation influence the ways people live.

 Target Reading Skill

Preview and Predict Before you read, make a prediction or a guess about what you will be learning. Predicting is another way to set a purpose for reading. It will help you remember what you read. Follow these steps: (1) Preview the section title, objectives, headings, and table on the pages in Section 2. (2) Predict something you might learn about Latin America. Based on your preview, you will probably predict that you will learn more about Latin America's climate and plants.

List two facts that you predict you will learn about Latin America's climate and plants.

_____

As you read, check your predictions. How correct were they? If they were not very accurate, try to pay closer attention when you preview.

Vocabulary Strategy

Using Context Clues to Determine Meaning You will probably come across words you haven't seen before when you read. Sometimes you can pick up clues about the meaning of an unfamiliar word by reading the words, phrases, and sentences that surround it. The underlined words in the sentences below give clues to the meaning of the word *dense*.

The Amazon rain forest is *dense* with plants and trees. The plant life is so crowded that almost no sunlight reaches the ground.

Unfamiliar Word	Clues	Meaning
dense	so crowded no sunlight	thick, close together crowded

Chapter 1 Section 2 **9**

Section Summary pages provide an easy-to-read summary of each section.

Provides a summary of the section's most important ideas.

Large blue headings correspond to large red headings in your textbook.

This checkmark tells you when to answer the Reading Check question.

Key Terms, in blue within the summary, are defined at the bottom of the page.

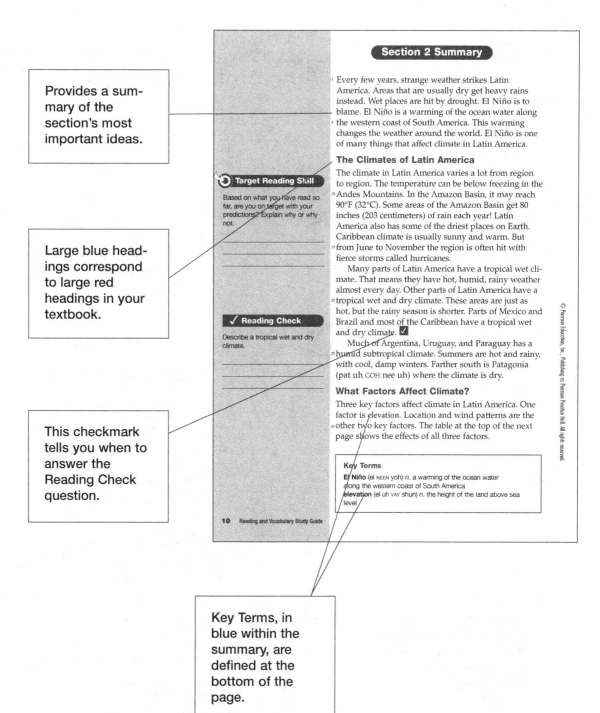

Section 2 Summary

Every few years, strange weather strikes Latin America. Areas that are usually dry get heavy rains instead. Wet places are hit by drought. El Niño is to blame. El Niño is a warming of the ocean water along the western coast of South America. This warming changes the weather around the world. El Niño is one of many things that affect climate in Latin America.

The Climates of Latin America

The climate in Latin America varies a lot from region to region. The temperature can be below freezing in the Andes Mountains. In the Amazon Basin, it may reach 90°F (32°C). Some areas of the Amazon Basin get 80 inches (203 centimeters) of rain each year! Latin America also has some of the driest places on Earth. Caribbean climate is usually sunny and warm. But from June to November the region is often hit with fierce storms called hurricanes.

Many parts of Latin America have a tropical wet climate. That means they have hot, humid, rainy weather almost every day. Other parts of Latin America have a tropical wet and dry climate. These areas are just as hot, but the rainy season is shorter. Parts of Mexico and Brazil and most of the Caribbean have a tropical wet and dry climate. ☑

Much of Argentina, Uruguay, and Paraguay has a humid subtropical climate. Summers are hot and rainy, with cool, damp winters. Farther south is Patagonia (pat uh GOH nee uh) where the climate is dry.

What Factors Affect Climate?

Three key factors affect climate in Latin America. One factor is elevation. Location and wind patterns are the other two key factors. The table at the top of the next page shows the effects of all three factors.

Key Terms

El Niño (el NEEN yoh) *n.* a warming of the ocean water along the western coast of South America
elevation (el uh VAY shun) *n.* the height of the land above sea level

Target Reading Skill

Based on what you have read so far, are you on target with your predictions? Explain why or why not.

✓ Reading Check

Describe a tropical wet and dry climate.

Questions and activities in the margin help you take notes on main ideas, and practice the Target Reading Skill and Vocabulary Strategy.

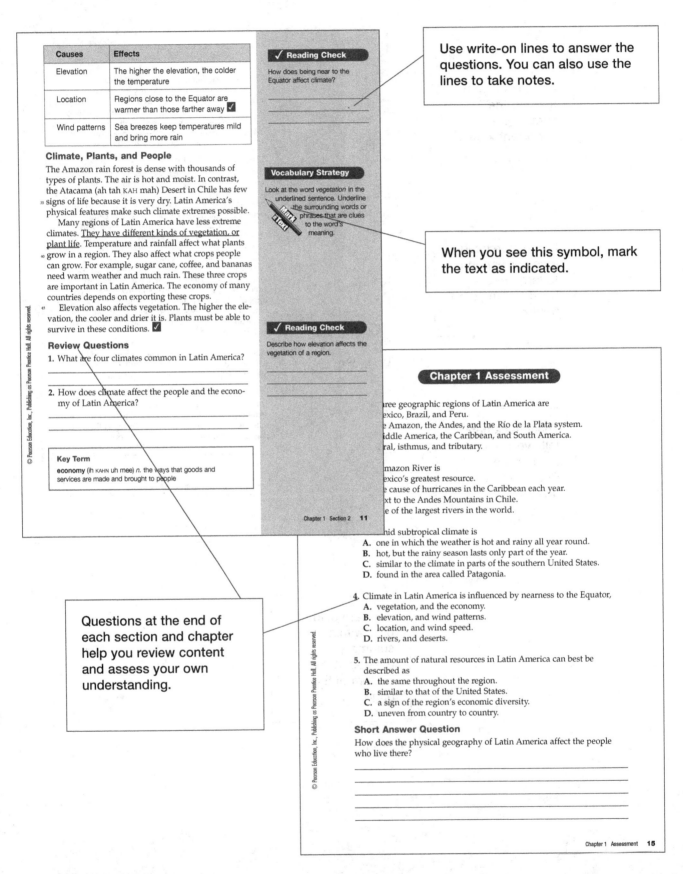

Causes	Effects
Elevation	The higher the elevation, the colder the temperature
Location	Regions close to the Equator are warmer than those farther away ☑
Wind patterns	Sea breezes keep temperatures mild and bring more rain

Climate, Plants, and People

The Amazon rain forest is dense with thousands of types of plants. The air is hot and moist. In contrast, the Atacama (ah tah KAH mah) Desert in Chile has few
₃₅ signs of life because it is very dry. Latin America's physical features make such climate extremes possible.

Many regions of Latin America have less extreme climates. They have different kinds of vegetation, or plant life. Temperature and rainfall affect what plants
₄₀ grow in a region. They also affect what crops people can grow. For example, sugar cane, coffee, and bananas need warm weather and much rain. These three crops are important in Latin America. The economy of many countries depends on exporting these crops.
₄₅ Elevation also affects vegetation. The higher the elevation, the cooler and drier it is. Plants must be able to survive in these conditions. ☑

Review Questions

1. What are four climates common in Latin America?

_____

2. How does climate affect the people and the economy of Latin America?

_____

_____

> **Key Term**
> **economy** (ih KAHN uh mee) *n.* the ways that goods and services are made and brought to people

✓ Reading Check

How does being near to the Equator affect climate?

_____

_____

Vocabulary Strategy

Look at the word *vegetation* in the underlined sentence. Underline the surrounding words or phrases that are clues to the word's meaning.

✓ Reading Check

Describe how elevation affects the vegetation of a region.

_____

_____

> Use write-on lines to answer the questions. You can also use the lines to take notes.

> When you see this symbol, mark the text as indicated.

Chapter 1 Assessment

...ree geographic regions of Latin America are
...exico, Brazil, and Peru.
...e Amazon, the Andes, and the Río de la Plata system.
...iddle America, the Caribbean, and South America.
...ral, isthmus, and tributary.

...mazon River is
...exico's greatest resource.
...e cause of hurricanes in the Caribbean each year.
...xt to the Andes Mountains in Chile.
...e of the largest rivers in the world.

...id subtropical climate is
A. one in which the weather is hot and rainy all year round.
B. hot, but the rainy season lasts only part of the year.
C. similar to the climate in parts of the southern United States.
D. found in the area called Patagonia.

4. Climate in Latin America is influenced by nearness to the Equator,
A. vegetation, and the economy.
B. elevation, and wind patterns.
C. location, and wind speed.
D. rivers, and deserts.

5. The amount of natural resources in Latin America can best be described as
A. the same throughout the region.
B. similar to that of the United States.
C. a sign of the region's economic diversity.
D. uneven from country to country.

Short Answer Question

How does the physical geography of Latin America affect the people who live there?

_____

_____

_____

_____

> Questions at the end of each section and chapter help you review content and assess your own understanding.

Foundations of Geography

Prepare to Read

Section 1
The Five Themes of Geography

Objectives

1. Learn about the study of Earth.
2. Discover five ways to look at Earth.

Target Reading Skill

Reread or Read Ahead Have you ever replayed a scene from a video or DVD so you could figure out what was going on? Rereading a passage is like doing this. Sometimes you may not understand a sentence or a paragraph the first time you read it. When this happens, go back and read it again. Sometimes you may need to reread it two or more times.

Reading ahead can help you understand something you are not sure of in the text. If you do not understand a word or passage, keep reading. The word or idea may be explained later.

For example, when you first see the word *degrees* under the heading "Five Ways to Look at Earth," you may not understand what it means. Most people think of how hot or cold something is when they read that word. If you read ahead, you will see that *degrees* is also a unit for measuring angles.

Vocabulary Strategy

Using Context Clues Words work together to explain meaning. The meaning of a word may depend on the words around it, or context. The context gives you clues to a word's meaning.

Try this example. Say that you do not understand the meaning of the word *movement* in the following passage:

> The theme of movement tells you how people, goods, and ideas get from one place to another.

You could ask yourself: "What information does the passage give me about the word?" Answer: "I know that movement is how people, goods, and ideas get from one place to another. This tells me that movement must be a way of getting from place to place."

Section 1 Summary

The Study of Earth and Five Ways to Look at Earth

1 **Geography** is the study of Earth. Five themes help geographers keep track of information about Earth and its people. These themes are: 1. location 2. regions 3. place 4. movement 5. human-environment interaction. They

5 help us see where things are, and why they are there. ✓

1. Geographers study a place by finding its **location**. Geographers use **cardinal directions** to describe north, south, east, and west.

Another way to describe location is to use latitude

10 and longitude. **Latitude** is the distance north or south of the Equator. **Longitude** is the distance east or west of the Prime Meridian. Latitude and longitude are measured in degrees.

The Equator is the parallel around the middle of the globe.

The Equator, at 0° latitude, circles Earth midway between the North and South poles.

A line of longitude.

The Prime Meridian, at 0° longitude, runs through Greenwich, England.

Lines of latitude, also called **parallels**, are east-west

15 circles around the globe. The latitude at 0 degrees (0°) is the Equator. Suppose you could cut Earth in half at the Equator. Each half of Earth is called a **hemisphere**. The Equator divides Earth into Northern and Southern hemispheres.

Key Terms

geography (jee AHG ru fee) *n.* the study of Earth
cardinal directions (KAHR duh nul duh REK shunz) *n.* the directions north, east, south, or west
latitude (LAT uh tood) *n.* the distance north or south of Earth's Equator, in degrees
longitude (LAHN juh tood) *n.* distance east or west of the Prime Meridian, in degrees
parallel (PA ruh lel) *n.* a line of latitude
hemisphere (HEM ih sfeer) *n.* half of Earth

Lines of longitude, also called **meridians**, run north and south. The Prime Meridian is the line of longitude that marks 0° of longitude. It divides Earth into Eastern and Western hemispheres.

Lines of longitude and latitude form a global grid. 25 Think of a tic-tac-toe game or a Bingo card. Geographers use this grid to state absolute location. The absolute location of a place is its exact address. For example, Savannah, Georgia, is located at 32° north latitude and 81° west longitude.

30 **2.** When places have something in common such as people, history, climate, or land, geographers call them **regions**. For example, the state you live in is a region because there is one government that unites the whole state.

35 **3.** Geographers also study **place**. Place includes both human and physical features at a specific location. You might say that the land is hilly. That is a physical feature. Or you might talk about how many people live in a place. That is a human feature.

40 **4.** The theme of **movement** tells you how people, goods, and ideas get from one place to another. For example, soccer is a popular game in parts of the United States. People who play soccer have moved here from other countries. This theme helps you understand how and why things change. ✓

45 **5.** The last theme is **human-environment interaction**. It looks at how people change the world around them. It also looks at how the environment changes people.

Review Questions

1. What do geographers study?

_____

2. What is a hemisphere?

_____

_____

Target Reading Skill

Read ahead to see what kinds of things regions can have in common. Pick two to write down.

1. _____

2. _____

✓ Reading Check

What kinds of things go from one place to another in the theme of movement?

_____

_____

_____

Vocabulary Strategy

What does the word *environment* mean in the underlined sentence? Circle the words in this paragraph that could help you learn what *environment* means and write a definition below

_____

_____

Key Terms

meridian (muh RID ee un) *n.* a line of longitude

Prepare to Read

Section 2
The Geographer's Tools

Objectives

1. Find out how maps and globes show information about Earth's surface.
2. See how mapmakers show Earth's round surface on flat maps.
3. Learn how to read maps.

Target Reading Skill

Paraphrase When you paraphrase, you put something into your own words. If you can put something into your own words, it means that you understand what you have read. Paraphrasing will also help you remember what you have read.

For example, look at the first paragraph under the heading "Globes and Maps." You could paraphrase it this way:

A globe is the best way to show Earth. The main difference is the size.

As you read, paraphrase the information following each heading.

Vocabulary Strategy

Using Context to Clarify Meaning When you come across a word that you do not know, you may not need to look it up in a dictionary. In this workbook, key terms appear in blue. The definitions of the terms are in a box at the bottom of the page. If you stop to look at the definition, you interrupt your reading. Instead, continue to read to the end of the paragraph. See if you can figure out what the word means from the words around it. Then look at the definition at the bottom of the page to see how close you were. Finally, reread the paragraph to make sure you understood what you read.

Globes and Maps

1 The best way to show Earth is to use a globe. A globe is a model of Earth with the same round shape. Using globes, mapmakers can show Earth's continents and oceans much as they really are. The only difference is 5 the **scale**.

There is a problem with globes, though. A globe big enough to show the streets of your town would be huge. It would be too big to put in your pocket.

Because of that problem, people use flat maps. But maps have problems, too. Earth is round. A map is flat. It is impossible to show Earth on a flat surface without **distortion**. Something will look too large or too small. Or it will be in the wrong place. Mapmakers have found ways to limit these distortions. ✓

15 Where do mapmakers get the information they need to make a map? To make a map, mapmakers measure the ground. They also use photographs taken from planes and satellite images. Satellite images are pictures of Earth's surface taken from a satellite. Both 20 provide current information about Earth's surface.

Geographers also use computer software. A **Geographic information system**, or GIS, is useful to governments and businesses as well.

Getting It All on the Map

In 1569, a mapmaker named Gerardus Mercator (juh 25 RAHR dus mur KAY tur) made a map for sailors. Mercator wanted to make a map that would help sailors find land. His map showed directions accurately. But sizes and distances were distorted. The Mercator **projection** is still used today.

✓ Reading Check

What are the advantages and disadvantages of two ways of showing Earth's surface?

Globes

Advantage: _____

_____

Disadvantage: _____

_____

Maps

Advantage: _____

_____

Disadvantage: _____

_____

Key Terms

scale (SKAYL) *n.* relative size
distortion (dih STAWR shun) *n.* loss of accuracy
Geographic information systems (jee uh GRAF ik in fur MAY shun sis tumz) *n.* computer-based systems that provide information about locations
projection (proh JEK shun) *n.* a way to map Earth on a flat surface

³⁰ On a globe, the lines of longitude meet at the poles. To make a flat map, Mercator had to stretch the spaces between the lines of longitude. On the map, land near the Equator was about the right size. But land areas near the poles became much larger. <u>Geographers call</u> ³⁵ <u>the Mercator projection a conformal map.</u> It shows correct shapes, but not true distances or sizes.

Another kind of map is named for its designer, Arthur Robinson. The Robinson projection shows most distances, sizes, and shapes accurately. Even so, there ⁴⁰ are distortions, especially around the edges of the map. It is one of the most popular maps today. ✓

Reading Maps

All maps have the same basic parts. They have a **compass rose** that shows ⁴⁵ direction. They have a scale bar. It shows how distances on the map compare to actual distances on the land. And they have a **key**, or legend. It explains the ⁵⁰ map's symbols and shading. ✓

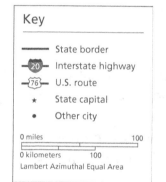

Key

——— State border

—⟨20⟩— Interstate highway

—⟨76⟩— U.S. route

★ State capital

• Other city

0 miles   100

0 kilometers   100

Lambert Azimuthal Equal Area

Review Questions

1. Where do mapmakers get the information they need to make a map?

_____

_____

2. Which map projection would a sailor most likely use?

_____

_____

Key Terms

compass rose (KUM pus rohz) *n.* a diagram of a compass showing direction

key (kee) *n.* the part of a map that explains the symbols

1. Which of the following is NOT a tool a geographer would use to study location?
   A. cardinal directions
   B. climate
   C. lines of latitude
   D. degrees

2. The theme geographers use to group places that have something in common is
   A. location.
   B. regions.
   C. place.
   D. movement.

3. What disadvantages do all flat maps share?
   A. They have some sort of distortion.
   B. They are hard to carry.
   C. There are few sources to create them.
   D. They can only show areas at a small scale.

4. Which of the following do mapmakers use to make maps?
   A. ground surveys
   B. aerial photographs and satellite images
   C. Geographic information systems
   D. all of the above

5. What basic parts do all maps share?
   A. compass rose
   B. scale
   C. key
   D. all of the above

Short Answer Question

Which would be more helpful for studying the exact shapes of continents, a globe or a map? Why?

_____

_____

_____

_____

CHAPTER 2

Prepare to Read

Section 1 Our Planet, Earth

Objectives

1. Learn about Earth's movement around the sun.
2. Explore seasons and latitude.

Target Reading Skill

Use Context Clues What should you do when you come across a word you don't know? Or, what if the word looks familiar, but its meaning is unclear to you? Then, look for clues to help you. Context clues are the words, phrases, and sentences around the unfamiliar word.

The word *revolution* is on the next page. Maybe the last time you saw that word it meant a rebellion. In this section, it means something very different. Use the context clues to help you figure out the meaning of revolution.

Vocabulary Strategy

Recognize Signal Words Signal words are words or phrases that prepare you for what is coming next. They are like road signs that tell drivers what to look for on the road ahead. In this section you will learn how Earth travels around the sun. You will also learn how the movement of Earth causes day, night, and the different seasons. Look out for signal words and phrases such as *then, next, as a result, for this reason,* and *as.* They will help you understand how one thing, such as the movement of Earth, leads to another thing, such as why it is morning in New York hours before it is morning in Utah.

Earth and the Sun

1 The sun is about 93 million miles (150 million kilometers) away. But it still provides Earth with heat and light. If you were to trace the path that Earth makes as it moves around the sun, your finger would trace a cir-
5 cle. Instead of saying Earth circles the sun, we say that Earth **orbits** the sun. It takes one year to complete one **revolution** around the sun.

As Earth orbits the sun, it also turns on its **axis**. Each **rotation** takes about 24 hours. As Earth rotates, it is
10 night on the side away from the sun. As that side turns toward the sun, the sun appears to rise. It is daytime on the side of Earth that faces the sun. As that side turns away from the sun, the sun appears to set. ✓

Earth rotates toward the east, so the day starts earli-
15 er in the east. Governments have divided the world into standard time zones. Time zones are usually one hour apart.

Seasons and Latitude

Imagine sticking a pencil through an orange. The pencil is the axis, the orange is Earth. If you tilt or lean the
20 pencil, then the orange tilts too. Earth is tilted on its axis. At different times in Earth's orbit, the Northern Hemisphere may be tilted toward or away from the sun. At other times, neither hemisphere is tilted toward or away from the sun. Earth has seasons because it is
25 tilted during the revolutions.

Let's call the eraser end of the pencil the Northern Hemisphere and the sharpened end the Southern Hemisphere. For several months of the year as Earth orbits the sun, the Northern Hemisphere (eraser end) is
30 tilted toward the sun. The Northern Hemisphere

✓ Reading Check

Explain why it is day on one side of Earth and night on the other side.

_____

_____

_____

↻ Target Reading Skill

Read the underlined sentence. Circle words in the context that tell you what *tilted* means. Write a definition on the lines below.

tilted: _____

_____

_____

Key Terms

orbit (AWR bit) *n.* path one body makes as it circles around another
revolution (rev uh LOO shun) *n.* circular motion
axis (AK sis) *n.* an imaginary line through Earth between the North and South poles, around which Earth turns
rotation (roh TAY shun) *n.* a complete turn

receives lots of direct sunlight. That creates spring and summer in the Northern Hemisphere. At the same time, the Southern Hemisphere (the sharpened end) is tilted away from the sun. The Southern Hemisphere
35 receives indirect sunlight, creating fall and winter in the Southern Hemisphere.

When the Northern Hemisphere is tilted toward the sun, the Southern Hemisphere is tilted away. For this reason, the seasons are reversed in the Southern Hemisphere.

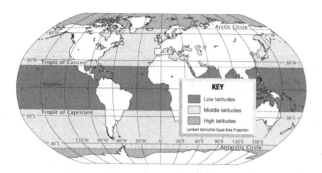

How far a place is from the Equator influences the temperature of a place. Remember that lines of latitude circle Earth above and below the Equator. The areas between the Tropic of Cancer and the Tropic of
45 Capricorn receive fairly direct sunlight all year. Weather is usually hot.

The areas above the Arctic Circle and below the Antarctic Circle get indirect sun. They are cool or very cold all year.
50 The areas between the high and low latitudes are the middle latitudes. In summer, they get fairly direct sunlight. In winter, they get indirect sunlight. This means they have four seasons. Summers are hot, winters are cold, and spring and fall are in between. ✓

Review Questions

1. What is the rotation of Earth?

_____

_____

2. How do Earth's tilt and orbit cause the seasons?

_____

_____

_____

Vocabulary Strategy

In the bracketed paragraph, a signal phrase is used to show effect. Find the signal phrase and circle it. What effect is explained?

_____

_____

_____

✓ Reading Check

How does latitude influence temperature?

_____

_____

_____

Objectives

1. Learn about the planet Earth.
2. Explore the forces inside Earth.
3. Explore the forces on Earth's surface.

Target Reading Skill

Use Context Clues When you come across a word you don't know, you can often use context to figure out its meaning. Context clues can be a definition, an example, an explanation, or even what you already know about the subject.

The phrase *Ring of Fire* appears in this section. Which box in the graphic organizer will help you the most as you try to figure out the meaning of *Ring of Fire?*

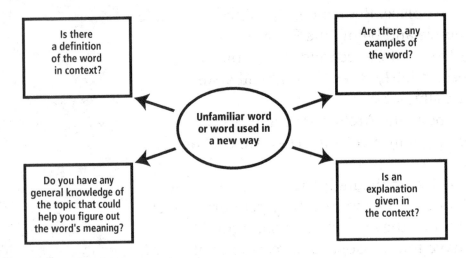

Vocabulary Strategy

Recognize Signal Words When someone drives on a road or highway, road signs can help them know whether to drive fast or slowly, when traffic will merge, and what to watch out for on the road ahead. Recognizing signal words is a lot like reading road signs. Signal words tell you what to expect.

Some signal words show different kinds of relationships, such as contrast. Contrast shows the difference between things or ideas.

Signal words that show contrast include *but, however, not, on the other hand, even though, yet,* and *despite.*

Section 2 Summary

Understanding Earth

1 Deep inside Earth is a **core** of hot metal. Around that is a second layer called the **mantle**. A third layer floating on top of the mantle is called the **crust**. The surface, or top of the crust, includes Earth's land areas and ocean

5 floors. Powerful forces shape and change Earth. ☑

Most of Earth's surface is not land however. It is water. In fact, water covers more than 70 percent of Earth. The oceans hold about 97 percent of Earth's water. That means that most of Earth's water is salty.

10 Most of the fresh water is frozen. People can use only a small part of Earth's fresh water. It comes from lakes, rivers, and ground water. They receive water from rain.

<u>Above Earth's surface is the atmosphere, a thick layer of gases.</u> The atmosphere contains oxygen that

15 people and animals need to breathe. It also has the gas that plants need.

Earth's land surface comes in all shapes and sizes. Mountains, volcanoes, hills, plateaus, and plains are landforms found on the top of the crust. Mountains

20 rise more than 2,000 feet (610 meters) above sea level. A volcano is a kind of mountain. Hills are lower and less steep than mountains. A plateau is a large, mostly flat area that rises above the land around it. Plains are large areas of flat or gently rolling land.

Forces Inside Earth

25 Extreme heat deep inside Earth is always changing the way Earth looks on the surface. It makes rocks rise toward the surface. Streams of hot **magma** push up Earth's crust to form volcanoes. Volcanoes pour out molten rock, or lava, from inside Earth.

30 Streams of hot magma may also push the crust apart along openings called seams. These seams separate

---

✓ Reading Check

Which layer of Earth contains all of its landforms?

_____

_____

_____

⟳ Target Reading Skill

If you do not know what the word *atmosphere* means, notice that a definition follows the phrase in the underlined sentence. What does *atmosphere* mean?

_____

_____

_____

Key Terms

core (kawr) *n.* the sphere of very hot metal at the center of Earth
mantle (MAN tul) *n.* the thick layer around Earth's core
crust (krust) *n.* the thin, rocky layer on Earth's surface
magma (MAG muh) *n.* soft, nearly molten rock

huge blocks of crust called **plates**. A plate may include continents or parts of continents. A plate also includes part of the ocean floor.

35 Sometimes, where two plates meet, molten rock explodes to the surface through a volcano. A good example of this is the Ring of Fire. It is a string of volcanoes near the plates that form the Pacific Ocean. Volcanoes can form at other places, too.

40 When two plates push together, the crust cracks and splinters. These cracks are called faults. When blocks of crust rub against each other along faults, they release energy in the form of earthquakes.

Scientists now know that the forces inside Earth are 45 powerful enough to move continents. They know that the continents were once close together. Magma works to move Earth's plates and continents. ✓

Forces on Earth's Surface

Forces inside Earth slowly build up Earth's crust. But two forces slowly wear down the surface. **Weathering** is one force. Water, ice, and living things like lichens on rocks slowly break rocks into tiny pieces. Weathering helps create soil. Soil is made up of tiny pieces of rock mixed with decaying animal and plant matter.

Erosion also reshapes Earth's surface and land-
55 forms. Water and wind carry soil downstream or downwind to create new landforms. Plains are often made of soil carried by rivers. ✓

Review Questions

1. What are Earth's three main layers?

_____

_____

2. How is erosion different from weathering?

_____

_____

Key Terms

plate (playt) *n.* a huge block of Earth's crust
weathering (WETH ur ing) *n.* a process that breaks rocks down into small pieces
erosion (ee ROH zhun) *n.* the removal of small pieces of rock by water, ice, or wind

Prepare to Read

Section 3
Climate and Weather

Objectives

1. Learn about weather and climate.
2. Explore latitude, landforms, and precipitation.
3. Discover how oceans affect climate.

Target Reading Skill

Use Context Clues When you read, you sometimes come across a word you don't know. Sometimes the word you don't know is used in comparison with a word or a group of words you *do* know. These word clues and your own general knowledge can help you figure out what the word means without having to look it up.

Look at this sentence:

The kindling burned more quickly than the other pieces of wood.

Here, the word *kindling* is compared to <u>other pieces of wood.</u> Reading the sentence will help you figure out the meaning of the new word.

Vocabulary Strategy

Recognize Signal Words Signal words are words or phrases that give you clues or directions when reading. Sometimes a signal word or phrase will alert you that two or more things are being compared. Here are some words that can signal a comparison.

also	like	same as
as well as	more	similar to
both	same	too
in the same way	just as	less

Weather or Climate?

1 Do you check the weather before you get ready for school? Most people need to know the **weather** before they get dressed. They need to know two things. The first is temperature, the second is precipitation. The 5 **temperature** is how hot or cold the air is. **Precipitation** is water that falls to the ground as rain, sleet, hail, or snow. Weather is not the same as climate. Weather is what people feel from day to day. **Climate** is the average weather from year to year. ✔

Why Climates Vary

10 Earth has many climates. Some climates are so hot that people almost always wear summer clothes. In some climates, snow stays on the ground most of the year. Climate depends on location. Places in low latitudes, or the tropics, have hot climates. This is because they are 15 closer to the Equator and get direct sunlight. Places in the high latitudes, or polar regions, have cold climates. That is because their sunlight is indirect. ✔

Air and water spread heat around Earth as they move. Without wind and water, places in the tropics 20 would overheat. Oceans take longer than land to heat up and cool down. This makes land near oceans have mild temperatures.

Oceans and Climates

An ocean current is like a huge river in the ocean. Ocean currents move across great distances. The cur- 25 rents are huge rivers of warm and cold water. Usually, warm water flows away from the Equator. Cold water moves toward the Equator.

Key Terms

weather (WETH ur) *n.* the condition of the air and sky from day to day

temperature (TEM pur uh chur) *n.* how hot or cold the air is

precipitation (pree sip uh TAY shun) *n.* water that falls to the ground as rain, sleet, hail, or snow

climate (KLY mut) *n.* the average weather over many years

Ocean currents help make climates milder. A warm current can make a cool place warmer. A cold current can make a warm place cooler. The warm Gulf Stream gives Western Europe a milder climate than it would if the current was not near. In the same way, the cold Peru Current keeps Antofagasta, Chile, cooler than it would otherwise be.

35 Oceans and lakes affect climate in other ways, too. Water takes longer to heat or cool than land. In summer, wind blowing over water cools the nearby land. In the winter, water helps keep nearby land by the shore warmer than inland areas. ☑

Raging Storms

40 Wind and water can make climates milder. They can also create dangerous storms. **Tropical cyclones** are a good example. Similar storms that form over the Atlantic Ocean are usually called hurricanes. Their winds can reach speeds of more than 100 miles (160 45 kilometers) per hour. Hurricanes push huge amounts of water onto land, destroying homes and towns.

Tornadoes are like funnels of wind. They can reach 200 miles (320 kilometers) per hour. The swirling winds wreck almost everything in their path. They are 50 just as dangerous as hurricanes. But they affect much smaller areas. ☑

Other storms are less dangerous. In winter, blizzards dump snow on parts of North America. Heavy rainstorms and thunderstorms happen in the spring 55 and summer.

Review Questions

1. What kind of climate occurs near the Equator?

_____

_____

2. How does the ocean influence the temperature of land near it?

_____

_____

Key Terms

tropical cyclone (TRAHP ih kul SY klohn) *n.* an intense wind and rain storm that forms over oceans in the tropics

Vocabulary Strategy

Mark the Text

In the bracketed paragraph, a signal phrase is used to make a comparison. Find the phrase and circle it. What is being compared here?

_____

_____

✓ Reading Check

During the summer, are places near the ocean hotter or cooler than places inland?

_____

_____

✓ Reading Check

Which storms cover larger areas, hurricanes or tornadoes?

_____

_____

_____

Prepare to Read

Section 4
How Climate Affects Vegetation

Objectives

1. Investigate climate and vegetation.
2. Explore Earth's vegetation regions.
3. Study vertical climate zones.

Target Reading Skill

Use Context Clues What can you do when you see a word used in an unfamiliar way? Of course, you could look the word up in a dictionary. But often you can get a good idea of what the word means from the words around it.

Textbooks often give examples of new words or ideas. You can tell the meaning of the word from the examples. In the sentence below, the meaning of the word *scrub* is given by the examples in italics:

Scrub includes *bushes and small trees.*

Did you figure out that *scrub* is a word that describes types of plants?

Vocabulary Strategy

Recognize Signal Words Signal words are words or phrases that give you clues or directions when reading. They tell you that what is coming next will be different in some way from what you have just read.

Sometimes a signal word or phrase will help you recognize a cause or effect.

Words that signal causes:	Words that signal effects:
because	as a result
if	so
since	then
on account of	therefore

Section 4 Summary

Climate and Vegetation

1 These are the five major types of climate: tropical, dry, temperate marine, temperate continental, and polar. Every climate has its own types of natural **vegetation**. That is because different plants need different amounts
5 of water and sunlight and different temperatures to live. ✓

You can probably guess that a **tropical climate** is hot! Some tropical climates also get rain all year long. You would find a tropical rain forest in this climate.
10 Other tropical climates get less rain. In those climates there is more grass and fewer trees.

Dry climates have very hot summers and mild winters. Because dry climates get little rain, few plants can grow there. Semidry climates get just enough rain to grow scrub, including bushes and small trees.

Temperate marine climates are usually near a coastline. There are three types: Mediterranean, marine west coast, and humid subtropical. All have mild winters. The marine west coast and humid subtropical climates
20 get lots of rain. The Mediterranean climates get less rain and have Mediterranean vegetation.

The summers in **temperate continental climates** can be hot. But the winters are very cold. Grasslands and forests grow in these climates.
25 **Polar climates** are always cold. Summers are short and cool there. Winters are long and very cold. In the polar climates you find the **tundra** and ice caps.

Earth's Vegetation Regions

Vegetation depends on climate. But other things, such as soil, also affect vegetation. Geographers have
30 grouped vegetation into several regions. We will study just a few of them here.

Key Terms

vegetation (vej uh TAY shun) *n.* plants that grow in a region
tundra (TUN druh) *n.* an area of cold climate and low-lying vegetation

What types of vegetation grow in deserts?

_____

_____

_____

↻ **Target Reading Skill**

Underline the words in the bracketed paragraph that help you to figure out the meaning of the term *coniferous forest*. Then complete the following sentence:

Trees in coniferous forests have

_____.

What is the meaning of the word coniferous? What context clues helped you figure out the meaning? Write the context clues on the line below.

_____

_____

✓ **Reading Check**

How does vegetation change with elevation?

_____

_____

Tropical Rain Forest Plentiful sunlight, heat, and rain cause thousands of plants to grow. The trees grow so tall and close together they form a **canopy** high in
35 the air. Smaller plants grow in the shade.

Tropical Savanna Some tropical areas have less rain. They have a landscape of grasslands and scattered trees known as **savanna**.

Desert Scrub Some very dry areas have just enough
40 rain to support plant growth called **desert scrub**. ✓

Deciduous forest Several different climates support forests of **deciduous trees**. Many people enjoy the changing colors of leaves in the fall.

Coniferous forest Trees with needles instead of leaves can grow in climates that are a little drier than those needed by leafy trees. **Coniferous trees** get their name from the cones they produce.

Vertical Climate Zones

Mountains have vertical climate zones. That means that climate and vegetation depend on how high the
50 mountain is. In a tropical region, plants that need a tropical climate will grow only near the bottom of a mountain. Farther up you will find plants that can grow in a temperate climate. Near the top you will only find plants that grow in a polar climate. ✓

Review Questions

1. What are the five main types of climate?

_____

_____

2. What landform has a vertical climate zone?

_____

_____

Key Terms

canopy (KAN uh pea) *n.* the layer formed by the uppermost branches of a rain forest
savanna (suh VAN uh) *n.* a parklike combination of grasslands and scattered trees
desert scrub (DEZ urt skrub) *n.* desert plants that need little water
deciduous trees (dee SIJ oo us treez) *n.* trees that lose their leaves seasonally
coniferous trees (koh NIF ur us treez) *n.* trees that produce cones to carry seeds

1. When it is summer in the Northern Hemisphere, it is
   _____ in the Southern Hemisphere.
   A. summer
   B. winter
   C. spring
   D. fall

2. The layers of Earth include
   A. core, water, crust.
   B. volcanoes, mountains, plateaus.
   C. lava, magma, plates.
   D. core, mantle, crust.

3. Weathering is caused by
   A. water.
   B. ice.
   C. lichens.
   D. all of the above

4. Which of the following influences climate?
   A. latitude
   B. longitude
   C. the Prime Meridian
   D. tornadoes

5. In which vegetation region would you find trees that lose their leaves
   seasonally?
   A. tropical rain forest
   B. coniferous forest
   C. deciduous forest
   D. tundra

Short Answer Question

Why do some coastal cities in the tropics stay cool?

_____

_____

_____

_____

_____

Prepare to Read

Section 1 Population

Objectives

1. Learn about population distribution.
2. Explore population density.
3. Investigate population growth.

Target Reading Skill

Comparison and Contrast Have you ever played the game where you try to find the differences between two pictures? The pictures seem to be the same, but if you look closely, you can find little differences. Sometimes the differences are easy to spot. Other times you really have to work at it.

Playing that game is similar to comparing and contrasting as you read. It is easy to see the difference between the terms *birthrate* and *death rate*. But terms like *population density* and *population distribution* will require a little more work.

Vocabulary Strategy

Recognize Roots When you add letters in front or to the end of a root word, you create a new word. You use roots all the time without even thinking about it. When you write, "I watched a movie last night," you knew to add *-ed* to *watch* to create *watched*.

The word *density* appears in this section. The root word is *dense*. The letters *-ity* have been added. But the word isn't spelled *denseity*! It is spelled *density*. Sometimes the root word changes when you add letters. See if you can find more examples as you read. *Hint:* There is one in the first sentence of the next page.

Section 1 Summary

Population Distribution

1 The way Earth's **population** is spread out is called **population distribution**. People tend to live in uneven clusters on Earth's surface. **Demography** tries to explain why populations change and why population 5 distribution is uneven.

People usually don't move without a good reason. As long as people can make a living where they are, they usually stay there. That means that regions with large populations tend to keep them.

10 In the past, most people lived on farms where they grew their own food. Therefore, more people lived in places that had good climates for growing crops. After about 1800, things changed. Railroads and steamships made traveling long distances much easier. People 15 moved to cities to work in factories and offices instead of working on farms. ✓

Population Density

How do you find out how crowded a place really is? Find out how many people live in an area. Then divide that number by the area's square miles or square kilo- 20 meters. That will give you the **population density**. Remember, population distribution tells you the actual number of people in an area. Population density tells you the average number of people in an area.

Some places are more crowded, or have a higher 25 population density than others. For example, Japan has a high population density, while Canada has a low population density. ✓

✓ Reading Check

What happened to make people move to the cities after 1800?

_____

_____

_____

⟳ Target Reading Skill

How is population density different from population distribution?

_____

_____

_____

✓ Reading Check

Which country is more crowded, Japan or Canada? How do you know?

_____

_____

_____

Key Terms

population (pahp yuh LAY shun) *n.* total number of people in an area
population distribution (pahp yoo LAY shun dis truh byoo shun) *n.* the way the population is spread out over an area
demography (dih MAH gruh fee) *n.* the science that studies population distribution and change
population density (pahp yuh LAY shun DEN suh tee) *n.* the average number of people per square mile or square kilometer

Population Growth

For thousands of years, the world's population grew slowly. Food supplies were scarce. People lived without clean water and waste removal. Millions died of diseases. Although the **birthrate** was high, so was the **death rate**. The life expectancy, or the average length of people's lives, was short.

Today, death rates have dropped sharply. In some countries, birthrates have increased. As a result, populations have grown very fast. At the same time, people live longer than ever. Scientific progress caused much of this change. See the chart below to learn more. ✓

✓ **Reading Check**

Why have populations risen rapidly in recent years?

_____

_____

_____

Scientific Progress	
Changes in health and medicine	Green Revolution—improvements in farming methods
Clean drinking water / Vaccines and medicine	Ways to grow more food / Ways to grow food with less water

People in many countries still face big problems. Some nations do not have enough fresh water. In parts of Asia and Africa, the population is growing faster than the food supply.

The way people live can be hurt by population growth. There are shortages of jobs, schools, and housing. Public services like transportation and sanitation are inadequate. Forests are disappearing. This causes still more problems.

Review Questions

1. How did the Green Revolution increase population?

_____

_____

2. List problems caused by population growth.

_____

_____

Key Terms

birthrate (BURTH rayt) *n.* the number of live births each year per 1,000 people

death rate (deth rayt) *n.* the number of deaths each year per 1,000 people

Prepare to Read

Section 2 Migration

Objectives

1. Learn about migration, or people's movement from one region to another.
2. Investigate urbanization, or people's movement to cities.

Target Reading Skill

Identify Contrasts Contrast is the way that things are different from each other. Some contrasts are easy to see. For example, it is easy to see how the city is different from the country. The city has more buildings, more people. The country has more plants and trees.

Ideas can be contrasted too. Sometimes it is harder to see the difference in ideas. On the next page you will read about the push-pull theory. Think about how the word *push* means something very different than the word *pull.* This will help you understand the push-pull theory.

Vocabulary Strategy

Find Roots Often, letters are added to the beginning or end of a word. The word the letters are added to is the root word. Sometimes the added letters will completely change the meaning of the root word.

For example, in this section you will study voluntary migration. This is a phrase that means "people choose to migrate." But add the letters *in-* to *voluntary* and you get something very different. *Involuntary migration* is a term that describes people who are forced to move.

Section 2 Summary

Why People Migrate

[1] For thousands of years, people have moved to new places. This movement is called **migration**. **Immigrants** are people who move into one country from another.

Some people choose to move. This is called voluntary migration. Today, most people move by their own choice. The push-pull theory explains voluntary migration. It says that difficulties "push" people to leave. At the same time, the hope for a better life "pulls" them to a new country. ☑

Here is an example of the push-pull theory. Many years ago, 1.5 million people left Ireland for the United States. Disease had destroyed Ireland's main crop, potatoes. Hunger pushed people to migrate. Job opportunities pulled Irish families to the United States.

Today, the main sources of migration are countries where many people are poor or there are few jobs. Sometimes, wars have made life dangerous and difficult. Also, some governments limit people's freedom. These problems push people to leave. They are pulled by the possibility of good jobs or political freedom.

Sometimes people are forced to move. This is known as involuntary migration. In the 1800s, the British sent prisoners to Australia to serve their sentences. War also forces people to migrate to escape death or danger.

The biggest involuntary migration may have been the slave trade. From the 1500s to the 1800s, millions of Africans were enslaved and taken to European colonies in North and South America.

Key Terms

migration (my GRAY shun) *n.* the movement of people from one place or region to another

immigrants (IM uh grunts) *n.* people who move into one country from another

---

Urbanization

30 Millions of people in many countries have moved to cities from farms and small villages. As a result, some cities have grown <u>enormously</u> in recent years. The movement of people to cities and the growth of cities is called <u>urbanization</u>.

35 In Europe and North America, the growth of industry created jobs. People moved to cities for jobs in factories and offices. Today, people in Europe and North America are moving out of cities into suburbs. Most people in suburbs rely on cars for <u>transportation</u>. More 40 cars mean increased pollution. But people still move to suburbs so they can own homes.

In Asia, Africa, and Latin America, people are still moving from the countryside to <u>growing</u> cities. Indonesia is an example. In the past, people lived in 45 **rural** areas. Recently, many Indonesians have moved to **urban** areas. The capital has grown from 3.9 million people to 11 million people in thirty years. ✓

Often, too many people are moving to the city too fast. Cities cannot provide the things that people 50 need. There are <u>shortages</u> of housing, jobs, schools, and hospitals.

So why do people move to big cities? As hard as life is in the cities, it can be even harder in the countryside. Often, there are few jobs and not enough farmland. 55 Most migrants who move to the city want a better life for their families.

Review Questions

1. Name one push factor and one pull factor.

_____

_____

2. What is urbanization?

_____

_____

Key Terms

urbanization (ur bun ih ZAY shun) *n.* the movement of people to cities, and the growth of cities
rural (ROOR uhl) *adj.* the countryside
urban (UR bun) *adj.* cities and towns

Vocabulary Strategy

Each of the underlined words in the part titled "Urbanization" contains another word that is its root. Circle the roots in these words. The root of the first word, *enormously*, is *enormous*.

✓ Reading Check

How is the population of urban areas changing in Africa, Asia, and Latin America?

_____

_____

_____

_____

Objectives

1. Examine different kinds of economies.
2. Investigate levels of economic development.
3. Study global trade patterns.

Target Reading Skill

Make Comparisons Comparing two or more situations lets you see how they are alike. It is often easier to understand new facts by comparing them with facts you already know. Sometimes one thing is compared to several other things.

In this section, you will read about developed nations and developing nations. As you read, compare how people live in developed and developing nations. What kinds of jobs do they have? What kinds of houses do they live in? Do people or machines do most of the work?

Vocabulary Strategy

Recognize Compound Words Compound words are made from two or more words. Compound words are like shortcuts. They make it easier to read or talk about things. For example, *workplace* is a compound word. You could say, "Describe the place where you work." Or, you could say, "Describe your workplace." If you know the meaning of the words that make up a compound word, you can often figure out the meaning of the compound word itself. Here are some compound words you will find in your reading.

sometimes	countryside
worldwide	anybody
healthcare	farmland

Section 3 Summary

Different Kinds of Economies

Economies differ from one country to another.
However, in every economy, there are **producers**, who
are the owners and workers who make products, and
consumers who buy and use products.

⁵   The owner of the workplace usually decides how
and what things will be made. But who are the owners? In some countries, the workplace belongs to private citizens. This economic system is called
capitalism. In others, the government owns most
¹⁰ workplaces. This is called **communism**.

Capitalism is also called a free-market economy.
Producers compete freely for consumers' business.
People may save money in banks, and invest money in
a business.

¹⁵   Under communism, the government controls the
prices of goods and services, what things are made,
and how much workers are paid. Today, only a few
nations practice communism. ☑

In some countries, the government owns some
²⁰ industries while others belong to private owners. This
system is sometimes called a mixed economy.

Levels of Economic Development

Three hundred years ago, most people did work by
hand. Then people invented machines to make goods.
They used energy instead of people and animals to run
²⁵ machines. This was a new form of technology.
Technology is a way of putting knowledge to practical
use. This change in the way people made goods was
called the Industrial Revolution.

Key Terms

economy (ih KAHN uh mee) *n.* a system in which people make,
exchange, and use things that have value

producers (pruh DOOS urz) *n.* owners and workers

consumers (kun SOOM urz) *n.* people who buy and use products

capitalism (KAP ut ul iz um) *n.* an economic system in which individuals own most businesses

communism (KAHM yoo niz um) *n.* an economic system in which
the central government owns farms, factories, and offices

Target Reading Skill

Compare producers and consumers. How are they different?

_____

_____

_____

✓ Reading Check

What are two differences between
capitalism and communism?

1. _____

_____

2. _____

_____

Vocabulary Strategy

The word *healthcare* is a compound word. What are the two root words of *healthcare* and what does each root word mean?

1. _____

   _____

2. _____

   _____

Use the meanings above to understand the meaning of healthcare. Write a definition for healthcare on the lines below.

Healthcare means:

_____

_____

✓ **Reading Check**

What do developing nations sell to developed nations?

_____

_____

_____

The Industrial Revolution divided the world into
30 **developed nations** and **developing nations**. People live differently in the two types of nations. Developed nations have more industries and a high level of technology. Developing nations have fewer industries and simpler technology. ✓
35   Only about one fifth of the world's people live in developed nations. These nations include the United States, Canada, Japan, and most of Europe. In these countries most people live in towns and cities. They work in offices and factories. Most people have enough
40 food and water. Most people can get an education and healthcare. Developed nations have some problems. Two of these problems are unemployment and pollution.
  Most of the people in the world live in developing nations. These nations are mainly in Africa, Asia, and
45 Latin America. Most people grow just enough food for themselves. People and animals do most of the work. There are many problems in these nations. They include disease, food shortages, and political unrest.

World Trade Patterns

Different countries have different economic strengths.
50 Countries trade with one another to get the things they want and need.
  Countries have grown to depend on one another. Developing nations tend to sell foods, natural resources, and simple industrial products. In return, they buy
55 high-technology goods from developed countries. ✓

Review Questions

1. How did the Industrial Revolution change the way people made things?

_____

_____

2. How do countries depend on one another?

_____

_____

Key Terms

developed nations (dih VEL upt NAY shunz) *n.* nations with many industries and advanced technology
developing nations (dih VEL up ing NAY shunz) *n.* nations with few industries and simple technology

Prepare to Read

Section 4 Political Systems

Objectives

1. Examine different types of states.
2. Investigate types of government.
3. Learn about alliances and international organizations.

Target Reading Skill

Use Contrast Signal Words Signal words are words or phrases that give you clues when reading.

There are different kinds of signal words. Certain words, such as *like* or *unlike, just as* or even the phrase *such as* in the beginning of this sentence can signal a comparison or contrast. This section contrasts several kinds of government. You will learn that some governments encourage people to participate, other governments do not.

In the sentence below, are the signal words signaling comparison or contrast?

Just as in an absolute monarchy, dictatorships do not allow people to participate in government.

Once you read the section you will know for sure!

Vocabulary Strategy

Find Roots Often, syllables or groups of syllables are added at the beginning or end of a word to make a new word.

In some cases, the spelling changes slightly when a word becomes a root. Often, a final *e* is dropped when a new ending is added to a word.

Here are some other examples from this section.

Root	Added letters	New word
make	-ing	making
share	-ing	sharing
simple	-y	simply

Target Reading Skill

The second sentence in the bracketed paragraph begins with the word *Some*. The fourth sentence begins with *Others*. These words signal a contrast. What contrast is made here?

_____

_____

✓ Reading Check

Name four kinds of states.

1. _____

2. _____

3. _____

4. _____

Vocabulary Strategy

Each of the four words below appear in the sections titled "Types of Government," and "International Organizations." Each contains a root that has had a spelling change before the ending was added. Write the full roots on the lines below.

1. earliest _____

2. dictator _____

3. alliance _____

4. organization _____

Types of States

1 When people lived in small groups, all adults took part in making group decisions. Today, nations are too large for everyone to take part in every decision. But they still need to be able to protect people. They need to be able to 5 solve problems. That is why we have **governments**.

A **state** is a region that shares a government. The entire United States can also be called a state. That's because it is a region that shares a federal government.

There are four kinds of states. Some regions are **dependencies**. They belong to another state. Others, like the United States, are **nation-states**, which are often simply called nations. Every place in the world where people live is a nation-state or dependency.

The first states formed in Southwest Asia more than 15 5,000 years ago. Early cities set up governments called **city-states**. Later, military leaders conquered several countries and ruled them as **empires**. ✓

Types of Government

Each state has a government. There are many different kinds of government. Some are controlled by one per-20 son. Others are controlled by all of the people.

The earliest governments were simple. People lived in small groups. They practiced **direct democracy**. All adults took part in decisions. In time, communities banded together into larger tribal groups. Members of 25 the tribe had a say in group decisions. But under **tribal rule,** chiefs or elders made the final decision.

Key Terms

government (GUV urn munt) *n.* a body that makes laws
state (stayt) *n.* a region that shares a government
dependency (dee PEN dun see) *n.* a region that belongs to another state
nation-state (NAY shun stayt) *n.* a state that is independent of other states
city-state (SIH tee stayt) *n.* a small city-centered state
empire (EM pyr) *n.* a state containing several countries

Until about 200 years ago, **absolute monarchy** was one of the most common forms of government. In that system, kings or queens have complete control. Today, 30 there are other countries where just one person rules. The leader is not a king or queen but a **dictator**. Dictators have complete control over a country. An **oligarchy** is a government controlled by a small group of people. The group may be the leaders of a political 35 party, a group of military officers, or even a group of religious leaders. In oligarchies and dictatorships, ordinary people have little say in decisions. ✓

Today, most monarchies are **constitutional monarchies**. The power of the king or queen is limited by 40 law. These nations have **constitutions** that define the government's power. **Representative democracies** are governments in which people elect representatives who create laws. If they do not like what a representative does, they can refuse to reelect that person.

International Organizations

45 Nations may agree to work together in an <u>alliance</u>. Members of an alliance are called allies. In some alliances, members agree to protect each other in case of attack. Some alliances, such as the European Union, are mainly economic.

50 The United Nations is an international organization that tries to resolve problems and promote peace. Almost all of the world's nations belong to the United Nations. It sponsors other international organizations with specific purposes, such as combating hunger or 55 promoting the well-being of children. ✓

Review Questions

1. What were the earliest types of states?

_____

_____

2. What is an alliance?

_____

_____

Key Terms

constitution (kahn stuh TOO shuhn) *n.* a set of laws that define and often limit a government's power

---

✓ **Reading Check**

Name two forms of government in which the leader has total control.

1. _____

_____

2. _____

_____

✓ **Reading Check**

What is the purpose of the United Nations?

_____

_____

_____

1. The number of people per square mile or square kilometer is a region's
   A. population.
   B. population density.
   C. population distribution.
   D. life expectancy.

2. People moving to a different region to seek better job opportunities is an example of
   A. urbanization.
   B. suburbanization.
   C. voluntary migration.
   D. involuntary migration.

3. In which of the following does the government control the prices of goods and services?
   A. developed countries
   B. developing countries
   C. capitalism
   D. communism

4. In the earliest societies, the form of government was
   A. direct democracy.
   B. representative democracy.
   C. absolute monarchy.
   D. constitutional monarch.

5. Today, most monarchies are
   A. absolute monarchies.
   B. dictatorships.
   C. oligarchies.
   D. constitutional monarchies.

Short Answer Question

What is the Green Revolution?

_____

_____

_____

_____

_____

CHAPTER 4

Prepare to Read

Section 1
Understanding Culture

Objectives

1. Learn about culture.
2. Explore how culture has developed.

Target Reading Skill

Understand Sequence History is a series of events. To help you understand history, list events in sequence, or the order in which they happened. Make a chart like the one below to help you. This one is about how culture developed. The first two events are filled in for you. Fill in the event that happens next when you come across it as you read. The arrows show how one event leads to another.

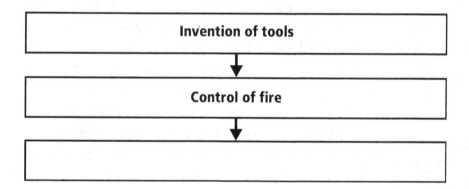

Vocabulary Strategy

Use Context Clues to Determine Meaning Context clues help you figure out the meaning of words. One way to use context clues is to imagine a blank space in place of the word you don't understand. Let's say you don't know the meaning of the word *institutions.* Read the paragraph below. There is a blank everywhere the word *institutions* would appear.

Before civilizations developed, people had simple _____. These were extended families and councils of elders. As people gathered in larger groups, they needed more complex _____. They developed religions. States needed armies, schools, and governments. Today, we have many different kinds of _____. They are important parts of our culture.

Did you figure out that *institutions* means organized groups of people?

What Is Culture?

[1] Culture is the way people live. It includes what people believe and the things they do everyday. It includes the language people speak and the clothes they wear.

Parents pass culture on to their children. Ideas and
[5] ways of doing things are called cultural traits. For example, in the United States, eating with a fork is a cultural trait. In Japan, people use chopsticks.

Some parts of a culture are easy to see. They include houses, food, and clothing. Things you cannot see or
[10] touch are also part of culture. They include spiritual beliefs, government, and ideas about right and wrong. Language is a very important part of culture.

Geographers want to know how the environment affects culture. Japan is a nation of mountainous
[15] islands, with very little farmland. So the Japanese use the sea for food. But the same environment may not lead to the same culture. Greece is also made of mountainous islands. The Greeks eat some fish. But they use mountainsides to get food. Goats and sheep graze
[20] there and provide food for the Greeks. ✓

The **cultural landscape** varies from place to place. In Indonesia, farmers have used technology to carve terraces into hillsides. On the plains of northern India, farmers have laid out broad, flat fields.

The Development of Culture

[25] Scientists think that early cultures went through four important steps. First was the invention of tools. Second was the control of fire. Third was the beginnings of farming. Fourth was the development of **civilizations.**

✓ Reading Check

Describe the way environment affects culture.

_____

_____

_____

Vocabulary Strategy

The word *landscape* has more than one meaning. You may already know one of its meanings. Circle the words in the bracketed paragraph that are context clues for *landscape*. What does it mean in this context?

_____

_____

_____

Key Terms

culture (KUL chur) *n.* the way of life of a people, including their beliefs and practices

cultural landscape (KUL chur ul LAND skayp) *n.* the parts of a people's environment that they have shaped and the technology they have used to shape it

civilization (sih vuh luh ZAY shun) *n.* an advanced culture with cities and a system of writing

Early people were hunters and gatherers. They traveled from place to place. As they traveled, they collected wild plants, hunted animals, and fished. Later, they learned to grow crops. They tamed wild animals to help them work or to use for food. Over time, people got more of their food from farming. This is called the Agricultural Revolution.

Farmers were able to grow more food than they needed. This meant that some people could work full time on crafts such as metalworking. They traded the things they made for food. People developed laws and government. To keep track of things, they developed writing. All these events together created the first civilizations. That was about 5,000 years ago. ✓

In time, farming and civilization spread throughout the world. Then, about 200 years ago, people invented power-driven machinery. This was the beginning of the Industrial Revolution. It led to the growth of cities, science, and highly advanced technologies.

Before the Agricultural Revolution, people had simple **institutions**. These were extended families and simple political institutions, such as councils of elders. As people gathered in larger groups, they needed more complex institutions. They developed religions. States needed schools, armies and governments. Today, we have many different kinds of institutions. They help to organize our culture.

Review Questions

1. List the events that led to the first civilizations.

_____

_____

2. What are two events of the Agricultural Revolution?

_____

_____

✓ **Reading Check**

What happened because farmers were able to grow more food than they needed?

_____

_____

_____

⟳ **Target Reading Skill**

What invention led to the Industrial Revolution?

_____

_____

Key Term

institution (in stuh TOO shun) *n.* a custom or organization with social, educational, or religious purposes

Prepare to Read

Section 2 Culture and Society

Objectives

1. Learn how people are organized into groups.
2. Look at language.
3. Explore the role of religion.

Target Reading Skill

Understand Sequence Throughout history, things change. You can show a sequence of changes by simply listing the changes. As you read this section, list some of the changes that have happened in societies. Here is an example for you.

Extended family **changed to** nuclear family.

Vocabulary Strategy

Use Context to Clarify Meaning Social studies textbooks often contain words that are new to you. These textbooks have context clues to help you figure out the meanings of words. Context refers to the words and sentences just before and after each new word. The clues can include examples, explanations, or definitions. As you read, use the graphic organizer as a guide to help you find the meaning of new words.

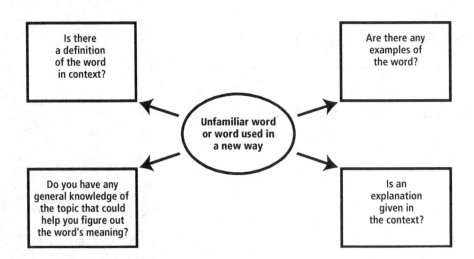

Section 2 Summary

How Society Is Organized

1 A group of people who share a culture is known as a **society**. A society may be as small as a single community. Or it may be as large as a nation. It may even be a group of nations. Every society has a **social structure**. 5 Smaller groups in a society work together. For example, teachers, doctors, and farmers are part of the social structure. Social structure helps people work together to meet basic needs.

The family is the basic, most important part of 10 every society. Families teach the customs and traditions of the culture to their children. ☑

Society is also organized into **social classes**. A person's place in society may come from wealth, land, ancestors, or education. In the past, it was often hard for people to move from one social class to another. Today, people in many societies can improve their position in society. They can get a good education, make more money, or marry into a higher class.

In some cultures, people think of family as a moth-20 er, father, and children. The **nuclear family** is common in the United States.

Other cultures have **extended families**. In addition to the parents and children, there are the children's wives and husbands. It also includes the children's 25 children. In extended families, older people often help care for the children. They are respected for their knowledge and experience. They pass on traditions. Extended families are not as common as they once were. As people move to cities, nuclear families are 30 becoming more common.

✓ Reading Check

What is the most important part of any society?

_____

_____

Target Reading Skill

In the past, it was hard for people to move from one social class to another. Read the bracketed paragraph to find out if that has changed. Has it? How?

_____

_____

_____

Key Terms

society (suh SY uh tee) *n.* a group of people sharing a culture
social structure (SOH shul STRUK chur) *n.* a pattern of organized relationships among groups of people within a society
social class (SOH shul klas) *n.* a grouping of people based on rank or status
nuclear family (NOO klee ur FAM uh lee) *n.* a mother, a father, and their children
extended family (ek STEN did FAM uh lee) *n.* a family that includes several generations

What does the word *ethics* mean? Use the graphic organizer on page 38 to help you figure out what it means. Then write a definition below.

_____

_____

_____

Language

All cultures have language. Cultures depend on language. People learn their cultures through language. ✓

Language describes the things that are important to that culture. For example, English has words for
35 Christian and Jewish beliefs. Other languages do not have words for these beliefs because their speakers are not Christian or Jewish. But they have words for the beliefs of their religion.

In some countries, people speak more than one lan-
40 guage. Canada has two official languages, English and French. In the United States, you usually hear English, but you can also hear Spanish, Chinese, and other languages. India has 16 official languages, but people there speak more than 800 languages!
45 A country can have more than one culture when its people speak different languages. This is because they may have different festivals or different customs. They talk about different things.

Religion

Religion is another important part of every culture. It helps people make sense of the world. It provides comfort and hope in hard times. It helps answer questions about life and death. And it guides people in ethics, or how to act toward others. People of the same religion may practice their religion differently. ✓
55 Religious beliefs vary. Members of some religions believe in one God. Members of others believe in more than one god. But all religions have prayers and rituals. Every religion celebrates important places and times. All religions expect people to treat one another
60 well and to behave properly.

Review Questions

1. What is the difference between an extended family and a nuclear family?

_____

_____

2. What do all religions expect people to do?

_____

_____

Prepare to Read

Section 3 Cultural Change

Objectives

1. Explore how cultures change.
2. Learn how ideas spread from one culture to another.

Target Reading Skill

Recognize Words That Signal Sequence Signal words are words or phrases that prepare you for what is coming next. They are like following the directions in a recipe for baking a cake. When baking, you need to pay attention to the order of when ingredients are added, how long to mix or bake, and when to ask an adult to take something out of the oven.

When you read, look for words such as *first, next, then, later, before,* or *at that time.* They signal the order in which the events took place.

Vocabulary Strategy

Use Context to Clarify Meaning Sometimes you may read a word you recognize, but you aren't sure about its meaning. Many words have more than one meaning. What a word means depends on its context. Look for clues in the surrounding words or sentences. For example, the word *matter* has many meanings. You will find what meaning the author had in mind by looking at the context.

Some examples of *matter* are listed in the chart below.

Word	Definitions	Examples
matter	what all things are made of	It was made up of organic matter.
	subject of concern	It was a personal matter.
	material that is spoken or written	This package contains only printed matter.
	trouble	What is the matter?
	to be important	My grades matter to me.

How Cultures Change

1 All cultures change over time. Just look at the culture of blue jeans. They were invented in the United States. At first, only Americans wore them. But today, jeans are popular all over the world. This culture of clothing
5 changed.

Cultures are always changing. Culture is an entire way of life. A change in one part changes other parts. Changes in the natural environment, technology, and ideas all affect culture.

10 New technologies change a culture. During the 1800s and early 1900s, industry grew and factories spread. Americans moved from the countryside to the cities. Because people had to walk to work, they had to live close to the factories. Cities grew as a result.

15 The invention of the car in the late 1800s changed all this. By 1920, many Americans had cars. People could live farther from their jobs and drive to work. The idea of owning a house with a yard became more popular. That led to the growth of suburbs since the
20 mid-1900s. A new culture based on car travel began. ✓

Technology has changed the culture in other ways. Radio and television brought entertainment and news into homes. Today, instant information is part of our culture. Computers change how and where people
25 work. They even help people live longer. Doctors use computers to treat patients.

Cultural change has been going on for a long time. Controlling fire helped people survive colder climates. When people started to farm, they could stay in one place. Before that, they moved about in search of wild plants and animals.

How Ideas Spread

The airplane has made it easier for people to move all over the world. When they move, they bring new kinds of clothing and tools with them. They also bring
35 new ideas.

✓ Reading Check

How did the invention of cars change culture?

_____

_____

_____

◎ Target Reading Skill

What do the words *Before that*, in the bracketed paragraph, tell you about the sequence of events? Place the events in the paragraph in the order they took place.

1. _____

2. _____

3. _____

Ideas can travel to new places in other ways. People may buy something from another culture then learn to make it themselves. <u>They may learn from other cultures through written matter.</u> This movement of customs and ideas is called **cultural diffusion**.

Baseball began as an American sport, but today it is played all over the world. That is an example of cultural diffusion. The Japanese love baseball. But they have changed the game to fit their culture. These changes are an example of **acculturation**. Americans value competition. They focus on winning. A baseball game isn't over until one team wins. In Japan, a game can end in a tie. The Japanese focus on how well the game is played, not on winning.

For thousands of years, cultures changed slowly. People, ideas, and goods moved by foot, or wagon, or boat. Now things go much faster. Faxes and computers send information almost instantly. Magazines and television bring ideas and information from all over the world to any home. When ideas are shared quickly, culture changes quickly. ✓

Change can help, but it can also hurt. If things change too fast, people may feel that they are losing their culture. It is hard to bring back lost traditions. People are working to preserve their own cultures before it is too late. They want to save their artistic traditions, religious beliefs, and wisdom for future generations.

Review Questions

1. How did the car change where people live?

_____

_____

2. List two ways in which ideas travel from one culture to another.

_____

_____

Key Terms

cultural diffusion (KUL chur ul dih FYOO zhun) *n.* the movement of customs and ideas

acculturation (uh kul chur AY shun) *n.* the process of accepting new ideas and fitting them into a culture

The word *matter* is used in the underlined sentence. Find it and circle it. How is it used here? Copy the correct definition from the chart at the beginning of this section.

_____

_____

_____

✓ Reading Check

Why do ideas spread faster today?

_____

_____

_____

Chapter 4 Assessment

1. Ideas and ways of doing things are called
   A. environment.
   B. cultural traits.
   C. cultural landscape.
   D. institutions.

2. What is the name for the change from hunting and gathering to growing more food than farmers need?
   A. the Invention of Tools
   B. the Agricultural Revolution
   C. the Development of Civilizations
   D. the Industrial Revolution

3. What is the most important part of every society?
   A. social classes
   B. governments
   C. the family
   D. nations

4. People learn their cultures mainly through
   A. schools.
   B. government.
   C. religion.
   D. language.

5. Which of the following cultural changes is a result of the invention of the car?
   A. the growth of suburbs
   B. the move from the countryside to the nation's cities
   C. the loss of valuable traditions
   D. the speeding up of cultural change

Short Answer Question

Explain how playing baseball in Japan is an example of acculturation.

_____

_____

_____

_____

_____

CHAPTER 5

Prepare to Read

Section 1 Natural Resources

Objectives

1. Learn about natural resources.
2. Investigate energy.

Target Reading Skill

Identify Main Ideas Good readers look for the main idea of what they read. The main idea is the most important point. It is the one that includes all the other points, or details. Sometimes the main idea is stated in a sentence at the beginning, middle, or end of the paragraph.

The headings in a textbook give you information about the main idea. Think about the headings as you read the section. Try turning headings into questions to help you find the main idea. As you read, ask yourself, "What is this about?"

The first heading on the next page is What Are Natural Resources? Which of the sentences that follow the heading is the main idea? *Hint:* It is the sentence that answers the question that the heading asks.

Vocabulary Strategy

Using Word Origins Many English words are made from Greek roots, or word parts. When scientists need a new word they often use Greek roots.

In this chapter, you will read the word *geothermal*. It is made up of two Greek roots:

geo (from *gaia*, which means *earth*) + *therm* (which means *heat*)

Now that you know its Greek roots, can you figure out what *geothermal* means?

Other English words that are related to these Greek roots are *geography*, and *thermostat*. See if you can answer this. What is the name of the instrument a doctor uses to see how high your temperature is when you have a fever?

What Are Natural Resources?

1 Everything that people use is made with **natural resources**. Natural resources are things like water, minerals, and plants.

People use some resources just as they are found in
5 nature. Fresh water is one of these. But most resources must be changed first. Resources that must be changed or worked are called **raw materials**. For example, trees are the raw materials for paper and wood.

The world is filled with natural resources. But not
10 all resources are alike. There are two main groups.

Renewable resources can be replaced. Some are replaced naturally because of the way Earth works. Water is one of these. Earth has a steady supply of water because of the water cycle.

Some types of energy are renewable resources. Solar energy is a renewable resource. No matter how much of the sun's energy we use, there will always be more. The same is true for geothermal energy.

Living things such as plants and animals are also
20 renewable resources. With proper planning, people can have a steady supply of living resources. For example, timber companies can plant new trees to replace the ones they cut down.

The second major group of resources is called **non-**
25 **renewable resources**. They include most nonliving things, such as metal ores, most minerals, natural gas, and petroleum. These cannot be replaced. Coal, natural gas, and petroleum are called fossil fuels. Scientists think they were created from the remains of prehistoric
30 living things. In time, these fuels will run out. ✓

Target Reading Skill

Which sentence directly states the main idea of the bracketed paragraph? Circle the sentence.

✓ Reading Check

What is the difference between renewable and nonrenewable resources?

_____

_____

Key Terms

natural resources (NACH ur ul REE sawr siz) *n.* useful materials found in the environment

raw materials (raw muh TIHR ee ulz) *n.* natural resources that must be worked to be useful

renewable resources (rih NOO uh bul REE sawr siz) *n.* natural resources that can be replaced

nonrenewable resources (nahn rih NOO uh bul REE sawr siz) *n.* natural resources that cannot be replaced

However, many metals, minerals, and plastics can be recycled. The resource can be reused. The material hasn't been replaced, but recycling means we will use less of the resource.

A Special Resource: Energy

35 Many natural resources are sources of energy. People use energy from fossil fuels. They also use energy from the wind and the sun. Dams use the power of falling water to make hydroelectric power.

People in every country need energy. But energy
40 resources are not spread evenly around the world. Some areas have many energy resources. Others have few.

Countries like Canada and Saudi Arabia have more energy resources than they need. They sell some to
45 other countries. Countries like Japan and the United States cannot make as much energy as they use. They have to buy energy from other countries. ☑

Every day, people use more and more energy. There are not enough fossil fuels to meet energy needs in the
50 future. This means that people will have to find other kinds of energy.

Here are some ideas. Wind and solar energy are available. Geothermal energy is energy from the heat of Earth's interior. It will not run out. Biomass, or plant material, is a renewable source of energy.

Atomic energy uses radioactive materials. They are not renewable, but they are plentiful. Radioactive materials can be dangerous. On the other hand, atomic energy does not pollute the air.

60 Fossil fuels will last longer if people use less energy. New technologies can help. You may have seen hybrid cars. They use less gas. If people use less energy now, there will be more energy in the future.

Review Questions

1. Why are trees considered a renewable resource?

_____

_____

2. List two ways that people can use less energy.

_____

_____

✓ Reading Check

Why do some countries have to buy energy?

_____

_____

_____

Vocabulary Strategy

The word *energy* comes from a Greek root that means *work* or *activity*. The bracketed paragraph describes several different kinds of energy. Pick one and write a sentence that describes how that form of energy works for us.

_____

_____

_____

_____

Prepare to Read

Section 2 Land Use

Objectives

1. Study the link between land use and culture.
2. Investigate the link between land use and economic activity.
3. Explore changes in land use.

Target Reading Skill

Identify Supporting Details The main idea of a paragraph or section is its most important point. The main idea is supported by details. Details explain the main idea. They may give additional facts or examples. They can tell you *what, where, why, how much,* or *how many.*

In the second paragraph on the next page, the first sentence states the main idea:

Even in similar environments, people may use land differently.

To find the details, ask yourself, "*How* do people use land differently?"

Vocabulary Strategy

Using Word Origins Many English words came from other languages. For example, many words have been made by combining Latin word parts. In fact, all of the key terms in this section are based on Latin words. We will look at one of them now. You can use a dictionary to find the Latin word parts of the others.

Let's take a closer look at the word *manufacturing*. It is made up of two Latin word parts:

manu ("hand") + *factura* ("making")

To manufacture means to make something by hand. What do you call a place where things are manufactured? *Hint:* The word begins with the Latin word part for *making.*

Section 2 Summary

Land Use and Culture

[1] How people use their land depends on their culture. People may use land differently because their cultures have developed in different **environments**. The Inuit live in a cold, arctic climate. It is too cold to grow crops. [5] The Inuit use their land mainly for hunting wild animals. The Japanese live in a warmer, wetter climate. Their main crop is rice. It grows well in Japan's climate.

Even in similar environments, people may use land differently. That is because they have different cultural [10] traits. Georgia has a climate like Japan. But farmers in Georgia don't grow rice. Instead, Georgians raise chickens and grow crops like peanuts. The Japanese eat rice at nearly every meal. But Americans eat more meat and peanut butter. ✓

[15] Cultures change landscapes. Thousands of years ago, Western Europe was covered with forests. Then farming cultures began to spread across the region. People cleared forests to use the land for farming. Today, most of the land is open fields and pastures.

[20] Different cultures respond differently to their environments. Much of the western United States has a dry climate. People use pipes and sprinklers to water crops. The Middle East also has a dry climate. But Middle Eastern farmers use qanats, or brick irrigation [25] channels, to water their crops. Both cultures live in similar environments. But they do things differently.

Land Use and Economic Activity

There are three ways of making a living. Geographers have grouped these ways into three stages or levels.

In the first stage, people use land and resources directly to make products. They may hunt, cut wood, mine, or fish. They may herd animals or raise crops. Most of the world's land is used for first-level activities. In developed countries, such as the United States, only a few people make a living in this way. ✓

Key Term

environment (en VY run munt) *n.* natural surroundings

Even though the climate in Georgia is good for growing rice, farmers in Georgia don't grow rice. Why?

_____

_____

_____

⟳ Target Reading Skill

List three details in the bracketed paragraph about first-level activities.

1. _____

_____

2. _____

_____

3. _____

_____

✓ **Reading Check**

How is most of the world's land used?

_____

_____

_____

At the second stage, people process the products of the first-level activities. For example, they turn trees into lumber, or wool from sheep into sweaters. Most second-level activity is **manufacturing**. Manufacturing is important in developed countries, especially in cities.

Third-level activities are also known as services. While services do not produce goods, services may help deliver or sell goods. Many businesses offer services. They include doctors, bankers, <u>automobile</u> repair workers, and clerks. Services are often found in cities, especially in developed countries.

Changes in Land Use

During **colonization**, the newcomers may change the landscape. If farmers move to an area without farms, they will create farms. As people find new ways of making a living, they will start using the land in new ways, too.

Crops such as wheat and grapes were unknown in the Americas before colonization. So were animals such as cows and chickens. When Europeans came, they cleared large areas for their crops and animals. ✓

Since the 1800s, **industrialization** has changed landscapes in many countries. Cities have grown around factories. Since 1900, suburbs have spread. The spread of cities and suburbs is known as sprawl.

Review Questions

1. What are second-level activities?

_____

_____

2. How are second-level activities different from third-level activities?

_____

_____

Key Terms

manufacturing (man yoo FAK chur ing) *n.* the large-scale production of goods by hand or by machine

colonization (kahl uh nuh ZAY shun) *n.* the movement of settlers and their culture to a new country

industrialization (in dus tree ul ih ZAY shun) *n.* the growth of machine-powered production in an economy

---

Vocabulary Strategy

The word *automobile* combines the Greek word *auto* ("self") and the Latin word *mobile* ("to move").

Try this one yourself. If a biography is the story of someone's life, what is an *autobiography*?

_____

_____

_____

✓ Reading Check

How did European colonization change the American landscape?

_____

_____

_____

Prepare to Read

Section 3
People's Effect on the Environment

Objectives

1. Investigate how first-level activities affect the environment.
2. Explore how second- and third-level activities affect the environment.

Target Reading Skill

Identify Implied Main Ideas Have you ever had a conversation with someone where you had to pay close attention to what they were saying? Maybe they were telling you all the details about a family event, but what they were actually talking about was how important their family is to them.

Sometimes reading is like that. The main idea is not stated directly. Instead, the details in a paragraph or section add up to a main idea. In a case like this, we say the main idea is implied. It is up to you to put the details together. You will then be able to see the main idea.

For example, the details in the first paragraph on the next page add up to this main idea:

First-level activities are necessary for human survival, but they reshape the environment.

Vocabulary Strategy

Using Word Origins Many English words have been made from Greek word parts. Some of these word parts are names for new inventions. For example, the ancient Greeks used the word part "tele" to mean *far off*. They used the word part "phone" to mean *sound*. We put those word parts together to give us *telephone*. Now that is something the ancient Greeks never imagined!

There are many other words that use each of these roots. Below is a partial list.

telecommunication	telescope
telecommute	television
telegraph	headphone
telemarketing	microphone

First-Level Activities

1 In first-level activities people use raw materials to get food and resources to live. In the process the environment changes. For example, crops replace wild plants.

As countries grow, new ways of farming are tried. 5 In the Great Plains of North America, farms have replaced land where buffalo roamed. In the Netherlands, people have drained wetlands to create dry farmland. Creating new farmland destroyed wild grasslands and wetlands. But the new land has fed 10 millions of people. ✓

Agriculture, forestry, and fishing provide resources that people need to live. But they sometimes hurt the environment. Wood is needed to build houses. But cutting down too many trees can lead to **deforestation**. 15 Animals that depend on the forest may also suffer. Deforestation can lead to a loss of **biodiversity**.

Farmers use fertilizers to grow crops. More people can be fed. But rain washes the chemicals into streams. This harms fish and the people who eat the fish.

20 The key is to find a balance. Around the world, people are working to find ways of meeting their needs without hurting the environment. One way is to plant tree farms. Or farmers can use natural methods to grow crops. Or they can use chemicals that will not 25 damage waterways. Fishers can catch fish that are more plentiful.

Second- and Third-Level Activities

Over the years industry, or second-level activities, and services, or third-level activities have changed deserts, prairies, and forests. These activities have created a landscape of cities, factories, offices, highways, and shopping malls.

✓ Reading Check

What is one way people have created new farmland?

_____

_____

_____

⟳ Target Reading Skill

In one sentence, state what all the details in the bracketed paragraph are about.

_____

_____

> **Key Terms**
>
> **deforestation** (dee fawr uh STAY shun) *n.* a loss of forest cover in a region
>
> **biodiversity** (by oh duh VUR suh tee) *n.* a richness of different kinds of living things in a region

Industrial and service activities provide most of the jobs in developed countries. The main purpose of some of these activities is to change the environment. **Civil**
35 **engineering** builds structures that change the landscape. For example, dams create lakes that cover large areas with water. They provide water for farms and cities. They also protect areas from flooding.

Other industrial and service activities have side
40 effects on the environment. Industries use large amounts of resources. They release industrial wastes into the environment. Service activities require the building of roads, telephone lines, and power lines. ✓

Industry is not the only source of **pollution**. Our
45 own trash may pollute the soil, water, or air. Exhaust from cars and trucks causes air pollution. Air pollution may cause harmful changes in our climate.

Working together, people can find solutions to these problems. One is to use more fuel-efficient cars. Cars
50 that burn less fuel create less air pollution. Renewable energy resources pollute less than fossil fuels.

Waste can be recycled to reduce the amount that must be burned or dumped. It also saves natural resources. For example, paper can be recycled. Then
55 fewer trees have to be cut down to make new paper.

Finding ways to solve environmental problems is one of the greatest challenges of our time.

Review Questions

1. How does deforestation hurt the environment?

_____

_____

2. List ways in which industrial and service activities change landscapes.

_____

_____

Key Terms

civil engineering (SIV ul en juh NIHR ing) *n.* technology for building structures that alter the landscape, such as dams, roads, and bridges

pollution (puh LOO shun) *n.* waste, usually man-made, that makes the air, water, or soil less clean

1. Resources that must be worked are called
   A. renewable resources.
   B. nonrenewable resources.
   C. recyclable materials.
   D. raw materials.

2. Which of the following is a renewable resource?
   A. water
   B. metal ore
   C. natural gas
   D. coal

3. Manufacturing is an example of
   A. a first-level activity.
   B. a second-level activity.
   C. a third-level activity.
   D. all of the above

4. Cutting down too many trees can lead to
   A. biodiversity.
   B. deforestation.
   C. pollution.
   D. loss of biomass.

5. In developed countries, most of the jobs are in
   A. agriculture.
   B. first-level activities.
   C. industrial and service activities.
   D. first- and third-level activities.

Short Answer Question

List three ways that people affect the environment.

_____

_____

_____

_____

_____

Europe and Russia

Prepare to Read

Section 1 Land and Water

Objectives

1. Learn about the size, location, and population of Europe and Russia.
2. Examine the major landforms of Europe and Russia.
3. Find out about the waterways of Europe and Russia.

Target Reading Skill

Set a Purpose for Reading When you set a purpose for reading, you give yourself a focus. Think of this focus, or purpose, as a pair of eyeglasses that will help you read more clearly.

Before you read this section, look at the objectives above, then flip through the next two pages and read the headings. Use this information to set a purpose for reading the section. What are you curious about? What would you like to know about the geography of Europe and Russia? Read to satisfy that curiosity—that's your purpose for reading.

Vocabulary Strategy

Using Context to Determine Meaning When you come across new words in your textbook, or in this workbook, they are often defined for you. Sometimes the definition appears in a separate sentence. Sometimes there may be a brief definition in the same sentence. The word *or* may be used to introduce the definition. Look at the following examples.

> The Central Uplands are a region of highlands, made up of mountains and plateaus. *Plateaus are large raised areas of mostly level land bordered on one or more sides by steep slopes or cliffs.*

> The people of the Netherlands created polders, or *patches of new land.*

The underlined words are defined in context. In these examples, the definitions appear in italics. Look for definitions in the context as you come across unfamiliar words in your reading.

Size, Location, and Population

Europe and Russia are parts of Eurasia. Eurasia is the world's largest landmass. It is made up of two continents—Europe and Asia. The country of Russia stretches over both continents. Much of Europe and nearly all of Russia are located farther north than the United States. ✓

Europe is a small continent, but it has 44 different countries. Most of these countries are small. Russia, on the other hand, is the largest country in the world. Most European countries have a much higher **population density** than most other countries in the world. Russia, on the other hand, has a very low population density.

Major Landforms

The continent of Europe forms a **peninsula**, or a body of land nearly surrounded by water. The European peninsula juts out into the Atlantic Ocean. Because of this, Europe has many good harbors. Much of Russia lies on the Arctic Ocean, which is frozen most of the year.

Europe has four major land regions. See the chart below to learn about these regions.

Europe's Land Regions	
Region	**Characteristics**
Northwestern Highlands	• in far north • old mountains with thin soil
North European Plains	• covers more than half of Europe • now best farmland and large cities
Central Uplands	• highlands made of mountains and plateaus • not good for farming, but has other uses
Alpine Mountain System	• in southern Europe • includes the Alps

Key Terms

population density (pahp yuh LAY shun DEN suh tee) *n.* the average number of people living in a square mile or a square kilometer

peninsula (puh NIN suh luh) *n.* a land area nearly surrounded by water

plateau (pla TOH) *n.* a large raised area of mostly level land bordered on one or more sides by steep slopes or cliffs

✓ **Reading Check**

What is the largest landmass in the world?

_____

_____

_____

Target Reading Skill

If your purpose is to learn about the geography of Europe and Russia, how does the chart help you meet your goal?

_____

_____

_____

Europe and western Russia share the North European Plains. Russia's largest cities and most of its industries are located there. The Ural Mountains are on the eastern border of the North European Plains. East of the Urals is a region known as Siberia. Few people live there because the climate is so harsh. ☑

Waterways of Europe and Russia

Rivers and lakes provide water and transportation. The Rhine River, Danube River, and Volga River are the major rivers of Europe and Russia.

The Rhine River starts in the Alps in Switzerland. The Rhine then winds through forests and plains. Canals and **tributaries** allow the Rhine to reach far into Western Europe.

The Danube is Europe's second-longest river. It begins in the Black Forest region of western Germany. It passes through nine countries and ends in the Black Sea of Central Europe.

The longest river in Europe is Russia's Volga River. It flows through western Russia and empties into the Caspian Sea. Unfortunately, the Volga River freezes for three months of each year. During the winter, it is not **navigable**, or clear enough for ships to travel through.

Europe has many rivers, but contains few lakes. Russia, on the other hand, has a huge number of lakes. Lake Baikal, the world's largest freshwater lake, is located in southern Russia. ☑

Review Questions

1. How does the land size of Europe differ from the land size of Russia?

_____

_____

2. Why is the Volga River not navigable year-round?

_____

_____

> **Key Terms**
>
> **tributary** (TRIB yoo tehr ee) *n.* a river or stream that flows into a larger river
> **navigable** (NAV ih guh bul) *adj.* wide and deep enough for ships to travel through

✓ Reading Check

Where is Siberia located?

_____

_____

_____

Vocabulary Strategy

The term *navigable* is defined in context. Circle its definition. *Hint:* Look for the word *or*.

✓ Reading Check

Where is the world's largest freshwater lake located?

_____

_____

_____

Prepare to Read

Section 2 Climate and Vegetation

Objectives

1. Find out about the wide range of climates in Europe and Russia.
2. Learn about the major climate regions of Europe and Russia.
3. Examine the natural vegetation regions of Europe and Russia.

Target Reading Skill

Predict Making predictions about what you will learn is one way to set a purpose for reading. It also helps you remember what you have read.

Before you begin reading, preview the section. Look at the section title and objectives above, then the headings. Also preview any maps. Then predict what the section will tell you. Based on your preview, you will probably predict that this section will tell you about the climate and vegetation of Europe and Russia.

List two facts that you expect to learn about the climate and vegetation of Europe and Russia.

Prediction 1: _____

Prediction 2: _____

As you read, check your predictions. Were they right? If they were not very accurate, you may need to pay closer attention while you preview the section.

Vocabulary Strategy

Using Context to Determine Meaning Sometimes a word might sound familiar, but its meaning is still a mystery to you. When this happens, it's time to put on your detective hat. Search for clues from the words, phrases, and sentences that surround the familiar-sounding word. Sometimes, a word with a very similar meaning is used nearby. Substitute the word *climate* for the underlined phrase in the paragraph below. Now do you know what *climate* means?

> An area's distance from an ocean or a sea helps explain its *climate*. Areas that are near an ocean or a sea usually have fairly mild <u>weather from year to year</u>. Areas that are far from the ocean often have more extreme weather.

Section 2 Summary

A Wide Range of Climates

Areas that are near an ocean or a sea have milder weather year-round than areas of the same latitude that are far from the ocean often have more extreme weather. Look at the map below and find the Gulf Stream. Notice that it becomes the North Atlantic Current as it crosses the Atlantic Ocean. This powerful ocean current brings mild weather to northwestern Europe by carrying warm water and winds from the Gulf of Mexico. Winds blowing across the ocean pick up moisture that turns into rain.

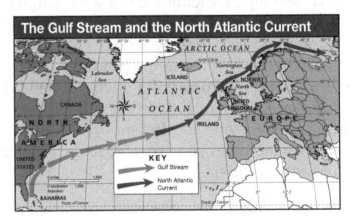

The Gulf Stream and the North Atlantic Current

In Europe, areas west of mountains receive a lot of rain. Areas east of mountains get less rain. The mountains cause this difference. As winds rise up a mountain, they cool and drop their moisture. The air is dry by the time it reaches the other side of the mountain. Areas on the side away from the wind are in a **rain shadow**. Oceans and mountains both affect the climates of Europe and Russia. ☑

Major Climate Regions

There are four main climate regions in Europe and Russia. The humid continental climate region has long, cold winters and hot summers. The subarctic climate region has short summers and long, cold winters. Subarctic regions include places like Irkutsk, Russia. The far north areas of Europe and Russia have an arctic climate.

Key Term

rain shadow (rayn SHAD oh) *n.* the area on the dry, sheltered side of a mountain, which receives little rainfall

---

It is very cold in these areas all year round. On the other hand, southeastern Europe and southwestern Russia have a semiarid climate. These areas have hot temperatures and very little rainfall. Europe also has three moderate climate regions that Russia does not have. ☑

Natural Vegetation Regions

There are also many different kinds of natural vegetation, or plant life, in Europe and Russia. The four main vegetation zones in the region are *forest*, *grassland*, *Mediterranean*, and *tundra*.

Much of Europe's vegetation is forest. Northern Europe has forests of large evergreen trees. Most of western and central Europe has forests of trees that lose their leaves in the fall. Russia also has many forests. The Taiga (TY guh) in Siberia is the world's largest forest. ☑

In Europe, grasslands once covered large parts of the North European Plain. Today, the land is used for farming. In Russia, the grasslands are called **steppes**. The soil of the steppes is rich and good for farming.

Mediterranean vegetation is a mix of trees, scrub, and smaller plants.

Northern parts of Europe and Russia have a cold, dry region called the **tundra**. No trees grow on the tundra, and the ground is covered with snow for most of the year. The ground contains **permafrost**. When the top layer thaws, grasses, mosses, and other plant life grow quickly.

Review Questions

1. What is the climate like in areas close to an ocean?

_____

_____

2. Name two vegetation zones of Europe and Russia.

_____

_____

Key Terms

steppes (steps) *n.* the grasslands of fertile soil in Russia
tundra (TUN druh) *n.* a cold, dry, treeless region covered with snow for most of the year
permafrost (PUR muh frawst) *n.* permanent layer of frozen ground below the top layer of soil.

✓ **Reading Check**

Name the four main climate regions of Europe and Russia.

_____

_____

_____

_____

✓ **Reading Check**

Where is the world's largest forest located?

_____

_____

_____

Vocabulary Strategy

From context clues, write a definition of the word *tundra*. Circle words or phrases in the text that helped you write your definition.

tundra means:

_____

_____

_____

Prepare to Read

Section 3
Resources and Land Use

Objectives

1. Learn about the natural resources of Western Europe.
2. Find out about the natural resources of Eastern Europe.
3. Examine Russia's natural resources.

Target Reading Skill

Preview and Ask Questions Before you read this section, preview the section objectives shown above. Then look at the title and headings on the next two pages to see what the section is about. What do you think are the most important concepts in this section? How can you tell?

After you preview the section, write two questions that will help you understand or remember important concepts or facts in the section. For example, you might ask yourself:

- What natural resources are located in Europe?
- What types of natural resources does Russia have?

Find the answers to your questions as you read.

Keep asking questions about what you think will come next. Does the text answer your questions? Were you able to predict what would be covered under each heading?

Vocabulary Strategy

Using Context to Determine Meaning Using context is like being a detective looking for clues. Sometimes you can pick up clues about an unfamiliar word's meaning from the words, phrases, and sentences around it. The underlined words in the paragraph below give clues to the meaning of the word *loess*.

> Over thousands of years, winds have deposited *loess* on the North European Plain. With this <u>rich, dustlike soil</u> and plenty of rain and moderate temperatures, European farmers grow abundant crops.

> Loess is a type of rich, dustlike soil. The underlined phrase told you that information.

Section 3 Summary

Resources of Western Europe

1 Western Europe is a wealthy region. It also helps lead the world's economic development. There are many reasons why this region has so much wealth and success. One reason is that Western Europe has many

5 natural resources. These natural resources include fertile soil, water, and fuels.

Soil is important for growing food. Much of Western Europe is covered with rich, fertile soil. Wind helps create the fertile soil of the North European Plain. Over

10 thousands of years, winds have deposited **loess** on the plain. Along with plenty of rain and moderate temperatures, this has helped European farmers grow abundant crops.

Water is another important resource in Western

15 Europe. People need water to drink and for farming. Water is also used to make electricity. The force of rushing water spins machines called turbines (TUR bynz). These turbines create **hydroelectric power.** ✔

Fossil fuels are another important natural resource.

20 Industries use fossil fuel deposits as a source of energy. The United Kingdom and Norway have many deposits of natural gas, oil, and coal. Long ago, remains of ancient plants and animals formed these deposits.

Resources of Eastern Europe

Eastern Europe has natural resources like those of West-

25 ern Europe. Ukraine, a large country in Eastern Europe, has coal deposits. It also has oil and natural gas. However, the most important resource in Ukraine is probably its soil. The region's black soil is very fertile. Because of the fertile soil, farming is very important in Ukraine. ✔

Key Terms

loess (LOH es) *n.* a type of rich, dustlike soil
hydroelectric power (hy droh ee LEK trik POW ur) *n.* the power generated by water-driven turbines
fossil fuel (FAHS ul FYOO ul) *n.* a source of energy that forms from the remains of ancient plants and animals

---

Target Reading Skill

Ask and answer a question about Western Europe's natural resources.

Question:

_____

_____

Answer:

_____

_____

✓ Reading Check

How is hydroelectric power generated?

_____

_____

_____

Vocabulary Strategy

Look at the term *fossil fuels* in the underlined sentences. The term is not defined for you. But there are clues to what it means. Circle the words or phrases that help you learn its meaning. In your own words, write down the meaning of the term.

_____

_____

_____

✓ Reading Check

What important natural resources are located in Ukraine?

_____

_____

_____

Resources of Russia

30   Russia has many more natural resources than the United States does. But Russia's harsh climate, huge size, and few navigable rivers have made it difficult to turn the country's resources into wealth. Russia has few places fit for farming. Most places lack one or more of 35 the key elements for farming: favorable climate, good soil, and plentiful water.

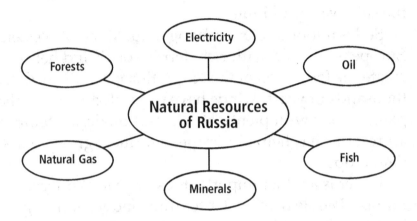

    Many of Russia's natural resources are located in Siberia, which is far away from the population and industrial centers of the country. Getting these resour- 40 ces from Siberia is not easy. Siberia's rivers flow away from major cities and are frozen part of the year. Pipelines carry oil and natural gas. Railroads carry coal. They have to transport these resources to the industrial centers in Russia. ✔

45   Collecting the natural resources causes another problem—protecting the environment. Some of the world's worst cases of pollution are found in Russia, especially in Siberia.

Review Questions

1. How is water used as a natural resource in Western Europe?

_____

_____

2. Why has Russia not been able to use its resources as effectively as Western Europe?

_____

_____

✓ Reading Check

Where are many of Russia's natural resources located?

_____

_____

_____

Chapter 6 Assessment

1. A land area nearly surrounded by water is known as a
   A. peninsula.
   B. plateau.
   C. tributary.
   D. loess.

2. Where are Russia's largest cities and most of its industries located?
   A. in the Northwestern Highlands
   B. in the North European Plains
   C. in the Central Uplands
   D. in the Alpine Mountain System

3. Which of the following describes the subarctic climate region of Europe and Russia?
   A. This region has hot temperatures and little rainfall.
   B. This region has long, cold winters and hot summers.
   C. This region has hot summers and mild, rainy winters.
   D. This region has short summers and long, cold winters.

4. What kind of plant life grows in the tundra?
   A. evergreen trees
   B. grasslands
   C. grasses and mosses
   D. a mix of trees, scrub, and smaller plants

5. Why has it been difficult for Russia to turn its natural resources into wealth?
   A. Russia has very few deposits of natural resources.
   B. Most of Russia's natural resources are located far away in Siberia.
   C. Many of its resources, such as the forests, were used up long ago.
   D. Pipelines to carry oil still need to be built.

Short Answer Question
How does the North Atlantic Current affect the climate of northwestern Europe?

_____

_____

_____

_____

Prepare to Read

Section 1
From Ancient Greece to the Middle Ages

Objectives

1. Learn how the heritage of ancient Greece influences life today.
2. Discover the glory of the ancient Roman Empire.
3. Learn about Europe in the Middle Ages.

Target Reading Skill

Reread Rereading is a strategy that can help you to understand words and ideas in the text. Rereading is like watching a video and rewinding the tape to see the action you missed.

If you do not understand a certain passage, reread it to look for connections among the words and sentences. Put together the facts that you do understand. See if you can find the main idea. For example, rereading the first paragraph on the next page can make it clear that the Greek idea of democracy influenced later civilizations.

Vocabulary Strategy

Using Word Parts Words are often made up of different parts. When you come across an unfamiliar word in your reading, you can figure out the meaning of the word by looking at its parts. Two types of word parts are prefixes and suffixes. A prefix is a word part attached to the beginning of a word. A suffix is a word part attached to the end of a word.

Take a close look at the parts that make up the word *independent*. The prefix *in-* means "not." The root *depend* means "rely." The suffix *–ent* means "one who does an action." From these word parts, you can figure out that *independent* means "one who does **not** depend or rely."

Here are some other common prefixes and suffixes, their meanings, and examples.

	Meaning	Examples
Prefixes		
un-	not	uncertainty, unable
trans-	across	translate, transport
Suffixes		
-ism	act or practice of	feudalism, manorialism
-ation	action or process	obligation, occupation

Section 1 Summary

The Greek Heritage

The ancient Greeks were Europe's first great thinkers, historians, poets, and writers. They invented new ideas about how the world worked and how people should live. One idea was democracy. In a **democracy**, citizens, not a king or other ruler, govern themselves. In ancient times, Greece had more than a hundred **city-states**. One of the most famous Greek city-states was Athens. Democracy in ancient Greece was not the same as the democracy we practice today in the United States. Still, the Greek belief that citizens should have a voice in their own government gave the people in later civilizations a great idea to build on.

Alexander the Great helped spread the ideas of the Greeks. He conquered many lands. In all his new lands, 15 he established Greek cities, the Greek language, and Greek ideas. At the time of Alexander's death, Greek culture linked the entire Mediterranean world. ✔

The Glory of Ancient Rome

The Roman Empire covered a huge area, and Romans built magnificent cities and structures. <u>They also built</u> 20 <u>one of the most outstanding transportation networks</u> <u>ever made.</u> Built over 2,000 years ago, many of these roads are still in use today.

For about 200 years, Rome was the most powerful state in Europe and in the Mediterranean. One of 25 Rome's greatest gifts to the world was a system of written laws.

Roman emperors allowed a certain amount of religious freedom as long as everyone obeyed Roman law. Those who didn't obey were often put to death. In 30 about A.D. 30, a spiritual leader named Jesus of Nazareth traveled and preached throughout the region. He

---

Key Terms

democracy (dih MAHK ruh see) *n.* a kind of government in which citizens govern themselves
city-state (SIH tee stayt) *n.* a city with its own government that was both a city and an independent state

---

Target Reading Skill

Reread the bracketed paragraph. What ancient Greek idea about government influenced people in later times?

_____

_____

_____

✓ Reading Check

Who was Alexander the Great?

_____

_____

_____

Vocabulary Strategy

What does the word *transportation* mean in the underlined sentence? The word contains a prefix and a suffix. Identify the different parts of the word and write them on the lines below. Use the chart on the previous page to help you. Finally, write the meaning of the word. *Hint: port* means "carry."

prefix _____

suffix _____

transportation means:

_____

became known as Jesus Christ. After the Romans put Jesus to death, his followers spread his teachings. They became known as Christians. At first, they were treated
35 poorly by the Romans. But later, when the emperor Constantine became a Christian, Christianity became the official religion of the Roman Empire.

Over time, the Roman Empire grew too large for one person to govern. It split into eastern and western
40 branches. The western branch collapsed in A.D. 476 when invaders attacked Rome. ✓

Europe in the Middle Ages

The collapse of the Roman Empire caused problems in western Europe. During the **Middle Ages**, Europeans needed a way to restore order and organize their society.
45 They developed **feudalism**. In this system, the king held the highest position. He promised to make sure his kingdom was safe. Nobles pledged loyalty to him. In return, they received land. Most people were serfs. They worked on the nobles' land. In return, they received
50 some crops and protection. This economic system is called manorialism. ✓

The eastern Roman Empire did not have feudal kingdoms. It stayed together as the Byzantine Empire until the 1400s. People there followed the Orthodox
55 Christian Church. The church was an important part of life in the Middle Ages. Religion helped give people a sense of security and community.

Review Questions

1. What were some of the important achievements of the ancient Romans?

_____

_____

2. How did manorialism work during the Middle Ages?

_____

_____

> **Key Terms**
>
> **Middle Ages** (MID ul AY juz) *n.* the time between the ancient and modern times, about A.D. 500–1500
> **feudalism** (FYOOD ul iz um) *n.* a system in which land was owned by lords but held by vassals in return for their loyalty

Prepare to Read

Section 2
Renaissance and the Age of Revolution

Objectives

1. Discover what the Renaissance was like at its peak.
2. Examine the effects of trade and strong rulers in the Renaissance.
3. Learn about revolutions in government and science in the 1600s and 1700s.

Target Reading Skill

Paraphrase When you paraphrase, you put something into your own words. Paraphrasing can help you understand what you have read. Putting ideas into your own words will also help you remember what you have read.

For example, read these two sentences: "Stories about Marco Polo's world travels were published in a book called *The Travels of Marco Polo.* Two hundred years later, Marco Polo's book inspired Christopher Columbus, another explorer." You could paraphrase the two sentences this way: "Marco Polo wrote about his world travels in a book that later inspired Christopher Columbus."

As you read, paraphrase the information following each heading. Use as few words as possible.

Vocabulary Strategy

Using Word Parts As you learned in the last section, a prefix is a word part attached to the beginning of a word to make a new word. The new word combines the meaning of the prefix with the meaning of the original word.

Some common prefixes are listed below, along with their meanings and examples. Learning to identify prefixes, and knowing what they mean, will help you figure out the meaning of unfamiliar words.

Prefix	Meaning	Example
re-	again, back	return, reappear
dis-	not	distrust, disbelief
ex-	out	explore, explain

Glories of the Renaissance

1 In the 1300s, new ideas that began in Italy swept across Europe. People had time and money to enjoy art and learning. This time period in European history is called the **Renaissance**.

Renaissance thinkers looked to the past to understand their world better. They re-examined the ideas of Greek and Roman thinkers. People learned from the art and literature of the ancient world.

Renaissance thinkers also began to think about 10 improving their world, rather than hoping for a better life after death. This new approach to knowledge was called humanism. Humanistic thinkers emphasized the importance of human nature. They believed in human abilities. Humanism affected every part of Renaissance 15 life, even the arts. During the Renaissance, people came to see art as a way to better understand life. Also, Renaissance ideas were able to spread more quickly because of the invention of the printing press in 1450. ✓

More Trade, Stronger Rulers

During the Renaissance, traders began to travel outside Europe more often. They made a lot of money by trading in gold, ivory, and slaves. Also, traders and merchants formed a new middle class. In 1492, Christopher Columbus landed in the Americas and claimed the lands for Spain. Other Spanish and European explorers raced to the Americas in search of wealth. Much of the wealth went to European **monarchs**. With this wealth, monarchies no longer needed feudal lords. Monarchs became even wealthier from taxes paid by this new middle class of merchants and traders. Kings, such as Louis XIV of France, seized complete power over their people. ✓

Vocabulary Strategy

The word below appears in the first bracketed paragraph. How does the prefix *re-* tell you what the Renaissance thinkers did to understand their world better? *Hint:* Use the chart on the previous page.

re-examined

_____

_____

_____

✓ Reading Check

How did humanism affect the arts?

_____

_____

_____

Target Reading Skill

Paraphrase the second bracketed paragraph. In your paraphrase, use as few words as possible to tell how trade increased and rulers became stronger.

_____

_____

_____

✓ Reading Check

What were two effects of trade in the Americas?

1._____

2._____

Key Terms

Renaissance (REN uh sahns) *n.* a period of European history that included the rebirth of interest in learning and art
monarch (MAHN urk) *n.* the ruler of a kingdom or empire

Revolutions in Government

The English Revolution
• People believed that kings should not have all the power. • Parliament went to war with the king, tried him in court, and had him put to death.

The American Revolution
• In 1776, the 13 **colonies** in North America rebelled against the British king because they felt the laws were unfair. • The colonists defeated the British and formed the United States.

The French Revolution
• In 1789, the French people used violence to overthrow their government. • The French Revolution created chaos in France. It also inspired new ideas about political and economic change. ✓

The 1600s and 1700s are often called the Age of Revolution. During this period of **revolution** the way Europeans thought and lived changed. It was the beginning of the modern age of science and democracy began.

✓ **Reading Check**

What revolutions took place during the 1600s and 1700s?

_____

_____

_____

Revolutions in Science

For centuries, religious faith had controlled how Europeans saw the world. The ideas of humanism and the Renaissance brought changes to the field of science as well as in government and the arts. Scientists began to observe nature carefully and record only what they saw. Then they based their theories on facts, instead of religious beliefs. This change in outlook is called the Scientific Revolution. Some of the greatest advances were in the fields of chemistry and medicine. Isaac Newton invented a new branch of mathematics called calculus (KAL kyoo lus). He also created a number of laws about how the moon and planets move. ✓

✓ **Reading Check**

What did Isaac Newton invent?

_____

_____

_____

Review Questions

1. What was humanism?

_____

_____

2. Why are the 1600s and 1700s called the Age of Revolution?

_____

_____

Key Terms

revolution (rev uh LOO shun) *n.* a far-reaching change
colony (KAHL uh nee) *n.* a territory ruled by another nation

Prepare to Read

Section 3
Industrial Revolution and Nationalism

Objectives

1. Learn how the Industrial Revolution changed peoples' lives.
2. Examine how nationalism and war can be related.

Target Reading Skill

Summarize Have you ever taken a message for someone? When you take a message, you jot down the most important information and leave out the minor details. Summarizing is a lot like taking a message. When you summarize, you use your own words to restate the main points. A good summary includes important events and details. It also keeps the main ideas or facts in the correct order. Like a message, a summary is also shorter than the original text. Read the following paragraph, then read the summary of the text.

Original paragraph:

Weaving, or making cloth from threads or yarns, is one of the oldest crafts in the world. It was also the first to take advantage of the inventions that fed the Industrial Revolution. First water, and then steam, powered the first textile factories and their machines.

Summary:

Weaving is one of the oldest crafts in the world. It was also the first to use the new inventions of the Industrial Revolution.

Vocabulary Strategy

Using Word Parts As you learned in the first section, a suffix is a word part attached to the end of a word to make a new word. The new word combines the meaning of the suffix with the meaning of the original word.

Some common suffixes are listed below, along with their meanings and examples. Learning to identify suffixes, and knowing what they mean, will help you figure out the meaning of unfamiliar words.

Suffix	Meaning	Example
-ism	act or practice of	imperialism, nationalism
-ive	inclined to	destructive, inventive
-ance	state or quality of	alliance

Section 3 Summary

The Industrial Revolution

In the 1800s, a revolution occurred in the ways goods were made and in the ways people lived. This life-changing period was called the **Industrial Revolution**. Before the 1800s, people made what they needed by hand. During the Industrial Revolution, goods started to be made by machines in factories.

The first machines were invented in Great Britain to speed up the weaving of **textiles**, or cloth products. Large factories housed the machines. In a factory, each worker had a specific job that he or she did over and over again. Goods could be made more quickly and cheaply.

The Industrial Revolution changed life in positive and negative ways. New inventions made everyday life easier. Transportation and communications improved. Many people, however, left their farms to work in factories. Cities grew rapidly. This meant that people lived in crowded and unclean conditions where diseases quickly spread. Workers earned low wages and worked in unsafe conditions.

The Industrial Revolution also spurred changes in government. Many European nations followed the policy of **imperialism**. That is, they took over other countries and turned them into colonies. European countries competed for new colonies in Africa and parts of Asia. Colonies provided the raw materials—such as cotton, wood, and metals—that industry needed. Because of this, the late 1800s are called the Age of Imperialism. ☑

Key Terms

Industrial Revolution (in DUS tree ul rev uh LOO shun) *n.* the life-changing period in the 1800s when products began to be made by machines in factories

textile (TEKS tyl) *n.* a cloth product

imperialism (im PIHR ee ul iz um) *n.* the pursuit of political and economic control over foreign territories

---

Target Reading Skill

Summarize the bracketed paragraph. Be sure to include the main point. Also include three important details about how the Industrial Revolution changed life.

Main point: _____

_____

_____

Detail: _____

_____

Detail: _____

_____

Detail: _____

_____

✓ Reading Check

Why are the late 1800s called the Age of Imperialism?

_____

_____

_____

Vocabulary Strategy

The words listed here are under-lined in your reading. Identify the meaning of the suffix in each of these words by using the chart on the first page of this section. Write it next to the word.

nationalism:

_____

destructive:

_____

alliances:

_____

Circle the suffix in each word when you come across it in your reading. Did knowing what the suffix meant help you determine what each word means?

✓ Reading Check

Which countries made up the Axis Powers?

_____

_____

_____

A Century of War and Nationalism

At the start of the 1900s, the people of Europe were filled with **nationalism**. They felt a sense of pride in their countries. Between 1900 and 1950, <u>nationalism</u> became a <u>destructive</u> force. It played a part in causing two world wars and the deaths of millions of people.

During the early 1900s, each European nation was afraid that another would invade its territory. To protect themselves, nations made **alliances** with one another. Each nation promised to protect its friends if someone attacked them. Europe was divided into two <u>alliances</u> when World War I started in 1914. On one side were Germany, Austria-Hungary, and Turkey. On the other side were Great Britain, France, and Russia. The war ended in 1918, after over 22 million people died.

In 1939, World War II broke out. On one side was an alliance called the Axis Powers—Germany, Italy, and Japan. The Allies—Great Britain, the Soviet Union, France, China, and the United States—opposed the Axis Powers. World War II was the most destructive war in history. It finally ended in 1945. The Allies had won. ✓

After World War II, much of Europe was in ruins. The Soviet Union and the United States emerged as the world's two superpowers. These nations had very different ideas about government and society. Europe split in half. Western Europe allied with the United States. Eastern Europe allied with the Soviet Union.

Review Questions

1. When and where did the Industrial Revolution begin?

_____

_____

2. Why did European nations form alliances in the early 1900s?

_____

_____

Key Terms

nationalism (NASH uh nul iz um) *n.* pride in one's country
alliance (uh LY uns) *n.* an agreement between countries to protect and defend each other

---

Section 4
Imperial Russia to the Soviet Union

Objectives

1. Discover how Russia built its empire.
2. Understand the fall of the Russian tsars.
3. Examine the rise and fall of the Soviet Union.
4. Learn the causes and effects of the Cold War.
5. Learn about the Russian Federation today.

Target Reading Skill

Read Ahead Reading ahead can help you understand something you are not sure of in the text. If you do not understand a word or passage, keep reading. The word or idea may be explained later. Sometimes a word is defined after it has been used.

When you read the sentence in this section that mentions Russia's westernization, you may not understand what westernization means. By reading ahead, you will find out that westernization is the adoption of Western culture. You will also find out that one of Russia's rulers, Peter the Great, wanted the Russian people to adopt Western customs. This will help you understand what westernization means.

Vocabulary Strategy

Using Word Parts Have you ever had to take something apart in order to put it back together again? Well, some words are made up of two words. These are called compound words. To figure out the meaning of a compound word, you'll need to break it into two parts. For example, if you did not know what *landowner* means, you could break it into: *land* and *owner*. A landowner is an owner of land.

Here are some common words that are made up of two words:

everyone	*seaport*	*breakup*
railroad	*farmland*	*superpower*

Section 4 Summary

Building a Vast Empire

In the 1540s, Ivan IV became the leader of Moscow. He called himself **tsar**, or emperor. Ivan IV expanded Moscow's territory to the south and east.

In 1613, Michael Romanov became tsar. The Romanovs continued expanding Russian territory throughout the 1600s. **Westernization** began when Peter the Great came to power in 1689. He brought Western European ideas and culture to Russia. He encouraged the Russian people to take on western customs. Peter believed that Russia needed good seaports to become a world power. He took over land on the Baltic and Black seas for this purpose. ☑

The Fall of the Tsars

Russia was becoming a powerful empire. But the lives of most Russian people had not improved. The Russians were divided into two groups—a few wealthy landowners and many very poor serfs. Some tsars tried to make reforms, but conditions never really got better. In 1894, Nicholas II became tsar. He would be the last Russian tsar. Unrest grew among peasants and workers. In 1905, thousands of workers marched to the Winter Palace and demanded change. Tsar Nicholas agreed to establish the Duma, a kind of congress. Some reforms were made, but the people wanted more. ☑

The Rise of the Soviet Union

In 1914, Russia entered World War I against Germany. Millions of Russian soldiers were killed or wounded. People ran out of food and fuel. In 1917, the Russian people rioted. Troops joined the uprising. Tsar Nicholas II was forced to give up his throne and was later killed.

✓ Reading Check

Why did Peter the Great want to control land on the Baltic and Black seas?

_____

_____

_____

✓ Reading Check

Why did thousands of workers march to the Winter Palace?

_____

_____

_____

Vocabulary Strategy

The compound word *uprising* appears in the bracketed paragraph. Draw a vertical line between the two parts of the word. Use the two word parts to figure out what *uprising* means. Write your definition on the lines below.

_____

_____

_____

Key Terms

tsar (zahr) *n.* Russian emperor
westernization (wes tur nuh ZAY shun) *n.* the adoption of Western European culture

A man named Lenin became the new leader of Russia. Earlier, the Russian government had put Lenin in prison for spreading **revolutionary** ideas. <u>Lenin caused changes in Russia.</u> He wanted to create a communist government. However, **communism** in Russia never lived up to the promises Lenin made. Instead, the government kept all of the power and wealth for itself. In 1922, Lenin created the Union of Soviet Socialist Republics (USSR), also called the Soviet Union. Josef Stalin became the next leader. He was a dictator with absolute power. He jailed and killed those who went against him. ✓

The Cold War

After World War II, relations between the United States and the Soviet Union were very tense. The Soviet Union wanted to spread communism. The United States was determined to stop it. This time of tension without any actual war is called the Cold War. ✓

By the early 1980s, most Soviet people had lost faith in communism. Several republics became independent. In 1991, the Soviet Union broke apart.

The Russian Federation

After the breakup, Russia changed its name to the Russian Federation. The Russian Federation has tried to build a western-style economy and to become more democratic. The transition has not been easy. ✓

Review Questions

1. What was the Cold War?

_____

_____

2. What changes has the Russian Federation made to the Russian government?

_____

_____

Key Terms

revolutionary (rev uh LOO shuh neh ree) *adj.* ideas that relate to or cause the overthrow of a government, or other great change
communism (KAHM yoo niz um) *n.* a political system in which the central government owns all farms, factories, and offices.

Target Reading Skill

The underlined sentence says that Lenin caused changes in Russia. Keep reading to see what that means.

What change did Lenin make to the Russian government?

_____

_____

_____

✓ Reading Check

What kind of leader was Josef Stalin?

_____

_____

_____

✓ Reading Check

Why was there tension between United States and the Soviet Union?

_____

_____

_____

✓ Reading Check

What country became the Russian Federation?

_____

_____

_____

Objectives

1. Learn about the history of the European Union.
2. Understand the purpose of the European Union.
3. Examine the structure of the European Union.
4. Find out what the future holds for the European Union.

Target Reading Skill

Reread or Read Ahead Is there a book you really like that you have read several times? Maybe you have gone to see a movie more than once. When you know the ending of a book or movie, and then read or watch it again, you often pick up more information. Maybe something that didn't make sense the first time makes sense the second or third time.

Rereading and reading ahead in a text works the same way. If something is unclear, it may be a good idea to read ahead first to see if the idea is made clear later on. If it still doesn't make sense, try going back and rereading the passage. See if you can find the main idea. Think about how the idea you don't understand relates to the main idea.

Vocabulary Strategy

Using Word Parts As you learned earlier, a prefix is a word part attached to the beginning of a word to make a new word. The new word combines the meaning of the prefix with the meaning of the original word.

Some common prefixes are listed below, along with their meanings and examples. Learning to identify prefixes, and knowing what they mean, will help you figure out the meaning of unfamiliar words.

Prefix	Meaning	Example
co-	together	coordinate, cooperate
pro-	for	propose, promote
inter-	between	intercept, interpret

At the end of World War II, Europe lay in ruins. Europeans needed to work together to rebuild their nations and make their economies strong again. In 1951, the idea of a European Union began to take shape in a small way. Six nations formed a group. They worked together to control their coal and steel industries. Over time, this small group grew into a much larger group with many more roles and responsibilities. Today, this group is called the European Union (EU) and has 27 member states. Many other countries are waiting to join.

History of the European Union

In 1957, the European Economic Community (EEC) was created. It gave the original group greater powers. Throughout the 1970s and 1980s, more and more nations wanted to join the EEC.

In 1992, the member nations signed the Maastricht Treaty. This treaty created the European Union (EU). The treaty also laid out plans for EU nations to adopt a single currency, or type of money. The currency is called the **euro**. In 2002, most EU nations began using euros. ✓

What Does the European Union Do?

The European Union promotes economic and social progress for member countries. Member countries are still independent nations. They have agreed to work together for the common good. EU nations can trade freely with one another without having to pay taxes on international trade. The EU has a **single market**, or a system in which goods, services, and money move. EU nations cooperate to create jobs. The EU also works to protect European culture.

Key Terms

euro (YUR oh) *n.* the official currency of the European Union
single market (SING ul MAHR ket) *n.* system in which goods, services, and capital move freely, with no barriers

---

✓ Reading Check

What is the currency of the European Union?

_____

_____

_____

Vocabulary Strategy

The words listed below appear in the bracketed paragraph. Circle the prefix in each word. Then write down what you think each word means, based on what you know about the prefix and the word root. *Hint:* Use the chart on the previous page.

Mark the Text

international

_____

cooperate

_____

🎯 **Target Reading Skill**

Read ahead to find out about the EU's three main policy institutions. Which one represents the interests of the whole EU community?

_____

_____

_____

✓ **Reading Check**

Which institution in the European Union looks after the goals of each individual EU nation?

_____

_____

_____

30 The EU creates laws that govern its member nations. A court called the Court of Justice makes sure that the EU's policies are applied fairly in every EU member nation. ✓

Structure of the European Union

The EU has three main policy-making institutions.
35 These institutions are the European Parliament, the Council of the European Union, and the European Commission.

The European Parliament makes most of the laws for the EU. The citizens of the EU elect its members. It
40 represents their interests.

The Council of the European Union is made up of the foreign ministers from individual EU nations. A **foreign minister** is a government official who is in charge of a nation's relations with other nations. Each
45 Council member looks after the goals of their individual country.

The European Commission looks after the goals of the whole EU community. Each EU nation sends representatives to the Commission, so that all are repre-
50 sented equally. ✓

Future of the European Union

In just 50 years, the EU has brought peace and prosperity to the almost 500 million people of Europe. As the EU grows, other nations want to join. To join, new members must accept existing EU laws, values, and policies.

Review Questions

1. What did the Maastricht Treaty establish?

_____

_____

2. What must new members of the EU accept before joining?

_____

_____

Key Term

foreign minister (FAWR in MIN is tur) *n.* a government official who is in charge of a nation's foreign affairs

---

Chapter 7 Assessment

1. What system brought order and security to people in the Middle Ages?
   A. democracy
   B. feudalism
   C. imperialism
   D. communism

2. A far-reaching change is known as a(n)
   A. alliance.
   B. renaissance.
   C. revolution.
   D. colony.

3. Which of these is true of the Industrial Revolution?
   A. It caused a rebirth of interest in learning and art.
   B. It prompted many countries to form alliances for protection and security.
   C. It changed how goods were made and how people lived and worked.
   D. It caused the overthrow of European governments.

4. Who was the first Russian leader to begin westernization?
   A. Ivan IV
   B. Josef Stalin
   C. Lenin
   D. Peter the Great

5. In a single-market system, goods, services and money are
   A. able to move freely with no barriers.
   B. a country's property and are shared equally.
   C. paid to the king in return for protection.
   D. dependent on a country's single resource.

Short Answer Question

1. What changes occurred in Russia after the breakup of the Soviet Union?
   _____
   _____
   _____
   _____

Objectives

1. Find out how industry has led to the growth of cities and increased wealth.
2. Learn about the cultural centers of Western Europe.
3. Understand how open borders affect life in Western Europe.

Target Reading Skill

Identify Main Ideas Have you ever asked someone, "What's your point?" By asking that, you were trying to find the main idea. Good readers look for the main ideas of what they read. To help you find the main idea of a paragraph, read it through once. Then ask yourself what the paragraph is about. Do all the sentences focus on the same subject? What are the sentences saying about that subject? If you can answer these questions, you've found the main idea. Sometimes the main idea is stated directly in the first sentence or two.

The main idea of the paragraph below is underlined:

<u>When people travel in Europe, they are often heading for a city.</u> People travel from small towns and villages to cities to find jobs. Some people go to cities to attend school. People also travel to cities to enjoy cultural attractions.

As you read, look for the main ideas of paragraphs.

Vocabulary Strategy

Recognizing Roots The main part of a word is its root. For example, the root of the word *spectator* is *-spect-*, which means "see." When the root is a complete word, it is called a base word. *West*, for example, is the base word of *western*.

When you see a new word, look at it closely. Look for a root or base word that you already know. If you know the meaning of a base word or a word's root, you have a clue to the meaning of the word. See the table below for examples.

Roots	Meanings	Words	Meanings
-soph	wise	sophisticated	wise in the ways of the world
-loc-	a place	locate	find a place
Base Words	**Meanings**	**Words**	**Meanings**
major	great or greater	majority	more than half of a total
prosper	thrive or grow	prosperous	successful or wealthy

Section 1 Summary

In Western Europe, high-speed trains have made travel between countries easy and fast. Europeans can be in another country in just a few hours. Being able to move so easily through Western Europe has affected the culture.

Growth of Industry

Most Western European countries are prosperous. This prosperity is based on strong economies. Industry and services have caused this growth.

Farming used to play the biggest role in the economy of Western Europe. About 200 years ago, most people had to work on farms. They grew their own food. Over time, inventors created new and better farm machines. With these advances, farms could produce more and better crops with fewer laborers. This change took place around the same time as the Industrial Revolution. As fewer farm workers were needed, the need for industrial workers grew. Many people began moving to cities, where factories were located.

After World War II, **urbanization**, or the movement of people toward cities, sped up rapidly. The region's industries became stronger than ever. Even more people left the country to work in cities.

Today, the majority of Western Europeans work in factories or in jobs where they provide a service. Most Western European workers earn good wages and have a comfortable life. ✓

Centers of Culture

When people travel in Europe, they are often heading for a city. People travel from small towns and villages to cities to find jobs. Some people move to cities to go to school. People also travel to cities to enjoy cultural attractions.

Key Term

urbanization (ur bun ih ZAY shun) *n.* the movement of populations toward cities

---

Vocabulary Strategy

Each of the underlined words on this page contains a base word. Circle the base words you find within these words.

Target Reading Skill

Which sentence states the main idea of the bracketed paragraph? Underline the sentence.

✓ Reading Check

Where do most Western Europeans work today?

_____

_____

_____

Most Western European cities are a mix of old and new. Public buildings and houses from the Middle Ages are common. They stand next to modern build-
35 ings. Each city in Western Europe is different from every other city. Paris, the capital of France, attracts scholars, writers, and artists from all over the world. The German city of Berlin attracts many visitors to its theaters and museums.

40 Life in Western Europe is good now, but it was not always that way. In the 1800s and 1900s, millions of Western Europeans left Europe. After World War II, industry grew and workers were needed. People from other countries began moving to Western Europe to fill
45 those jobs. Today, about 6 percent of workers in Western Europe are **immigrants**, or people who moved to one country from another. Most of the immigrants in Western Europe are from North Africa, Eastern Europe, South Asia, and the Middle East. ☑

Open Borders

50 Most European countries are small and close together. People, ideas, goods, and raw materials can travel quickly between countries. The policies of the European Union have helped create this situation. The open borders, as well as the speed of travel, have helped
55 Western Europe become more prosperous. ☑

Review Questions

1. What is Western Europe's prosperity based on?

_____

_____

2. When people travel in Europe, why are they often heading for a city?

_____

_____

Key Term

immigrant (IM uh grunt) *n.* a person who moves to one country from another

---

✓ **Reading Check**

Why did people from other countries begin moving to Western Europe after World War II?

_____

_____

_____

🎯 **Target Reading Skill**

Which sentence states the main idea under the heading "Open Borders"? Underline the sentence.

✓ **Reading Check**

Name two things that can be transported quickly in Western Europe.

1._____

_____

2._____

_____

Prepare to Read

Section 2
The Cultures of Eastern Europe

Objectives

1. Learn about the different ethnic groups in Eastern Europe.
2. Understand the impact of foreign domination on the region.
3. Find out about ethnic conflict in Eastern Europe.
4. Learn about Eastern Europe's cultural centers.

Target Reading Skill

Identify Supporting Details The main idea of a paragraph or section is its most important point. The main idea is supported by details. Details give more information. They often tell you *what, where, why, how much,* or *how many* about the main idea.

Look at the following paragraph. The main idea is underlined once. The supporting details are underlined twice. The supporting details tell why and how the single Slavic language changed and what Slavic languages are spoken today.

> Many languages in Eastern Europe originally came from one Slavic language. Two thousand years ago, there was only one Slavic language. As the Slavs separated, different Slavic languages developed. Today, about ten Slavic languages are spoken in Eastern Europe. These include Czech, Polish, and Russian.

Vocabulary Strategy

Using Roots and Suffixes As you learned in the previous section, the main part of a word is its root or base word. *Europe*, for example, is the base word of *European*. The suffix *–an* means "of or relating to." So, European means "of or relating to Europe." A number of different suffixes have the same meaning as *–an*. These include *–ese* and *–ish*. As you read this section, use roots and suffixes to help you identify Eastern Europe's ethnic groups.

The bracketed paragraph describes Slavic cultures. What details in the paragraph give examples of the culture of the Slavs? Identify two supporting details.

_____

_____

_____

_____

✓ Reading Check

What are three Slavic languages spoken in Eastern Europe?

_____

_____

_____

There are few mountains or other natural barriers between the countries of Eastern Europe and their neighbors. For this reason, movement through much of the region has always been easy. Different groups of people have entered or crossed this region for thousands of years. This movement from place to place is called **migration**. It is still happening today.

Eastern Europe's Ethnic Groups

The Slavs (slahvz) were one of the groups that migrated across Eastern Europe long ago. Today, descendants of Slavs make up most of Eastern Europe's **ethnic groups**. Two thousand years ago, there was one Slavic language. As the Slavs separated, different Slavic languages developed. Today, about ten Slavic languages are spoken in Eastern Europe. They include Czech, Polish, and Russian. There are also many different **dialects** in some Slavic languages. ✓

Slavs also practice different religions. Most follow the Eastern Orthodox faith or are Roman Catholic. Others may be Protestant or Muslim.

Some countries in Eastern Europe are almost entirely Slavic, such as Poland and the Czech Republic. Many other ethnic groups also live in Eastern Europe. Almost all of the people of Hungary belong to an ethnic group called the Magyars (MAG yarhz). In Romania, most people are Romanians. In Albania, most people are Albanians. Roma, or gypsies, and Germans live in several countries of Eastern Europe.

Foreign Domination

Eastern Europe is a region with a history of foreign domination. Most of Eastern Europe came under Soviet control following World War II. Communist leaders, influenced

---

Key Terms

migration (my GRAY shun) *n.* movement from place to place
ethnic group (ETH nik groop) *n.* a group of people who share the same ancestors, culture, language, or religion
dialect (DY uh lekt) *n.* a version of a language found only in a certain region

by the Soviet Union, led the governments of most Eastern European countries. They took private land, punished people for criticizing the government, and discouraged traditional expressions of culture such as religion. ✓

Ethnic Conflict

35 In some Eastern European countries, people of different ethnic groups live together peacefully. In other places, there have been conflicts between ethnic groups.

In <u>Czechoslovakia</u>, the two main ethnic groups were the Czechs and the Slovaks. After World War II, the 40 Soviet Union controlled Czechoslovakia. Communists took over the country. Groups protested against communism. The protests led to a return to democracy. However, Czechs and Slovaks disagreed about how to run the new government. Czechoslovakia peacefully 45 split into two countries in 1993. They are called the Czech Republic and Slovakia.

Ethnic differences also led to the breakup of Yugoslavia in the early 1990s. This breakup was violent. ✓

European Centers of Culture

Eastern Europe's cities are important centers of life and 50 culture. They have grown quickly since the fall of communism.

Two European Cities

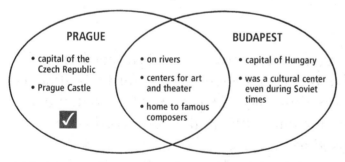

PRAGUE
- capital of the Czech Republic
- Prague Castle
  ✓

- on rivers
- centers for art and theater
- home to famous composers

BUDAPEST
- capital of Hungary
- was a cultural center even during Soviet times

Review Questions

1. Why has movement throughout much of Eastern Europe always been easy?

_____

_____

2. What has contributed to the growth of Eastern Europe's cities?

_____

_____

✓ **Reading Check**

How did Soviet policies affect the people of Eastern Europe?

_____

_____

Vocabulary Strategy

Circle the two roots you recognize in the underlined word on this page. Use the roots to identify the two main ethnic groups.

_____

_____

✓ **Reading Check**

What was one difference between the breakup of Yugoslavia and Czechoslovakia?

_____

_____

_____

✓ **Reading Check**

What is the capital of the Czech Republic?

_____

_____

Prepare to Read

Section 3
The Cultures of the Russian Federation

Objectives

1. Learn about Russia's ethnic groups.
2. Find out about Russia's culture and its educational system.

Target Reading Skill

Identify Main Ideas Sometimes the main idea is not stated directly. Instead, all the details in a paragraph or section add up to a main idea. It is up to you to add up the details, and then state the main idea in your own words.

Carefully read the details given in the paragraph below.

In the Soviet Union, the government tried to prevent people from practicing religion. In 1991, the Soviet Union collapsed. Hundreds of churches in Moscow reopened their doors. The return to religion can be seen in places of worship across all of Russia.

You could state the main idea this way:

After the Soviet Union collapsed, people returned to practicing religion all across Russia.

Vocabulary Strategy

Using Roots and Suffixes As you've learned, a suffix is a word part attached to the end of a word to make a new word. The word it is attached to is called the root or base word. When a suffix is added to a root, the new word that is formed has a new meaning. Often, the new word is an adjective or adverb, a word used to describe something.

Some common suffixes are listed below, along with their meanings and examples. Pay close attention to suffixes in this section when you're reading about St. Petersburg.

Suffix	Meaning	Example
-al, -ic	relating to	monumental, artistic
-ful, -ous	full of	joyful, wondrous
-ly	in what manner	elegantly, slowly

Section 3 Summary

Russia's Ethnic Groups

The Russian Orthodox religion is part of the Russian **heritage**. Heritage is the customs and practices that are passed from one generation to the next. Russia's ethnic culture is also part of the Russian heritage. More than 80 percent of Russian citizens are Russian Slavs. Most of these people speak the Russian language. They live in western parts of the Russian Federation. ☑

More than 60 non-Russian ethnic groups live in Russia. For example, Armenians and Mongolians live along Russia's southern edges. Some ethnic groups speak languages other than Russian. They also follow different religions.

The Soviet Union used to be made up of many republics. Some of the republics have different ethnic groups as the majority. When the Soviet Union came apart, some non-Russian republics formed their own countries. Other ethnic groups remained part of Russia, sometimes against their will. Independence movements have caused ethnic tensions. The Russian Federation has tried to keep the country together.

Russian Culture and Education

Many great artists come from Russia. Russians have produced outstanding buildings, fine paintings, great plays, and beautiful art objects.

The Soviet government only allowed people to create art that supported their **propaganda** efforts. Propaganda is the spread of ideas designed to support some cause or to hurt an opposing cause. When the Soviet Union collapsed, the Russian people began to create art freely once more. ☑

Key Terms

heritage (HEHR uh tij) *n.* the customs and practices passed from one generation to the next

propaganda (prahp uh GAN duh) *n.* the spread of ideas designed to support a cause or hurt an opposing cause

---

✓ Reading Check

What is Russia's largest ethnic group?

_____

_____

◎ Target Reading Skill

Read the details in the bracketed paragraph. Then state the main idea in one sentence in your own words.

_____

_____

_____

✓ Reading Check

Why did the creation of new works of art nearly stop under Soviet communism?

_____

_____

_____

St. Petersburg is an important center of Russian culture. It was founded by Peter the Great in 1703. His goal was to create a Russian city as <u>beautiful</u> as any Western European city. The Neva (nyeh vah) River winds <u>gracefully</u> through the city. On the river's bank is the Winter Palace. It is one of St. Petersburg's grandest sights. It was the winter home of Russia's tsars. It is now an art museum.

The Russian Federation provides free public schooling for children between ages 6 and 17. When students finish ninth grade, they can go to a secondary school or a vocational school for more education if they want. Schools used to teach only the official Soviet point of view. Today, Russia's schools are updating their courses.

These changes show that Russia is trying to recover the riches of its past even as it prepares for a new future. Religion and art, two important parts of Russia's cultural heritage, can now be freely expressed. And Russia's young people, unlike their parents, can grow up deciding their futures for themselves.

Vocabulary Strategy

Two underlined words describe St. Petersburg and the Neva River. Circle the suffixes in the words. One word has two suffixes. What do each of these words mean? *Hint:* Look at the chart at the beginning of this section.

beautiful:

_____

_____

gracefully:

_____

_____

Review Questions

1. What does Russia's artistic heritage include?

_____

_____

_____

2. What city is an important center of Russian culture?

_____

_____

_____

Chapter 8 Assessment

1. What increased rapidly in Western Europe after World War II?
   A. ethnic conflict
   B. farming
   C. unemployment
   D. urbanization

2. A group of people who share the same ancestors, culture, language, or religion is known as a(n)
   A. annex.
   B. heritage.
   C. ethnic group.
   D. immigrant group.

3. Today, most of Eastern Europe's ethnic groups are descendants of
   A. Albanians.
   B. Slavs.
   C. Germans.
   D. Magyars.

4. In which Eastern European country did different ethnic groups agree on a peaceful division of the country?
   A. Yugoslavia
   B. Macedonia
   C. Albania
   D. Czechoslovakia

5. How many ethnic groups does Russia have?
   A. more than 60
   B. only one
   C. twelve
   D. fewer than 20

Short Answer Question

Why is it easy to move between Western European countries?

_____

_____

_____

Prepare to Read

Section 1
The United Kingdom: Democracy and Monarchy

Objectives

1. Examine the regions that make up England, Great Britain, and the United Kingdom.
2. Learn about the United Kingdom's democratic heritage.
3. Find out how the United Kingdom combines democracy and monarchy.
4. Understand why trade is important to the United Kingdom.

Target Reading Skill

Use Context Clues Sometimes you may come across a word you don't understand. When this happens, try becoming a detective and looking for clues in the context—the surrounding words, sentences, and paragraphs. These context clues will help you understand the meaning of the unfamiliar word.

For example, you know the words *crown* and *jewels*, but you may not know what the term *crown jewels* means. Context clues in the following paragraph will help you understand the meaning of the term.

> The jewels are kept under guard in the Tower of London. The priceless collection includes crowns worn by the kings and queens of England. After a long wait, the tourists finally reach the amazing jewels. Their eyes widen at the sight of huge diamonds, bright-red rubies, and cool, blue sapphires.

Vocabulary Strategy

Recognizing Word Origins Another way to figure out the meaning of a word you don't know is by looking at its parts. If you know the meaning of the root of a word, you are already close to figuring out the whole word's meaning. The root of a word often comes from another language. The roots of many English words, for example, come from Greek and Latin.

The word *democracy* comes from the Greek root *demos*, which means "common people." Based on the meaning of the root, what kind of government do you think a democracy is? You'll be reading about two different kinds of government in this section—democracy and monarchy.

Section 1 Summary

Regions of the United Kingdom

The nation located on the British Isles has been called many different names. Some names are England, Great Britain, and the United Kingdom. Each name has a particular meaning.

England is a region inside of the United Kingdom. Once England was made of small kingdoms. One kingdom grew stronger than the others and conquered other kingdoms. It unified England into a nation.

England started taking over its neighbors. It took over Wales in the 1500s. In the early 1700s, England and Scotland joined together. All of the countries on the island of Great Britain became one nation. Its name was changed to Great Britain. ✓

Next, Great Britain claimed its neighboring island, Ireland. Only Northern Ireland has stayed part of the United Kingdom. Together, England, Scotland, Wales, and Northern Ireland form the United Kingdom, or UK. The British government unifies these four regions.

A Democratic Heritage

Today, the United Kingdom is headed by Queen Elizabeth II. She is the country's monarch. The United Kingdom also has a strong democratic government. Its roots go back many centuries.

In 1215, a group of nobles forced King John to sign a document called the Magna Carta, or "Great Charter." The Magna Carta required that the king obey the laws of the land. ✓

The group of nobles became known as the Parliament. **Parliament** is the lawmaking body of the United Kingdom. It later included common people. People elect **representatives** to speak for them in Parliament. The modern Parliament governs the nation.

Key Terms

Parliament (PAHR luh munt) *n.* the lawmaking body of the United Kingdom

representative (rep ruh ZEN tuh tiv) *n.* a person who represents, or speaks for, a group of people

---

✓ Reading Check

What regions made up Great Britain?

_____

_____

_____

✓ Reading Check

What did the Magna Carta require?

_____

_____

_____

🎯 Target Reading Skill

What does the term *common people* mean in the underlined sentence? What clues can you find in the surrounding words or phrases? Don't overlook clues that show a contrast. Define *common people* below. Circle the words in this paragraph that helped you learn its meaning.

common people

_____

_____

_____

Vocabulary Strategy

The underlined word *monarchs* is made up of two word parts from the Greek language–the prefix *mono* and the root *arch*. *Mono* means "sole or alone." The root *arch* means "rule or govern." What do you think *monarchs* means?

_____

_____

_____

✓ Reading Check

What organization does the United Kingdom rely on for trade now?

_____

_____

A Changing Monarchy

British <u>monarchs</u> today do not have the power that they once did. They no longer make laws or collect taxes. The United Kingdom is now governed by a constitu-
35 tion. A **constitution** is a set of laws that describes how a government works. This makes the British government a **constitutional monarchy**. In the 1990s, Parliament started to hand over some of its power to lawmaking groups in three of the four regions. These groups,
40 such as the Northern Ireland Assembly, make laws that affect their particular region. This process is called devolution. Only England's laws are still all made by Parliament. ☑

The Importance of Trade

The United Kingdom is an island nation with few
45 natural resources. It trades with other nations for resources. Therefore, trade has always been important to the United Kingdom. In the 1500s, trade helped the British to build a large empire. The British Empire had colonies on six continents. After World War I and II, the
50 Empire lost all of its colonies.

Today, the United Kingdom has many strong industries. It no longer relies on its colonies to boost its economy. It joined the European Union in 1973. Now it is a leading member. ☑

Review Questions

1. What is the difference between the terms *Great Britain* and *United Kingdom*?

_____

_____

2. Why has trade always been important to the United Kingdom?

_____

_____

> **Key Terms**
>
> **constitution** (kahn stuh TOO shun) *n.* a set of laws that describes how a government works
> **constitutional monarchy** (kahn stuh TOO shuh nul MAHN ur kee) *n.* a government in which a monarch is the head of state but has limited powers

Prepare to Read

Section 2
France: Cultural Heritage and Diversity

Objectives

1. Find out why the French take pride in their traditional culture.
2. Learn about growing cultural diversity in France.

Target Reading Skill

Use Context Clues When you come across a word you don't understand, look for context clues. Clues to a word's meaning can often be found in the surrounding words, sentences, and paragraphs. Sometimes context clues will give a definition or explanation of a word. Watch out for these as you read.

In the following example, the underlined phrase helps explain what *Impressionist* means:

> French Impressionist artists such as Claude Monet created <u>new ways to paint light and shadow.</u>

Did you figure out that Impressionist artists are painters who focused on the effects of light in their work?

Vocabulary Strategy

Recognizing Word Origins There are many words that you use every day—such as, *menu*, *picnic*, and *umpire*—that originally came from the French language.

The word *encourage* comes from the French root *corage*, which means "courage." Based on the meaning of the French root, what do you think it means to encourage someone? *Hint:* The prefix *en-* means "to provide with." What does *encourage* mean?

Now try this one. The prefix *dis-* means "opposite or absence of." What do you think it means to discourage someone?

Target Reading Skill

The word *preserve* is not defined for you in the underlined sentence. What clues can you find in the surrounding words and phrases, and in the chart? Circle the words and phrases on this page that could help you learn what *preserve* means.

Vocabulary Strategy

The word *philosophy* is formed from the Greek roots *phil* and *soph*. The root *phil* means "love." The root *soph* means "wise." How do these roots help you figure out what *philosophy* means? Check the Key Term box below to see how close you are to figuring out the meaning of *philosophy*.

_____

_____

_____

✓ Reading Check

What are two examples of the influence of French culture on the rest of the world?

1._____

_____

2._____

_____

Section 2 Summary

Pride in French Culture

French people take great pride in their own culture. <u>Many French people want to preserve their traditional French culture.</u> See the table below for some of France's important contributions to culture.

French Culture

Language
• Some French people want to keep the French language from changing too much.
• The French Academy decides which words can be officially part of the French language.

Philosophy
• Baron de Montesquieu developed the idea that government should be divided into three branches.
• The ideas of Jean-Jacques Rousseau helped shape the United States Constitution.

The Arts
• Impressionist artists such as Claude Monet created new ways to paint light and shadow.
• Alexandre Dumas wrote historical novels that are still read today.

Architecture
• In the 1100s, the "Gothic" style of architecture developed in Paris.
• Stunning cathedrals, such as the Cathedral of Notre Dame, were built in the Gothic style.

Fashion
• In the 1700s, Russian aristocrats followed French fashion, used French manners, and spoke French.
• Paris is still a fashion center.

Fine Foods
• French-style cooking has been popular all over the world.
• Today, many of the world's best chefs are trained in France. ✓

Key Term

philosophy (fil LAHS uh fee) *n.* a system of ideas and beliefs

Diversity in France

Many French citizens believe French culture is both unique and valuable. Yet other cultures are affecting French culture more and more. The French language, for example, has picked up words from many other languages, including English and Hindi. Immigration is another big source of change.

In the late 1800s and early 1900s, many people from European countries immigrated to France. These immigrants came from cultures similar to that of France. They quickly adopted French culture.

After World War II, France needed many workers. The government urged people from other countries to move to France. The largest group came from Algeria, in North Africa. When the economy took a turn for the worse in the 1970s, many native French people started to resent immigrants. The government limited immigration. However, people still move to France.

Life in France can be difficult for immigrants. They sometimes face economic disadvantages and unfair treatment. The French government has promised to improve opportunities for immigrants.

Today, immigrants from Algeria, Morocco, and Tunisia bring African and Arab cultures with them. Their food, dress, and music are very different from those of traditional French culture. The same is true of immigrants from Asia and other regions. ✓

France is now a diverse society. France and its people are adapting to change. Most have come to value their diverse population.

✓ Reading Check

How are France's recent immigrants different from those of the past?

_____

_____

_____

Review Questions

1. Why do you think French people take great pride in their culture?

_____

_____

_____

2. How has French culture been affected by other cultures?

_____

_____

_____

Section 3
Sweden: A Welfare State

Objectives

1. Learn about Sweden's welfare state.
2. Find out how Sweden became a welfare state.
3. Examine possible solutions to Sweden's economic problems.

Target Reading Skill

Use Context Clues Sometimes a word you already know may be used in a different way. It may have a different meaning in the context of what you are reading. For example, you have probably heard of the word *welfare*. In this section, the word *welfare* may have a different meaning than the one you know. Try to figure out the difference in meaning by looking closely at context clues in the following sentences:

> A welfare system means something very different in Sweden than it does in the United States. The American welfare system helps people who are in great need—people who cannot afford medical care or food. The Swedish system helps everyone.

Vocabulary Strategy

Recognizing Word Origins The word *welfare* comes from the old English phrase, *wel faren*. The prefix *wel-* means "well" or "according to desire." The root *faren* means "to go" or "to fare." By putting these word parts together, you can figure out that *welfare* means "the condition of being well" or "the condition of health, happiness, and comfort." Have ever asked someone, "How's it going?" If you have, you were asking about their welfare.

Based on the meaning of the roots, what does it mean when you say "Farewell" to someone? What kind of experience do you hope that person will have in the future?

Section 3 Summary

A Welfare State

Sweden is a welfare state. <u>In a welfare state, the government provides many services and benefits either for free or for a very low cost.</u> The American welfare system helps people who are in great need—people who cannot afford medical care or food. The Swedish system helps everyone.

Sweden has a "cradle-to-grave" welfare system. That means that the government gives everyone basic services throughout their lives. When a child is born, the government pays for parents to stay home. The government pays for schooling and buys books and lunches for students. The government also pays for people to go to college. Every Swedish citizen can get free or inexpensive health care. When Swedish workers retire, the government sends money each month for them to live on. ✓

Swedish people believe that these welfare benefits are very important. They pay the highest taxes in Europe in order to have them.

Building a Welfare State

In its early history, Sweden was ruled by a king or queen. Over time, the monarch gave the people more and more power. Today, Sweden is a constitutional monarchy. That means that there is still a monarchy, but the people make the laws. A poor economy led to the rise of Sweden's modern welfare state. By the late 1800s, industry had grown in the United States and most of Europe. But Sweden was far behind. Many people were very poor. Many Swedes moved to the United States in search of a better life. In 1932, a political party called the Social Democrats came to power. They promised a better life for Swedes. The Social Democrats made Sweden into a welfare state. At the same time, Sweden became an industrial country. The economy grew stronger. ✓

Key Term

welfare state (WEL fayr stayt) *n.* a country in which many services and benefits are paid for by the government

---

Target Reading Skill

What does the word *benefits* mean in the underlined sentence? What clues can you find in the surrounding words, phrases, or sentences? Circle the words and phrases in this section that could help you learn what *benefits* means.

Hint: Look in the next paragraph.

✓ Reading Check

What is a "cradle-to-grave" system?

_____

_____

_____

✓ Reading Check

Which political party created Sweden's welfare state?

_____

_____

Problems and Solutions

For decades, Sweden gave its citizens very generous
benefits. But that changed in the 1980s. Sweden's economy slowed down. To keep paying for benefits, the
government borrowed money. The **national debt**, or
the amount of money the government owed, grew very
large.

Sweden's aging population is another problem.
<u>Sweden has the highest proportion of retired people in
the world.</u> There are fewer workers because so many
people are retired. As a result, there is less tax money to
pay for benefits. Sweden's government is working to
solve these problems. In the 1990s, it reduced benefits.
This angered many Swedish voters.

Another solution would be for businesses to earn
more. Businesses could grow by making better use of
Sweden's natural resources. Sweden has iron ore and
produces steel. It also has fast rivers and waterfalls that
produce hydroelectric power. Sweden's large forests
support the timber industry. ✓

Another way to improve Sweden's economy would
be to make products faster. Most Swedish products
have high quality. But Swedes have not been able to
make goods as quickly and cheaply as other countries.
Improving the way things are made will help Sweden's
economy.

Review Questions

1. What benefits do Swedish citizens receive?

_____

_____

2. What are some of the economic challenges facing
   Sweden today?

_____

_____

> **Key Term**
> **national debt** (NASH uh nul det) *n.* the amount of money a
> government owes

Prepare to Read

Section 4
Italy: Northern and Southern Divisions

Objectives

1. Discover that there is another country within Italy called Vatican City.
2. Understand why there are divisions between northern and southern Italy.

Target Reading Skill

Use Context Clues After you use context clues to figure out the meaning of a word, look closely at the word itself for more clues. These clues can help you figure out if you were correct about the meaning of the word. For example, look at the word *guidance* in the following paragraph.

> Vatican City is the world headquarters of the Roman Catholic Church. The pope is its leader. Every day, Roman Catholics all over the world look to him for <u>guidance</u>.

The context clues in the paragraph tell you that the word has something to do with the leader. To double check, look at the word itself. You can recognize the word *guide* within *guidance*. Does this help you figure out what *guidance* means?

Vocabulary Strategy

Recognizing Word Origins As you know, many words and their roots come from other languages. The roots of many English words come from Greek and Latin.

The word *ancient* comes from the Latin root *ante*, which means "before." Based on the meaning of the root, you can figure out that the word *ancient* describes something that existed or happened in the past. When you read this section, you'll find out many things about the Vatican, including the fact that it has artwork from ancient Greece and Rome. You will know that these artworks are not modern but are from earlier times.

Target Reading Skill

Look at the word *headquarters* in the underlined sentence. Circle the context clues that help you understand why it refers to something important. Then look more closely at the word. You know that one meaning of *head* is "leader." One meaning of *quarters* is "a place where someone lives." What does *headquarters* mean?

_____

_____

✓ **Reading Check**

What is the Vatican?

_____

_____

_____

Vatican City

Vatican City, also called the Vatican, is a country within a country. It is located inside Rome, the capital of Italy. The Vatican is an independent city-state. A city-state is both a city and an independent country.

Vatican City is the world headquarters of the Roman Catholic Church. The pope is its leader. Every day, Roman Catholics all over the world look to him for guidance. Most Italians are Roman Catholic. Their religion unifies them. ✓

Every day, Catholics and non-Catholics visit the Vatican. Most visitors come to see St. Peter's Basilica. A **basilica** is a Roman Catholic church that is special because of its past. The Vatican's palace and art museums are also popular attractions. They have priceless collections of art. Some of the artwork is from ancient Greece and Rome.

The Sistine (SIS teen) Chapel is located inside the Vatican. It contains many famous paintings, sculptures, and other works of art. The famous artist Michelangelo painted religious scenes on the ceiling in the 1500s. It is the most famous ceiling in the world.

Divisions Between North and South

Roman Catholicism brings together about one billion people around the world. It also unites many Italians. Other things unite Italians. Most people living in Italy are ethnic Italians. Strong family ties are common among Italians.

There are also many differences among Italians. Italians in the north and Italians in the south live and work in different ways. For many years, there was no single Italy. Italy didn't unite into one country until the late 1800s.

Key Term

basilica (buh SIL ih kuh) *n.* a special style of Roman Catholic church that has special, high status because of age or history

Life in Northern and Southern Italy

	North	South
History	• Influenced by invaders from Western Europe. • Grew into city-states.	• Influenced by invaders from south and east. • Ruled by feudal kingdoms; large numbers of peasants worked the land.
Economy	• Has many international businesses and most of Italy's **manufacturing** industries. • More prosperous. • After World War II, the economy boomed in the large cities and industrial centers.	• Mostly agricultural • Fishing also important. • After World War II, agriculture-based economy failed to thrive. • Italy's government tried to help the south by introducing **land reform.** • The government also built roads and new irrigation systems here.
Politics	• <u>In the 1990s, a party called the Northern League called for northern Italy to secede and form its own country.</u>	• In recent elections the Northern League has not done well.

✓

Review Questions

1. Name three things that unite Italians.

_____

_____

_____

2. Name three differences between life in northern Italy and life in southern Italy.

_____

_____

_____

Key Terms

manufacturing (man yoo FAK chur ing) *n.* the process of turning raw materials into finished products

land reform (land ree FAWRM) *n.* the process of dividing large properties into smaller ones

✓ Reading Check

Which part of Italy is mostly agricultural?

_____

_____

_____

Prepare to Read

Section 5
Germany: A Unified Nation

Objectives

1. Learn about Germany's past.
2. Find out how Germany became reunited.

Target Reading Skill

Use Context Clues Sometimes you cannot determine the meaning of a word until you have read several paragraphs. When this happens, you need to play detective just a little bit longer and dig a little bit deeper for clues. After you first come across an unfamiliar word, jot down some ideas about its meaning. As you read and reread the paragraphs that provide its context, adjust the word's definition until you are certain of it.

Vocabulary Strategy

Recognizing Word Origins The Latin language has given us many words that are used in English. The word *protest* comes from two Latin words. If you break the word *protest* into its two Latin parts—prefix and root—you'll be able to figure out its meaning. Especially if you know that the prefix *pro-* means "for" or "forth, in public." The root of *protest* is *test*, which comes from *testari*, which means "to be a witness." When you read this section, you'll learn that people living in East Germany declared in public their strong feelings against communism. What do you think *protest* means?

Section 5 Summary

Germany's Past

¹ Germany lost World War I in 1918. The winning countries made Germany pay billions of dollars as punishment for attacking other countries. The German economy fell apart. Germans became desperate. A man
⁵ named Adolf Hitler promised to make Germany great again. By 1933, Hitler was dictator of Germany.

Hitler blamed Germany's economic problems on Jews. He claimed that Jews, Roma, and other ethnic groups in Germany were not as good as other Germans.
¹⁰ He claimed that the German ethnic group was better than other groups—and that they should rule Europe.

Hitler attacked neighboring countries. His actions started World War II. By the end of the war, Europe was in ruins. The Germans had kept countless Jews and
¹⁵ others in concentration camps. Millions of people were murdered in these camps. Many of these people were Jews. <u>This horrible mass murder of six million Jews is called the Holocaust</u>.

At the end of the war, the winning countries broke
²⁰ Germany into two parts. The Federal Republic of Germany, also known as West Germany, was a democratic country. The German Democratic Republic, or East Germany, was communist. Berlin, the capital, was in East Germany. Half of the city, however, was part of
²⁵ West Germany. The Berlin Wall separated the two parts of Berlin. It was a symbol of a divided world. ✓

During the Cold War, the United States and democratic countries in Western Europe opposed communism. Soviet Union troops stayed in Eastern European
³⁰ countries to make sure that they stayed communist. The Cold War had many effects on Europe. Cold War borders separated families and friends. People who escaped to the West suffered because they could not see the family they left behind. East Germans had to obey
³⁵ the communist government without asking questions.

Key Term

Holocaust (HAHL uh kawst) *n.* the mass murder of six million Jews

---

Target Reading Skill

Find the underlined word *horrible* in the third paragraph. Jot down some ideas about what you think the word means.

_____

_____

_____

Reread the paragraph and circle words and phrases that help you to be more certain of the meaning of the word *horrible*. Then readjust your definition.

_____

_____

✓ Reading Check

Which part of Germany was a democratic country—East or West?

_____

_____

In the late 1980s, changes in the Soviet Union weakened the East German government. Some East Germans began to escape to West Germany. Others began protesting in the streets. On November 9, 1989, huge
40 crowds of people began to take the Berlin Wall apart piece by piece. East Germans continued to protest against the government. Less than a year later, the two Germanies united into one country again.

Germany Reunited

Most Germans were thrilled about the fall of the Berlin
45 Wall. The cultures of East and West Germany had stayed alike in many ways, even though they had been separate countries. Still, **reunification** would not be easy.

The East German economy was very weak. To help the economy, the government sold the state-owned
50 factories to private companies. They modernized factories and businesses. They cleaned up <u>toxic</u> waste sites. Germans in the west had to spend a lot of money to do this. But, Germans in the east now enjoy a much better **standard of living** than they did under communism.

55 Berlin reunited too. In 1999, Berlin became the nation's capital once more. Germans believed that Berlin's location would help unify the country. ✓

Despite the high cost of reunification, Germany still has one of the world's strongest economies. It is a
60 powerful member of the European Union.

Review Questions

1. How was Germany punished after World War I?

_____

_____

2. How did East Germany change after reunification?

_____

_____

> **Key Terms**
>
> **reunification** (ree yoo nih fih KAY shun) *n.* the process of becoming unified again
> **standard of living** (STAN durd uv LIV ing) *n.* the level of comfort in terms of the goods and services that people have

Chapter 9 Assessment

1. A government in which a monarch is the head of state but has limited powers is called a(n)
   A. absolute monarchy.
   B. constitutional monarchy.
   C. monarchy.
   D. democracy.

2. Which style of architecture began in Paris during the 1100s?
   A. classical
   B. Renaissance
   C. French Academic
   D. Gothic

3. Which country is a welfare state?
   A. Italy
   B. Germany
   C. Sweden
   D. France

4. Which of the following is true of southern Italy?
   A. It has many large cities.
   B. It is mostly agricultural.
   C. It is a center of manufacturing.
   D. It is ruled by feudal kingdoms.

5. The Holocaust refers to
   A. the end of World War II.
   B. the collapse of the Germany economy.
   C. the horrible mass murder of six million Jews.
   D. the reunification of Germany.

Short Answer Question

What steps did the reunified German government take to improve the economy in former East Germany?

_____

_____

_____

_____

Section 1
Poland: Preserving Tradition Amidst Change

Objectives

1. Find out about Polish traditions.
2. Learn about economic changes that have taken place in Poland since the collapse of communism.
3. Understand the future challenges that Poland faces.

Target Reading Skill

Compare and Contrast When you compare, you look for the similarities between things. When you contrast, you look for the differences between things. Comparing and contrasting can help you sort out information. As you read, compare and contrast Polish life under communism and after communism. Use a chart like the one below.

Polish Life

Under Communism	After Communism
•	•
•	•

Vocabulary Strategy

Using Context Clues When you come across a new word, you'll often find that it is defined for you in context. Context means the nearby words and sentences. Sometimes the definition appears in a separate sentence. Sometimes there may be a brief definition in the same sentence. Sometimes, the word *or* is used to introduce the definition. Look at the following examples.

Underline Unemployment is high in Poland. Therefore, many *people are without jobs*.

There are many shrines, or *holy places*, all over Poland.

The underlined words are defined in context. In these examples, brief definitions appear in italics. Look for definitions in the context as you come across unfamiliar words in your reading.

Section 1 Summary

In the Middle Ages, Poland was the largest state in Europe. By the late 1700s, it was divided up. After World War II, a harsh communist government was set up in Poland by the Soviet Union. Poles regained their freedom when the communist government fell in 1989.

Tradition in Poland

Catholicism has been at the center of Polish tradition for centuries. The communist government tried to discourage Catholicism. But the Polish people remained devoted to the Roman Catholic Church.

Today, most Poles are Catholic. Poles practice Catholicism in their own distinctive way. Polish Catholics felt great pride in 1978, when a Pole was selected as pope of the Catholic Church. Pope John Paul II made the world more aware of Poland and its struggle under communism. ✓

A minority of Poles are Orthodox. Polish Orthodox religious life has its own traditions. You can see orthodox **shrines**, or holy places, all over Poland.

A small minority of Poles are Jewish. Most of Poland's 3 million Jews were killed during the Holocaust.

The Polish language has also stood the test of time. The communists forced Polish schoolchildren to learn Russian, the main language of the Soviet Union. Today, Polish is spoken by the majority of the population. It helps to unite Poland.

Great Economic Changes

Poland has been very successful in making the change from communism to **capitalism**. On January 1, 1990, Polish leaders ended the government's control over the prices people paid for goods. They also made sure that taxes and wages remained the same. A year later, Poland set up a stock market.

✓ Reading Check

What is the religion of most Poles?

_____

_____

Target Reading Skill

Reread the bracketed paragraphs. Identify two parts of Polish life that remained the same, even under communism.

_____

_____

Key Terms

shrine (shryn) *n.* a holy place
capitalism (KAP ut ul iz um) *n.* an economic system in which businesses are privately owned

Many foreigners began to invest their money in Poland. Foreign investment has strengthened the Polish economy. Also, small private businesses opened. Some were only booths on the street. As these businesses made money, they took over stores. Today, more than two million private businesses are run by **entrepreneurs**.

The change to capitalism was good for consumers, but hard on farmers. Under communism, the government always bought farm products and kept the prices high. This provided farmers with a reliable income. After communism, prices dropped. ☑

Future Challenges

The Polish people still face many challenges. During the communist era, pollution destroyed much of the forests in southern Poland. Pollution also increased rates of diseases, such as cancer. Poland has reduced many forms of pollution, but more needs to be done.

Poland also faces a high unemployment rate. Under communism, the government made sure that people had jobs. Under capitalism, there is no such <u>guarantee</u>, or assurance. Many Poles move to other places in Europe to find work. Others hope that membership in the European Union will bring more investment into Poland and create more jobs. ☑

Review Questions

1. What measures did Polish leaders take to change the economy from communism to capitalism?

_____

_____

2. What major challenges does Poland still face today?

_____

_____

> **Key Term**
>
> **entrepreneur** (ahn truh pruh NOOR) *n.* a person who develops original ideas in order to start new businesses

✓ **Reading Check**

Why did farm products sell at a higher price under communism?

_____

_____

Vocabulary Strategy

The word *guarantee* is defined in context. Circle its definition. *Hint:* Look for the word *or*. Also look for an explanation of *guaranteed* **before** the word. Underline that explanation.

✓ **Reading Check**

Why is unemployment a problem for Poland?

_____

_____

_____

Prepare to Read

Section 2
New Balkan Nations: A Region Tries to Rebuild

Objectives

1. Identify the groups of people who live in the Balkans.
2. Understand how Yugoslavia was created and how it broke up.
3. Identify issues that these Balkan nations face in the future.

Target Reading Skill

Make Comparisons Comparing two or more situations helps you to see how they are alike. This section is about six countries that have many things in common. But there are also differences. As you read this section, compare the six nations by considering their histories, economies, cultures, and challenges. What languages do people speak? What religion do they follow? What kinds of jobs do the people have? Create a chart like the one started below to keep track of these details.

Countries			
Language			
Religion			

Vocabulary Strategy

Using Context Clues When you come across a word you don't understand, you need to become a detective and look for context clues. Clues to a word's meaning can be found in the surrounding words, sentences, and paragraphs. These context clues will help you understand the meaning of the unfamiliar word.

In the following example, the underlined phrase helps explain what ethnic conflict is:

From the beginning, ethnic conflict was a problem. <u>Tensions between different ethnic groups</u>, such as ethnic Macedonians and Albanians, had existed for a long time.

Land of Many Peoples

The Balkan Peninsula—also called the Balkans—is located in southeastern Europe. This section discusses the six Balkan countries that used to make up the nation of Yugoslavia: Serbia, Montenegro, Bosnia and Herzegovina, Macedonia, Croatia, and Slovenia.

There are many ethnic groups in the Balkans. Many people in the Balkans speak related Slavic languages. For example, the Serbian, Croatian, and Bosnian languages are as similar as American English and British English.

Religion may be the most important difference among Balkan peoples. Most of them are Christian: either Orthodox Christian or Roman Catholic. Bosnians are mostly Muslim. ✓

The Creation of Yugoslavia

Yugoslavia was formed in 1918 after World War I ended. The new nation joined together many ethnic and religious groups. These groups disagreed about how the country should be governed. Yugoslavia was divided into republics. Its largest republic was Serbia. Serbia held the most power, and ran the national government. Other groups resented Serbian control.

After World War II, Josip Broz Tito became head of the government. He changed Yugoslavia into a communist state like the Soviet Union. But he also developed his own policies. For example, he traded with Western countries in order to strengthen Yugoslavia's economy. The economy under Tito grew.

Tito's rule reduced tensions among ethnic groups. That helped unify Yugoslavia. After Tito's death in 1980, various ethnic groups struggled for power. ✓

Yugoslavia Breaks Up

In 1989, communism began to crumble in Eastern Europe. Many people blamed the Serbs for Yugoslavia's problems. Some republics wanted to govern themselves.

In 1990, Slovenes and Croats began to pull away

✓ **Reading Check**

How are ethnic groups in the Balkans similar?

_____

_____

_____

🎯 **Target Reading Skill**

Read the bracketed paragraphs. What is one difference in Yugoslavia after Tito became head of government?

_____

_____

_____

_____

✓ **Reading Check**

What event led to a power struggle in Yugoslavia?

_____

_____

_____

from Yugoslavia. Slovenia said it had the right to **secede** from, or leave, Yugoslavia. Serbia recognized Slovenia's independence. But in Croatia war erupted. The United Nations sent peacekeepers to the area. It also imposed an **embargo** on Yugoslavia.

Tensions grew in Bosnia and Herzegovina among different ethnic groups. In 1992, a **civil war** began. The UN, NATO, and United States worked to get the Serbs, Croats, and Bosnian Muslims to sign a peace treaty.

Conflict also broke out in the Serbian province of Kosovo. The population of Kosovo is about 90 percent Albanian. In the old Yugoslavia, Albanians in Kosovo were <u>autonomous</u>. They made decisions for themselves. Yugoslavian President Slobodan Milosevic took away Kosovo's freedoms. The Albanians rebelled, and Serb forces attacked them. NATO stepped in, and a peace agreement was signed in 1999. ✓

The Region's Future

The United States and Europe placed **economic sanctions** on Yugoslavia. They lifted the sanctions when a court of the United Nations put Milosevic on trial for war crimes. The two remaining republics of Yugoslavia changed their name to Serbia and Montenegro. In 2006, Montenegro declared independence from Serbia. ✓

Review Questions

1. Which six Balkan nations made up Yugoslavia?

_____

_____

2. When was Yugoslavia created? When did its government turn to communism?

_____

_____

Key Terms

secede (sih SEED) *v.* to leave a group, especially a political group or a nation

embargo (em BAHR go) *n.* a ban on trade

civil war (sih vul wawr) *n.* a war between groups of people within the same nation.

economic sanctions (ek uh NAHM ik SANGK shunz) *n.* actions to limit trade with nations that have violated international laws

---

Vocabulary Strategy

What do you think it means to be "autonomous"? The word *autonomous* is defined in context. Circle its definition. *Hint:* Look in the sentence that follows where the word appears.

✓ Reading Check

To which ethnic group do most of the people of Kosovo belong?

_____

_____

✓ Reading Check

Why was Milosevic put on trial?

_____

_____

Prepare to Read

Section 3
Ukraine: Independence and Beyond

Objectives

1. Understand how Ukraine's history has been shaped by foreign rule.
2. Explain the major issues Ukrainians have faced since independence.
3. Describe life in Ukraine today.

Target Reading Skill

Compare and Contrast Have you ever played the game where you try to find the differences between two pictures? The pictures seem to be the same, but if you look closely, you can find little differences. Sometimes the differences are easy to spot. Other times you really have to work at it.

In this section you will read about farms in the Ukraine before and during Soviet rule. If you read closely, you will learn that they were different kinds of farms.

As you read this section, compare and contrast life in Ukraine before and during Soviet rule.

Vocabulary Strategy

Using Context Clues Words work together to explain meaning. The meaning of a word may depend on its context—the other words and sentences that surround it. The context gives you clues to a word's meaning.

For example, the word *occupation* appears in the heading at the top of the next page. You might be familiar with one meaning of this word, "job." You may also recall that to occupy a house means to live in it. *Occupation* has a different meaning in this context. Look at the context clues underlined in the following paragraph. Use them and your knowledge of the word's other meanings to figure out what *occupation* means in this context.

> For hundreds of years, Ukraine was <u>ruled</u> by its more <u>powerful neighbors</u>. Ukraine lies between the nations of Europe and Russia. In fact, the name Ukraine means "borderland." Ukraine's location makes it <u>open to invasion</u>.

A History of Occupation

1 For hundreds of years, Ukraine was ruled by its more powerful neighbors. Ukraine lies between the nations of Europe and Russia. In fact, the name Ukraine means "borderland." Ukraine's location makes it open to
5 invasion.

Ukraine's vast natural resources have attracted invaders. At one time or another, Poland, Czechoslovakia, Romania, and Germany have occupied areas of Ukraine. Russia, later the Soviet Union, ruled Ukraine
10 between the late 1700s and 1991.

Under Soviet rule, Ukrainian industries grew. Ukrainian mines supplied much of the iron ore, coal, and other minerals for Soviet industries. Ships used Ukraine's ports on the Black Sea to bring goods into and
15 out of the Soviet Union. The Soviets also used Ukraine's rivers to ship goods.

Ukraine was once one of Europe's largest grain producing regions. It was called the breadbasket of Europe. Why is Ukraine's farmland so productive? Over half of the country is covered by a rich, black soil called **chernozem**. When the Soviet Union took control of Ukraine in 1922, Ukrainian farmers were forced to supply the rest of the Soviet Union with food. By the end of the 1980s, they were producing one fourth of the grain and meat eaten in the Soviet Union. ✓

In order to produce the food, Soviet rulers took land away from Ukrainian farmers and created huge government-controlled farms called **collectives**. Farmers had to work on these collectives or work in new factories. All the crops from the collectives went to the government. Millions of Ukrainians died of hunger. Over the years, however, life improved on the farms.

✓ Reading Check

Why was "the breadbasket of Europe" a good nickname for Ukraine?

_____

_____

_____

🎯 Target Reading Skill

Reread the bracketed paragraphs. How did life for Ukrainian farmers change under Soviet rule?

_____

_____

_____

Key Terms

chernozem (CHEHR nuh zem) *n.* rich, black soil
collective (kuh LEK tiv) *n.* a huge government-controlled farm

Independence Brings Challenges

In 1991, Ukraine won its independence from the Soviet Union. First, the new country had to decide how to
35 build up its economy. Ukrainians had to learn how to start new businesses. They also needed to learn how to make consumer goods. Finally, they had to improve their agricultural production by breaking up the collective farm system.

40 They also had to choose a language. Under Soviet rule, the official language was Russian. With independence, Ukrainian was made the official language.

Ukraine is still recovering from a terrible event that happened during the Soviet period. In 1986, an explosion
45 rocked the Chernobyl (chehr NOH bul) nuclear power plant. Radioactive materials filled the air. Many people died. More than 100,000 people had to be moved out of the area. It was no longer safe to live there. Even today, much of Ukraine's soil and water is poisoned. <u>More than
50 32,000 square miles of farmland are contaminated.</u> ✓

Life in Ukraine

Independence has brought changes to life in Ukraine. For example, the capital, Kiev, is often jammed with people enjoying parks, stores, and restaurants. Since independence, new magazines and newspapers have
55 become available. East of Kiev, the city of Kharkiv is the busiest industrial center in the nation and a lively cultural center. The land's great resources and the people's ability to work together should help Ukrainians make independence succeed. ✓

Review Questions

1. Who controlled Ukraine until 1991?

_____

_____

2. What issues faced Ukraine after independence?

_____

_____

_____

Vocabulary Strategy

What does the word *contaminated* mean in the underlined sentence? What clues can you find in the surrounding sentences? Circle the words and phrases in this paragraph that could help you learn what *contaminated* means.

✓ Reading Check

What were the results of the disaster at Chernobyl?

_____

_____

_____

✓ Reading Check

What is Ukraine's busiest industrial center?

_____

_____

Prepare to Read

Section 4
Russia: A Huge Country Takes a New Path

Objectives

1. Investigate the changes that capitalism has brought to Russia.
2. Understand the cultural traditions that have endured throughout Russia.
3. Identify issues that create challenges for Russians.

Target Reading Skill

Identify Contrasts When you contrast two things, you identify ways that they are different from each other. Some contrasts are easy to see. For example, it is easy to see how the city is different from the country. The city has more buildings and more people. The country has more wilderness or farms.

In this section you will read about the city of Moscow, and a huge area of Russia called Siberia. Some differences will be easy to spot, but you may have to look hard to spot them all!

Vocabulary Strategy

Using Context Clues Sometimes you can pick up clues about the meaning of an unfamiliar word from its context: the words, phrases, and sentences around it. The underlined words in the paragraph below give clues to the meaning of the word *frigid*.

Siberians have adapted to life in their <u>frigid</u> climate. Farmers work over-time to harvest crops before the <u>frost</u>. Some families hang huge pieces of meat from their porches. <u>Temperatures in winter are so cold</u> that the <u>meat freezes solid</u> and does not spoil.

The underlined context clues tell you that *frigid* means "extremely cold."

Emerging Capitalism

1 When the Soviet Union dissolved in 1991, the new Russian Federation had to find a new way to govern itself. It also struggled to change from communism to capitalism.

5 Moscow is the capital of Russia. When the Soviet Union first collapsed, business in Moscow boomed. **Investors** came from many different countries to make money in Moscow. Some investors became very wealthy. But not all Russians shared in this new 10 wealth. Salaries are low for most Russian workers. Many live in poverty.

Many Russians have been able to fulfill their dreams of starting their own businesses or factories. However, corruption prevents these business owners from keep-15 ing all they earn. Criminal gangs often force honest people who own businesses to pay them money. Laws to protect people are often not enforced.

In the 1990s, many Russians lost their life savings when banks failed and **inflation** rose. The economy 20 slowly recovered. Russians also have concerns about health care. Medical care used to be free. Now it is expensive. Hospitals do not have modern equipment.

Siberia has also been affected by the change to capitalism. It is a vast region in eastern Russia. It has 25 coal, gold, iron, oil, and natural gas. To get to and use these rich reserves, Soviets built mines, factories, and the Trans-Siberian railroad. Large cities grew up in this rural area. The communist government made sure that all workers had jobs and that farmers got good prices 30 for their crops. Today, Siberians worry about losing their jobs. On the other hand, Siberians are now able to buy their own homes. ✓

Vocabulary Strategy

What does the word *corruption* mean in the underlined sentence? What clues can you find in the surrounding words, phrases, and sentences? Circle context clues in this paragraph that could help you learn what *corruption* means.

_____

_____

✓ Reading Check

How has life in Siberia changed since the collapse of the communist government?

_____

_____

_____

Cultural Traditions Continue

The collapse of Soviet communism brought big changes to the lives of many Russians. But old Russian ways still survive, too.

Moscow is still the cultural center of the nation. Street vendors still sell traditional Russian crafts —right next to people selling electronic goods.

Much of Siberia is still rural. Change comes slowly there. Many log homes have no running water. But Siberians have adapted to life in their frigid climate. ☑

Uniting a Vast Nation

Russia is a huge country. It has more than 144 million people. Most are ethnic Russians. There are also many different ethnic groups who speak different languages and practice different religions. Some of them are tired of Russian rule.

Most of the people in the republic of Chechnya (CHECH nee uh) are Muslims. In 1991, Chechnya declared its independence from Russia. Russia did not want to lose control of this oil-rich republic, and sent troops there. Fighting continues between Chechnyan rebels and Russian troops.

In the early 2000s, Russia's economy began to improve. Yet problems remain. Russia has many natural resources. But Russia depends too heavily on sales of these materials, rather than on creating new jobs. If world prices are low, then Russia's economy suffers. ☑

Review Questions

1. How has the change to capitalism both helped and harmed ordinary Russians?

_____

_____

_____

2. Describe the war in Chechnya.

_____

_____

_____

🎯 Target Reading Skill

Read the paragraphs under the heading "Cultural Traditions Continue." What are two differences between life in Moscow and life in Siberia?

_____

_____

✓ Reading Check

Describe one Russian tradition that survives.

_____

_____

✓ Reading Check

Why is Russia's dependence on its natural resources a problem?

_____

_____

Chapter 10 Assessment

1. Traditions that help unite Poland include
   A. Catholicism.
   B. collective farms.
   C. the Russian language.
   D. foreign investment.

2. The Serbian province where Albanians rebelled is
   A. Yugoslavia.
   B. Slobodan Milosevic.
   C. Kosovo.
   D. Montenegro.

3. What makes Ukraine's farmland so productive?
   A. huge collectives
   B. rich black soil called chernozem
   C. new farming machinery
   D. corporate farming

4. Ukraine is still recovering from a disaster during the Soviet period. It is
   A. the starvation of millions of people on collectives.
   B. the pollution of ports and rivers by Soviet ships.
   C. the explosion of a nuclear power plant at Chernobyl.
   D. the depletion of its natural resources, such as iron and coal.

5. Russia's new economy depends too heavily on
   A. sales of its natural resources.
   B. foreign investments in business.
   C. businesses owned by wealthy, former government officials.
   D. development of large cities and factories in Siberia.

Short Answer Question

Compare how the change from communism to capitalism has affected Poland and Russia.

_____

_____

_____

_____

Africa

Objectives

1. Learn about Africa's four regions and its major landforms.
2. Find out about Africa's major rivers.

Target Reading Skill

Reread Have you ever replayed part of a movie so you could better understand what happened in that scene? Rereading is like that. Reading something again can help you understand a word or idea that you did not understand the first time.

When you reread, look for connections. First, find the facts that you do understand. Next, see if you can find the main idea. Then think about how the idea you do not understand connects to the main idea. Is that idea more clear now?

Vocabulary Strategy

Using Context Clues All words have at least one meaning. Sometimes, you can learn what a word means from its context. A word's context is the other words and sentences that surround it. You can often find clues to a word's meaning in its context.

Try this example. Say that you do not know the meaning of the word *history* in the following sentence:

History began when people started to keep written records of their experiences.

You could ask yourself: "What information does the sentence give me about the word?" Answer: "I know that history began when people started to keep written records of their experiences. This tells me that history must be the written record of human experience."

Section 1 Summary

Africa's Regions and Landforms

Africa has more than 50 countries. The continent also has four regions: North Africa, West Africa, East Africa, and Central and Southern Africa. <u>Each region of Africa has several types of climates and landforms.</u>

North Africa has rocky mountains and the world's largest desert, the Sahara (suh HA ruh). **West Africa** has the most people. It is mostly grassland. The soil there is good for farming. **East Africa** has many mountains, a few **plateaus**, grasslands, and hills. Much of **Central and Southern Africa** is flat or hilly grassland. It also has rain forests, mountains, swamps, and deserts.

Africa is often called the plateau continent. That is because much of it is flat and has a high **elevation**. Not all of Africa is flat, though. All four regions have mountains. The highest are in East Africa. ✓

A strip of coastal plain runs along much of Africa's coast. This land is dry and sandy in some places. In other places, it is marshy and moist. In the West African country of Ghana, the coastal strip is only about 5 miles (8 kilometers) wide. It ends in a long, steep slope. At the top of the slope, there is a plateau.

Mount Kilimanjaro, Africa's highest mountain, is in East Africa. It is on the edge of the Great Rift Valley. This valley was formed millions of years ago. The continents pulled apart and left a **rift** that is 4,000 miles (6,400 kilometers) long. Most of Africa's major lakes are located in or near the Great Rift Valley.

Africa's Rivers

Africa has four large rivers: the Nile (nyl), the Congo (KAHN goh), the Zambezi (zam BEE zee), and the Niger (NY jur). Parts of these rivers can be used for travel. But waterfalls and steep rapids keep ships from sailing the whole way between Africa's interior and the coast.

Key Terms

plateau (pla TOH) *n.* a large, flat area that rises above the surrounding land; has at least one side that is steep

elevation (el uh VAY shun) *n.* the height of land above or below sea level

rift (rift) *n.* a deep crack in Earth's surface

Vocabulary Strategy

What does the word *landforms* mean in the underlined sentence? What clues can you find in the words, phrases, or sentences that follow it? Circle the words that help you understand what *landforms* means.

✓ Reading Check

Why is Africa called the plateau continent?

_____

_____

_____

Target Reading Skill

Reread to understand what *Africa's interior* means. When you read the paragraph at the left again, look for connections to other words.

Lengths of Africa's Major Rivers	
1. Nile River	more than 4,000 miles (6,400 kilometers)
2. Congo River	2,900 miles (4,677 kilometers)
3. Niger River	2,600 miles (4,180 kilometers)
4. Zambezi River	2,200 miles (3,540 kilometers)

The **Nile** is the longest river in the world. It is almost twice as long as the Mississippi River. The White Nile is
35 in Sudan. The Blue Nile is in Ethiopia. These two rivers are **tributaries** of the Nile. After they combine to form the Nile, it flows north into the Mediterranean Sea.

People have farmed the land along the Nile for thousands of years. Yearly floods provided water for crops.
40 They also left behind a layer of silt, or tiny pieces of rock and dirt. The silt made the soil **fertile**. In the 1960s, Egypt built the Aswan High Dam on the Nile. A lake, called Lake Nasser, was created behind the dam. Water from Lake Nasser is used to water crops in the desert. Because
45 of the dam, the Nile no longer floods. ☑

The **Congo River** flows through the rain forests of Central Africa. Hundreds of tributaries flow into the Congo River. People farm along the river. They also catch many kinds of fish.
50 The **Niger** flows north from Guinea, then bends south. It provides water for farms in the valley around it. Many people make their living fishing in the Niger.

The **Zambezi** is in Southern Africa. About halfway to where it pours into the Indian Ocean, the Zambezi
55 plunges into a canyon. This creates the spectacular waterfall known as Victoria Falls.

Review Questions

1. Name the four regions of Africa.

_____

_____

2. Which river includes Victoria Falls?

_____

_____

Key Terms

tributary (TRIB yoo tehr ee) *n.* a river or stream that flows into a larger river
fertile (FUR tul) *adj.* rich in the substances plants need to grow well

✓ **Reading Check**

What effect has the Aswan High Dam had on the waters of the Nile?

_____

_____

_____

Prepare to Read

Section 2
Climate and Vegetation

Objectives

1. Discover the factors that influence Africa's climate.
2. Learn the characteristics of each of Africa's vegetation regions.
3. Find out how climate can affect the health of people in Africa.

Target Reading Skill

Paraphrase Say your parents ask what you learned in school one day. You might repeat everything your teacher said. Or you might paraphrase. That means putting something into your own words.

If you can put something you read into your own words, it shows that you understand what you read. Paraphrasing will also help you remember what you read.

For example, you could paraphrase the second paragraph under the heading "What Influences Climate?" this way:

The seasons north of the Equator are the opposite of the seasons south of the Equator.

As you read this section, paraphrase the information that follows each heading.

Vocabulary Strategy

Using Context to Determine Meaning Using context is like being a detective looking for clues. Sometimes you can pick up clues about the meaning of an unfamiliar word from the words, phrases, and sentences around it. The underlined words in the paragraph below give clues to the meaning of the word *nomad*.

Most of the people who live in the desert are **nomads**. They move from place to place in search of water for themselves and their animals. When they reach an oasis, nomads may pitch their tents and stay for several days. But eventually, they move on.

Did you figure out that a nomad is a person who travels from place to place instead of settling in one place for good?

Section 2 Summary

What Influences Climate?

Three factors influence climate: distance from the Equator, elevation, and nearness to large bodies of water and large landforms.

The Equator runs through the middle of Africa. Regions near the Equator are usually hot and have a tropical climate. Most of Africa is in a tropical climate region. North of the Equator, winter and summer take place at the same time as in the United States. South of the Equator, the seasons are reversed. That means that July in South Africa is in the middle of winter.

Higher elevations tend to be cooler. For example, Mount Kilimanjaro is close to the Equator. But its peak stays cold all year because it is so high. ✓

Comparing Ethiopia and Somalia helps show the effects of elevation on climate. They are about the same distance from the Equator but have different climates.

Ethiopia is on a very high plateau. It has mild temperatures and plenty of rain. The rain allows farmers in Ethiopia to grow a wide range of crops. Therefore, many farmers there do not **irrigate** their crops. When the country goes through a **drought**, crops and animals are much harder to raise.

Somalia is at a much lower elevation than Ethiopia. Its climate is hot and dry. Farming is possible only near a river or near an **oasis**, where crops can be irrigated.

Rainfall varies greatly from one region of Africa to another. Parts of the west coast get a lot of rain. But in parts of the Sahara, rain may not fall for several years.

Vegetation Regions of Africa

Africa has different vegetation regions. There are rain forests in West and Central Africa that cover one fifth of the continent. In rain forest regions, rain falls often. Many types of trees, plants, and animals live there.

Vocabulary Strategy

Look at the word *reversed* in the underlined sentence. The term is not defined for you. But there are clues about what it means. Circle the words or phrases in the paragraph that help you learn its meaning.

✓ Reading Check

How are elevation and the climate of a place connected?

_____

_____

_____

Key Terms

irrigate (IHR uh gayt) **v.** to supply with water through a ditch, pipe, channel, or sprinkler

drought (drowt) **n.** a long period of little or no rain

oasis (oh AY sis) **n.** a fertile place in a desert where there is water and vegetation

Some people in rain forest regions live in cities or towns. Others cut down the trees to grow crops such as cacao (kuh KAY oh) and cassava. But clearing the trees threatens the survival of these forests.

The most common vegetation in Africa is tropical **savanna**. Tall grasses, bushes, and scattered trees grow in the savanna region. It is home to large herd animals. It has only two seasons, dry and wet. ✓

Beyond the savanna lie the deserts. The Sahara covers most of North Africa. A region called the Sahel (sah HEL) lies along the southern edge of the Sahara. The Sahel is hot and dry. It receives a few inches of rain each year. Shrubs, grass, and some trees grow there. The Namib and Kalahari deserts are in Southern Africa.

Most of the people who live in Africa's deserts are **nomads**. Desert nomads move around. Many herd animals such as camels. They also take part in trade.

Climate and Health

Throughout Africa, there are places that present health risks to farm animals and people. Many insects that carry diseases live in the wet rain forests. Even in the grasslands, disease and illness take their toll.

The tsetse (TSET see) fly lives in parts of Africa. Its bite can kill cattle and cause a disease called sleeping sickness in humans. ✓

Mosquitoes live in warm, moist climates. Those that have a disease called malaria can spread it to humans by biting them.

Review Questions

1. Name three factors that influence climate.

_____

_____

2. In which vegetation region does rain fall often?

_____

_____

Key Terms

savanna (suh VAN uh) *n.* a region of tall grasses with scattered trees

nomad (NOH mad) *n.* a person who has no permanent, settled home and who instead moves from place to place

✓ Reading Check

What kinds of vegetation grow in Africa's savanna region?

_____

_____

_____

Target Reading Skill

Use your own words to paraphrase the bracketed paragraph. What would be a good way to restate *take their toll?*

Hint: you might say "disease and illness cause serious problems" in your own words.

_____

_____

_____

✓ Reading Check

What problems does the tsetse fly cause?

_____

_____

_____

Prepare to Read

Section 3
Resources and Land Use

Objectives

1. Discover the ways in which Africans make use of their agricultural resources.
2. Learn about the mineral and energy resources found in Africa.
3. Find out what African countries are doing to improve their economic health.

Target Reading Skill

Summarize When you summarize what you have read, you tell a shorter version of it. Your summary should focus on the most important points. You may leave out the smaller details. When you summarize, keep the main ideas or facts in the correct order so they still make sense.

Read the following sentence: "Hardwood trees grow in all four regions of Africa. People earn money by cutting them down and selling them." You could summarize it like this: "In Africa, people are cutting down trees for money."

As you read, pause from time to time to summarize the main ideas about Africa's resources and land use.

Vocabulary Strategy

Using Context Clues to Determine Meaning Many words have more than one meaning. You may not always be sure how a word is being used. If that happens, try using context clues to figure out which meaning of the word is being used. For example, in the sentences below, the word *back* is used in two different ways.

He wrote his answers on the **back** of the worksheet.

By using context clues, you can figure out that in this sentence, *back* means "other side."

She asked her friends to **back** her decision.

By using context clues, you can figure out that in this sentence, *back* means "support."

Section 3 Summary

Agricultural Resources

1　Most Africans are farmers. Some of these farmers live in areas with fertile soil and much rain. But most of them live on land with poor soil or too little rain for easy farming.

5　Much of Africa's land is used for **subsistence farming**. Subsistence farmers may sell or trade a few crops for other items they need. But mainly they use their crops to feed their families.

Subsistence farmers grow different crops in different regions of Africa. For example, in North Africa, subsistence farmers raise barley, wheat, and dates. They also irrigate fields to grow fruits and vegetables.

In countries where there is dry tropical savanna, subsistence farmers grow grains. Where there is more rainfall, farmers also grow vegetables, fruits, and root crops. Root crops include yams and cassava. Corn and rice are important crops in West Africa. People in many African cultures fish or raise goats or poultry. ✓

Farmers in all regions of Africa grow **cash crops**. In Ivory Coast, Ghana, and Cameroon, they grow coffee and cacao beans. In Kenya, Tanzania (tan zuh NEE uh), Malawi (MAH lah wee), Zimbabwe, and Mozambique, tea is one of the cash crops.

In recent years, more and more farmers have planted cash crops. This means that less land is planted with crops that can meet a family's needs. At times, this causes problems in Africa. When cash crops have failed, some Africans have not had enough food. Also, sometimes the prices of cash crops drop. Then families earn less money that they can use to buy what they need.

Hardwood trees grow in all four regions of Africa. People can earn money by cutting them down and

---

Key Terms

subsistence farming (sub SIS tuns FAHR ming) *n.* raising just enough crops to support one's family
cash crop (kash krahp) *n.* a crop that is raised to be sold

The word *poor* has several meanings. What is its meaning in this context?

_____

_____

✓ Reading Check

What are some of the crops that subsistence farmers grow in different parts of Africa?

_____

_____

_____

Target Reading Skill

To summarize the bracketed paragraph, first state the main points. An important point is that more African farmers have started to plant cash crops. Which point follows that one?

_____

_____

selling them. Thousands of acres of trees have been cut down. Several countries are planting trees so that they
35 do not run out of this valuable resource.

Natural Resources

Each African country has its own **economy**. As you have read, farming is an important part of many African economies. The same is true of mining.

Parts of Africa are rich in mineral resources. Some
40 countries have large amounts of petroleum. It is used to make oil and gasoline. Libya, Algeria, Nigeria, Cameroon, Gabon, and Angola all produce a lot of oil. Ghana is a country that exports a lot of gold. African countries also produce the following mineral resources: copper,
45 silver, uranium, titanium, and diamonds. ☑

Improving Economic Health

Most of Africa's workers are farmers. When a nation's economy depends on one kind of industry, it is called a specialized economy. ☑
50 For Africa to have a strong economy, farms must receive enough rain for crops to grow. Also, farmers must sell crops for high enough prices to make money. The African countries are trying to **diversify** because these things may not always happen. This means they are trying to produce many kinds of crops, raw materi-
55 als, and manufactured goods. That way, if one cash crop fails, a country's economy is not as hurt as it would be if that were the country's only industry.

Review Questions

1. What two types of farming are practiced in Africa?

_____

_____

2. Name three mineral resources of Africa.

_____

_____

> **Key Terms**
>
> **economy** (ih KAHN uh mee) *n.* a system for producing, distributing, using, and owning goods and services
> **diversify** (duh VUR suh fy) *v.* to add variety to; to expand a country's economy by increasing the variety of goods produced

1. Mount Kilimanjaro and the Great Rift Valley are located in
   A. West Africa.
   B. North Africa.
   C. East Africa.
   D. Southern Africa.

2. Africa's longest river is
   A. the Nile.
   B. the Congo.
   C. the Niger.
   D. the Zambezi.

3. In which kind of climate region does much of Africa lie?
   A. continental
   B. highland
   C. tropical
   D. equatorial

4. Which kind of vegetation covers more of Africa than any other?
   A. tropical rain forest
   B. savanna
   C. desert
   D. Sahel

5. How do most Africans make their living?
   A. mining
   B. manufacturing
   C. fishing or hunting
   D. farming

Short Answer Question

What do elevation and distance from the Equator have to do with climate?

_____

_____

_____

_____

Objectives

1. Examine the ways in which the survival skills of early Africans changed over time.
2. Find out about early civilizations that arose along the Nile River.
3. Learn about the Bantu migrations.

Target Reading Skill

Set a Purpose for Reading Reading a textbook is different from reading a novel or the newspaper. To read to learn effectively, you must preview and set a purpose for your reading.

Before you read this section, take a moment to preview it. Look at the section title "African Beginnings" and the objectives. Now flip through the next two pages. Read the headings. They tell you about the section's contents. They tell you what to expect to learn from each section. As you preview, use this information to give yourself a reason to read the section. Are you curious about anything in the section? Maybe you want to learn about survival skills. Read to satisfy that curiosity—that's your purpose for reading.

Vocabulary Strategy

Using Context to Clarify Meaning When you come across difficult words in your text, they are often defined for you. Sometimes the definition appears in a separate sentence. Other times there is a brief definition in the same sentence. The word *or* is often used to introduce the definition. In the following examples, brief definitions appear in italics.

migrate, or *move from one place to settle in another*

domesticate, or *adapt wild plants or animals and breed them for human use*

a civilization is a *society that has cities, a central government, and social classes*

The definitions of the underlined words are part of their context. Look for definitions in the context as you come across unfamiliar words in your reading.

Section 1 Summary

Changing Survival Skills

Our early human ancestors were hunter-gatherers. They survived by hunting animals and gathering food such as fruits, nuts, and roots. In addition to meat, animals provided skins and fur to wear and use for shelter. Early human ancestors made tools from wood, animal bone, and stone. When our ancestors first used stone tools, a time period called the Stone Age began. ☑

Between 10,000 and 6,000 years ago, some hunter-gatherers began to farm and to herd animals. Farming in Africa probably began in North Africa, which was less dry than it is now.

The first farmers probably grew grains. Later, people began to **domesticate** plants. They did this by using only seeds from strong plants, not weak ones. They also began to domesticate some wild animals.

By domesticating plants and animals, people could control their food supply. They did not have to travel to look for food. They could settle in one place. Most early farmers settled on fertile land near a river or other source of water. Some communities were now able to produce more food than was needed. This allowed some people to do work other than farming.

Civilizations on the Nile

After hundreds of thousands of years, some Stone Age groups became **civilizations**. In a civilization, there are cities and a government. Also groups of people with similar backgrounds, wealth, and ways of living form social classes. And architecture, writing, and art usually develop. A few thousand years ago, two important civilizations grew up along the Nile River. They were Egypt and Nubia. Both began as early farming communities. ☑

Key Terms

domesticate (duh MES tih kayt) *v.* to raise plants or animals for human use

civilization (sih vuh luh ZAY shun) *n.* a society that has cities, a central government, and social classes and that usually has writing, art, and architecture

---

Vocabulary Strategy

The term *hieroglyphs* is defined in the context. Circle the definition.

Ancient Egypt was ruled by kings and queens. The kings were called pharaohs (FEHR ohz). The kings and queens were buried in tombs. Some of the tombs were large pyramids. Inside the tombs, people painted pictures of Egyptian life. They also painted <u>hieroglyphs</u> (HY ur oh glifs), or picture-writing symbols.

The kingdoms of Nubia began about 3100 B.C. One of the greatest was Napata. The Nubians of Napata conquered Egypt and ruled it for 60 years. A later Nubian kingdom was farther south, in Meroë (MEHR oh ee).

The Bantu Migrations

About 4,000 years ago, a group of people in Africa began to **migrate**. The people spoke Bantu (BAN too) languages. They left from the region that is now the border between Nigeria and Cameroon. The migration was one of the largest movements of people ever.

No one knows why the Bantu migrations began. Farming improvements may have caused the population to grow. Then people would need more land to farm. Whatever the reason, Bantu-speaking farmers spread across Central and Southern Africa. Their language soon became the one that most people spoke.

Today, there are hundreds of **ethnic groups** in Central and Southern Africa. Members of an ethnic group have a shared history or culture. They may also speak their own language. Most of the ethnic groups in Central and Southern Africa speak one of the many Bantu languages. That means more than 200 million people in the region are Bantu-speakers. ✓

✓ Reading Check

How many people in Central and Southern Africa speak Bantu languages today?

_____

_____

Review Questions

1. Where in Africa did farming most likely begin?

_____

_____

2. What were the Bantu migrations?

_____

_____

> **Key Terms**
>
> **migrate** (MY grayt) *v.* to move from one place to settle in another
> **ethnic group** (ETH nik groop) *n.* a group of people who share the same ancestors, culture, language, or religion

Prepare to Read

Section 2
Kingdoms, City-States, and Empires

Objectives

1. Learn how trade affected the development of early East African civilizations.
2. Examine the forces that shaped the history of the North African trading powers.
3. Find out how West African kingdoms gained wealth and power.

Predict Making predictions before you read helps you set a purpose for reading. It also helps you remember what you have read. First, preview the section. Look at the section title, objectives, and headings. Then use this information to predict what the section will be about. Based on your preview, you will probably predict that this section is about civilizations and trade in different regions in Africa.

List three regions of Africa that you expect to learn about in this section.

Prediction 1: _____

Prediction 2: _____

Prediction 3: _____

As you read, check your predictions. Were they right? If not, rewrite them as you learn more.

Vocabulary Strategy

Using Context to Clarify Meaning When you come across a word you do not know, you may not need to look it up in a dictionary. In this workbook, key terms appear in **blue**. The definitions are given at the bottom of the page. Stopping to look at the definition can interrupt your reading. Instead, continue reading through the end of the paragraph. See if you can figure out what the word means from its context. Clues can include examples and explanations. Then look at the definition at the bottom of the page to see how well you understood the word. Finally, reread the paragraph to make sure you understood everything you read.

East African Trading Civilizations

East Africa's early civilizations developed near coasts. They grew strong from trade. Their locations made trade possible with Arabia, India, and East Asia.

Around 1000 B.C., African and Arab traders began settling along the Red Sea. Later, the kingdom of Aksum was founded there. By the A.D. 200s, Aksum controlled trade from the Mediterranean Sea to India.

When goods are traded, often ideas are shared as well. In the A.D. 300s, news about Christianity spread. Many people in Aksum became Christian.

When Arabs took control of the region's trade in the A.D. 600s, Aksum lost power. At that time, trading cities were growing along the coast. Traders sailed to India and China with animal skins, ivory, and gold. They sailed back with cotton, silk, and porcelain. ✓

Trade brought change to the culture of coastal East Africa. Muslim traders introduced Islam to East Africa. A new language called <u>Swahili</u> developed. Today, Swahili is the most widely spoken Bantu language.

Some East African trading cities became powerful **city-states**. These included Malindi, Mombasa, and Kilwa. In the early 1500s, many city-states were conquered and destroyed by Europeans from Portugal. The Portuguese wanted to build their own trading empire.

Another great trading civilization arose south of the East African city-states and away from the coast. It was called Great Zimbabwe and it traded with East Africa.

North African Trading Powers

North Africa's location attracted sea traders. By 800 B.C., the Phoenicians had built the trading city of Carthage (KAHR thij). It became a powerful city-state. It controlled trade across the Mediterranean for centuries. It may have been the world's wealthiest city. In 146 B.C. the Roman Empire destroyed the city. ✓

✓ Reading Check

What kinds of goods traveled to and from East Africa?

_____

_____

_____

Vocabulary Strategy

Using context clues, write a definition of the word *Swahili*. Circle the words or phrases in the text that help you write your definition. Then compare your definition to the one in the Key Terms box.

_____

_____

_____

✓ Reading Check

For what purpose did the Phoenicians build Carthage?

_____

_____

_____

Key Terms

Swahili (swah HEE lee) *n.* a Bantu language spoken in much of East Africa; also an ethnic group

city-state (SIH tee stayt) *n.* a city that is also an independent state, with its own traditions, government, and laws

Under Roman rule, cities grew and roads were built
throughout North Africa. Christianity also spread. But in
A.D. 476, the Roman Empire collapsed. In the A.D. 600s,
the Arabs took control of North Africa. Their religion,
Islam, spread to North Africa and West Africa.

West African Kingdoms

In West Africa, kingdoms grew powerful from the
trade of salt and gold. People need salt to survive,
but there were no sources of salt in West Africa. However, there was gold. In North Africa, there was salt,
but no gold. Because of this, trade grew between North
Africa and West Africa. Controlling the trade brought
power to three West African kingdoms. To their south,
forest kingdoms also became wealthy from trade.

The first West African kingdom was Ghana. It's
kings grew rich from the taxes they charged on the salt
and gold that were traded in their land.

In the 1200s, a new power arose. It was Mali. Its
kings controlled the gold mines of the south and the
salt supplies of the north. Its most famous king was
Mansa Musa (MAHN sah MOO sah). ✓

Mansa Musa and many of his people were Muslim.
In 1324, Mansa Musa made a **pilgrimage** to Mecca, a
holy city in Arabia. On this journey, Mansa Musa set up
trade with other Muslim states and Europe.

In about 1332, the Songhai empire became West
Africa's most powerful kingdom. Its major trading city,
Tombouctou, was also a center of Muslim learning.
Invaders from North Africa defeated Songhai in 1591.

Review Questions

1. How did trade change coastal East Africa's culture?

_____

_____

2. How did West African kingdoms become wealthy?

_____

_____

Key Terms

pilgrimage (PIL gruh mij) *n.* a journey taken for a religious purpose
Tombouctou (tohm book TOO) *n.* a city in Mali near the Niger River

Target Reading Skill

Based on what you have read so
far, did you make good predictions? If not, revise or change your
predictions now.

New Prediction:

_____

_____

_____

✓ Reading Check

Who was Mansa Musa?

_____

_____

Section 3
European Conquest of Africa

Objectives

1. Discover what motivated Europeans to explore the African coast.
2. Find out how the Atlantic slave trade developed in the 1500s.
3. Learn how Europeans colonized regions of Africa.

Target Reading Skill

Ask Questions Before you read this section, preview the title and the objectives above. Then preview the headings. What do you predict will be the important ideas in the section?

Now write two questions that will help you understand or remember the ideas in the text. For example, you might ask yourself:

- Why did Europeans go to Africa?
- Which European countries colonized Africa?

Find the answers to your questions as you read. If what you read brings new questions to mind, write those down, too. Then see if the text answers all your questions.

Vocabulary Strategy

Using Context to Clarify Meaning When you read, you may come across a word you do not know. See if you can use the word's context to figure out what it means. The context may include examples or explanations.

Sometimes, you will only be able to get an idea of a word's meaning, not a true definition. When this happens, look the word up in a dictionary. Remember that the first definition listed may not be the right one. Look at each definition together with the context to find the one that works. Then reread the sentence where the word appeared. See how knowing the word's meaning makes the whole sentence clearer?

Section 3 Summary

Europeans on the Coast

In the mid-1400s, the Portuguese began sailing along West Africa's coast. They were searching for gold. They were used to getting gold from North Africans. Now Europeans wanted to trade with West Africans for their gold and their ivory.

Items Traded Between Europe and Africa	
Europe → Africa	**Africa → Europe**
Products copper, brass, clothing	**Products** gold, cotton, ivory, skins, metal objects
Food crops corn, cassava, yams	**Food crops** okra, watermelon, rice

But the situation changed. In 1498, three Portuguese ships sailed along Africa's east coast. The wealth of the city-states there amazed the Portuguese. They sent more ships to East Africa—this time to take over. Portugal controlled East Africa's coast until the 1600s. ☑

The Dutch, French, and English soon arrived in Africa, too. They set up trading posts on Africa's coasts. The Dutch built a trading post on the **Cape of Good Hope**. Soon, settlers arrived. They moved inland, building homes and farms. As Europeans spread out, the relationship between Africans and Europeans became worse. In particular, the slave trade that was developing was horrible for Africans.

The Atlantic Slave Trade

European settlers in the Americas needed workers for their mines and **plantations**. Instead of paying workers, the settlers wanted to use enslaved workers. At first, the settlers enslaved Native Americans. But many of them became sick and died. Others ran away. ☑

The settlers decided to enslave Africans instead. They knew that Africans were skilled farmers, miners, and metal workers. And, since they would be in unfamiliar lands, Africans could not escape easily.

Key Terms

Cape of Good Hope (kayp uv good hohp) *n.* the point of land at the southern end of Cape Peninsula, South Africa

plantation (plan TAY shun) *n.* a large farm that grows cash crops

Vocabulary Strategy

You may not know what *cassava* means in the chart. Circle the clues you find. Then look up the word in a dictionary and write the correct definition below.

_____

_____

✓ Reading Check

What happened when the Portuguese saw the East African city-states?

_____

_____

_____

✓ Reading Check

Why did the Europeans want to own slaves?

_____

_____

Choose one of the questions you asked earlier. Now answer your question based on what you have read.

Answer: _____

_____

_____

✓ Reading Check

Why were Europeans still interested in Africa after the slave trade had ended?

_____

_____

_____

By 1780, about 80,000 African slaves were being shipped across the Atlantic each year. They were not given enough food, water, or space. Up to one fifth of the slaves died during each journey.

Olaudah Equiano was luckier than most slaves. He was captured and sold at a slave auction in 1756, when he was 11. In time, he was able to buy his freedom. But for most slaves, freedom was only a dream.

Some native Africans grew rich from trading slaves. But overall, the slave trade was a disaster for Africa. West Africa lost many of its people. Families were torn apart. Many African societies broke down.

Europeans Colonize Africa

The African slave trade ended in the mid-1800s. But then Europeans began taking Africa's natural resources. They wanted the resources to run factories that were being built in Europe. ✓

European countries wanted to avoid going to war over Africa's resources. In 1884, European leaders set up rules for claiming African land. By 1900, Europeans had **colonized** much of Africa. People called the European competition for African land "the scramble for Africa." By 1914, only Ethiopia and Liberia were still free.

The scramble for Africa caused long-term problems. Africans had little power in the colonial governments. And the Europeans took the best land for themselves. They also encouraged conflicts between African groups.

Review Questions

1. What did the Portuguese want from West Africa?

_____

_____

2. How did the slave trade affect Africa?

_____

_____

Key Terms

Olaudah Equiano (oh LOW duh ek wee AHN oh) *n.* an antislavery activist who wrote an account of his enslavement
colonize (KAHL uh nyz) *v.* to settle in an area and take control of its government

Prepare to Read

Section 4
Independence and Its Challenges

Objectives

1. Learn about the growth of nationalism in Africa.
2. Find out about the effects of World War II on Africa and on the growing independence movement.
3. Examine the different challenges faced by African nations on their paths to independence.

Target Reading Skill

Use Prior Knowledge Prior knowledge is what you already know about a topic. Say a friend starts telling you about a field trip her class went on recently. You remember that your class went on that field trip last year. You start thinking about the things you learned on the trip. That is your prior knowledge about the topic. You use your prior knowledge to better understand your friend's experience.

Before you read, flip through this section. Write down what you already know about the topics. Connect what you learn to what you already knew.

Vocabulary Strategy

Using Context to Clarify Meaning Social studies textbooks often use words that you do not already know. To understand the meaning of these words, try using the context. The context is the words and sentences just before and after the word. Context clues can include examples, explanations, or definitions. As you read, use the graphic organizer to help you.

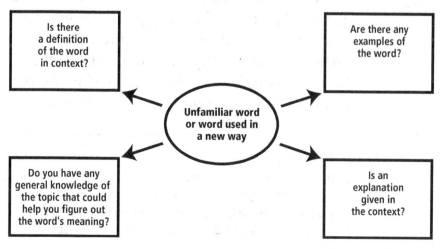

Section 4 Summary

The Growth of Nationalism

Many Africans dreamed of gaining independence from Europe. But most Europeans who ruled the African colonies did not view Africans as equals. Also, the colonial powers had set colony borders that combined many nations and ethnic groups. Some of the groups did not get along. African leaders saw that they would have to build unity and pride to end colonial rule.

Nationalism grew during the early 1900s. Africans in South Africa and in British West Africa formed new political parties. They wanted Africans to gain rights such as voting. ✓

During the 1920s, the **Pan-Africanism** movement began. Members of this movement believed that all Africans should work together for their rights and freedoms. Many people supported the movement.

One of the great Pan-African leaders was Léopold Senghor (lay oh POHLD sahn GAWR) of Senegal. He encouraged Africans to study their traditions and be proud of their culture. When Senegal became independent in 1960, Senghor was its first president.

Africa and World War II

During World War II, the Italians invaded Ethiopia. The Germans and the Italians also invaded North

The Allies
Great Britain
France
The United States

Africa, which was under British and French control. In response, thousands of African soldiers fought and died to help the Allies win World War II. ✓

African nations supported the Allies in other ways as well. Liberia and the Belgian Congo supplied rubber and other needed resources. Allied planes used African airfields to move supplies into Asia. In the end, World War II's focus on freedom inspired many Africans to fight for the freedom of their countries as well.

Key Terms

nationalism (NASH uh nul iz um) *n.* a feeling of pride in one's homeland; a group's identity as members of a nation

Pan-Africanism (pan AF rih kun iz um) *n.* the belief that all Africans should work together for their rights and freedoms

Different Paths to Independence

World War II weakened the economies of colonial powers such as France and Great Britain. The war also left people feeling unsure that colonialism should continue. In Britain, many people felt that the colonial empire was too expensive.

As more and more Africans demanded freedom, European countries began to give up their African colonies. Some countries did so peacefully. For example, Britain granted Ghana its independence. But Algeria, a French colony, had to fight for its freedom.

In the Gold Coast colony, Kwame Nkrumah (KWAH mee un KROO muh) led peaceful strikes and **boycotts** against British rule in the early 1950s. The British jailed Nkrumah several times. But the protests went on. In 1957, the people gained independence. The new country took the name Ghana. Nkrumah became its president.

The French thought of Algeria as part of France. Algerians disagreed. They were willing to fight to govern themselves. War began in 1954. In 1962, the Algerians won the war—and their independence. ✓

Many of the new African governments were not stable. In some, military leaders took control by force. Military governments do not always govern fairly. But many parts of Africa have a long history of **democracy**. In a democracy, citizens influence government decisions. Many Africans feel that it will take time to build stable countries. Today, most African countries are less than 50 years old.

Review Questions

1. When did nationalism in Africa begin to grow?

_____

_____

2. How did World War II help African independence?

_____

_____

> **Key Terms**
> **boycott** (BOY kaht) *n.* a refusal to buy or use certain products or services
> **democracy** (di MAHK ruh see) *n.* a government over which citizens exercise power

✓ **Reading Check**

How did Algeria gain independence?

_____

_____

_____

🎯 **Target Reading Skill**

Read the bracketed paragraph. What do you already know about democracy that can help you understand why it might take time to achieve?

_____

_____

_____

Prepare to Read

Section 5 Issues for Africa Today

Objectives

1. Learn about the economic issues faced by African nations today.
2. Find out about major social issues and how they affect Africans today.
3. Discover the ways in which Africa is facing current environmental challenges.

Predict Predicting what you will learn helps set your purpose for reading. It also helps you remember what you read. When you predict, you use two other reading skills: previewing and using prior knowledge.

For example, this section is titled "Issues in Africa Today." Read the objectives and the headings to preview the section. Then think about what you already know about Africa's history. This is your prior knowledge. Use all this information to predict some issues that Africa might face today.

As you read, connect what you read with your prediction. See if what you learn supports what you predicted you would learn. If not, revise your prediction as you read.

Vocabulary Strategy

Using Context to Clarify Meaning Sometimes you may read a word you recognize, but the word does not make sense to you. This is probably because most words have more than one meaning. What a word means depends on its context. Look for clues in the surrounding words or sentences to understand how the word is being used.

For example, the word *ground* has many meanings. You cannot know which meaning the author had in mind unless you look at the context. Some of the most common meanings are listed in the chart below.

Word	Meaning	Examples
ground	Earth's surface	It was good to stand on solid ground again.
	any piece of land	The students pitched their tents on the ground.
	(plural) lawn, garden, or other land surrounding a building	The grounds of the museum were beautiful.
	(plural) a reason or cause	What are your grounds for saying no?

Section 5 Summary

Economic Issues

Europeans ruling the colonies saw Africa as a place to find raw materials they needed. They did not see a need to build factories in Africa. Most African countries today have few factories and little manufacturing. Their economies are based on farming and mining. ☑

Farming is the main economic activity in Africa. Africans practice two kinds of farming. One kind is subsistence farming. Subsistence farmers try to raise the food their families need. The other kind is **commercial farming**. Commercial farmers grow cash crops to sell. Cash crops include coffee, cacao, and bananas.

Mining is also important in Africa. Many nations have a lot of minerals they can sell to other countries.

About 75 percent of African countries have specialized economies. That means they depend on exporting, or selling to another country, just one or two products. When prices for these products become low, it hurts those countries because they have few other ways to earn money. African countries are now trying to diversify their economies. That means exporting many more products. Countries can diversify by growing different crops or adding new industries.

Africa faces the problem of having to feed more and more people. One way is to increase the size of crops. For example, since the late 1990s, West Africans have been planting **hybrid** rice. This rice combines the best parts of African and Asian rices. As a result, more rice is grown.

Social Issues

African children often need to work. When the children go to school, the family loses income. Because families know education can improve their children's lives, many are willing to go without that income.

✓ Reading Check

On which two activities are most African economies based?

_____

_____

⟳ Target Reading Skill

Make a prediction about whether African economies will remain based in farming and mining.

Prediction: _____

_____

_____

Keep reading to see if you are right.

Key Terms

commercial farming (kuh MUR shul FAHR ming) *n.* the large-scale production of crops for sale
hybrid (HY brid) *n.* a plant that is created by breeding different types of the same plant

Vocabulary Strategy

Find and circle the word *grounds* in the bracketed paragraph. How is it used here? Copy the correct definition from the chart at the beginning of this section.

_____

_____

_____

African communities really support their schools. Parents have helped build schools when a government could not do it alone. Also, many schools have too many students. In some cases, students take turns attending class. Students also often help keep their school and its grounds clean.

40 The schools are doing a good job. In all African countries, more people have become **literate**, or able to read and write, since independence.

Like education, health can be a challenge in Africa. For example, **life expectancy** differs from country to country. In Morocco, life expectancy is between 67 and 45 72 years. In Botswana, people only live about 32 years.

The main reason for low life expectancy in Africa is childhood disease. Insects and unclean drinking water help some diseases spread. And millions of Africans have been born with HIV, which causes AIDS. Mil-50 lions more adults have died of AIDS before age 50. ✓

The Environment

The countries of Africa face several environmental problems. There is not enough good farmland. About two thirds of Africa's land is desert or very dry. Farmers cannot count on receiving rain regularly.

55 Often people cut down trees to create more farmland or to sell the wood. But this causes the soil to erode or wear away. Then there is even less farmland. Without enough farmland, many Africans face starvation. Farmers have also tried to keep the soil from eroding by 60 planting trees in crop fields to hold the soil in place. ✓

Review Questions

1. Why do African nations diversify their economies?

_____

_____

2. What health issues do people face in Africa today ?

_____

_____

Key Terms

literate (LIT ur it) *adj.* able to read and write
life expectancy (lyf ek SPEK tun see) *n.* the average length of time a person can expect to live

Chapter 12 Assessment

1. In which region today do most of the ethnic groups speak a Bantu language?
   A. North Africa
   B. East Africa
   C. West Africa
   D. Central and Southern Africa

2. Which trading civilization was located in West Africa?
   A. Carthage
   B. Mombasa
   C. Mali
   D. Kilwa

3. The European colonization of Africa is sometimes called
   A. "the scramble for Africa."
   B. "the Atlantic slave trade."
   C. "the Pan-African movement."
   D. "the nationalist movement."

4. What were the beliefs of the Pan-African movement?
   A. that all Africans should be freed from slavery
   B. that all Africans should work together for their rights and freedoms
   C. that only Africans should live in Africa
   D. that Europeans should build factories in Africa

5. Which of the following is true about the number of Africans who are literate?
   A. Everyone in Africa is literate.
   B. The number of people who are literate has gone up since independence.
   C. The number of people who are literate has stayed the same since independence.
   D. The number of people who are literate has gone down since independence.

Short Answer Question

How did World War II help the movement for African independence?

_____

_____

_____

Prepare to Read

Section 1
The Cultures of North Africa

Objectives

1. Learn about the elements of culture.
2. Discover how Islam influences life in North Africa.
3. Find out about cultural change in North Africa.

Target Reading Skill

Make Comparisons There are many things you can compare—facts, ideas, objects, groups, or situations. Comparing two things helps you see how they are alike. It is often easier to understand new facts by comparing them with facts you already know. For example, read the following facts.

The Sahara covers about 3,500,000 square miles (9,064,965 square kilometers).

The Sahara is nearly as large as the entire United States.

The second fact compares the Sahara to something you already know—the United States. Can you better picture the size of the Sahara now?

Make comparisons to help you understand what you read in this section. Compare your own way of life to how people live in North Africa.

Vocabulary Strategy

Finding Roots A root is a word that is used to make another word. You make another word by adding a few letters to the beginning or end of the root. For example, the letters *un-* may be attached to the beginning of a word. Or the letters *-ing* may be attached to the end of the word. When you remove these added letters, you end up with the root.

Attached Letters	Word	Root
un-	unwell	well
-ing	doing	do

When you come across a new word, look at it closely. See if it contains any other words that you already know. Often, you can use the root inside a word to help you figure out the word's meaning.

The Elements of Culture

1 Culture has many parts. It includes food, clothing, homes, jobs, and language. It also includes things that are not easy to see. For example, culture includes the way people view their world and people's beliefs. ✔

5 Different cultures may have some things in common. People who live in different places may speak the same language, wear similar clothes, or live in the same kinds of houses. For example, in Morocco, Mexico, and the United States, there are people who live in houses
10 made of sun-dried clay.

Religion and Culture in North Africa

North Africa includes the countries of Egypt, Libya, Tunisia, Algeria, and Morocco. Its people have different backgrounds and ways of life. The Arabic language and the religion of Islam help bring the people together.

More than 95 percent of North Africans are Muslims. Muslims call God, *Allah* (AL uh). Islam was founded by Muhammad. Muslims believe that Muhammad was a prophet, or one who speaks for God.

Muslims consider the **Quran** to be the word of God.
20 The Quran contains many kinds of writing, including stories, promises, and instructions. It teaches about God, but is also a guide to living. The Quran forbids lying, stealing, and murder. It says Muslims may not gamble, eat pork, or drink alcohol.

25 Islamic law is based on the Quran. It governs many aspects of life, including family life, business, and government. Because so many North Africans are Muslims, Islamic law influences the cultures of the region.

Most North Africans are Arabs. The region is some-
30 times seen as a part of the Arab world. But there are other ethnic groups as well. The largest of them is the Berbers.

Key Terms

culture (KUL chur) *n.* the way of life of people who share similar customs and beliefs
Quran (KOO RAHN) *n.* the sacred book of Islam; also spelled *Koran*

Vocabulary Strategy

The words below appear on this page. Each of these words contains another word that is its root. Circle the words in the text as you come across them. Then underline the roots you find in these words.

Mark the Text

different

Arabic

instructions

government

✓ Reading Check

Name some parts of culture that are easy to see.

_____

_____

_____

Target Reading Skill

Read the bracketed paragraph. What do the different people of North Africa have in common?

_____

_____

_____

They live mainly in Algeria and Morocco. Most of them speak both Berber and Arabic. Almost all are Muslim. ✓

Many Berbers live in cities. Others live in small
35 villages in mountain areas. They live by herding and farming. Those who live in the Sahara herd and trade.

In parts of North Africa, people live in traditional ways, much like their parents and grandparents. In the cities, people live in both traditional and modern ways.

Cultural Change in North Africa

40 Culture changes all the time. For example, when people travel, they share their customs and ideas with others. They also learn about new ideas and customs. The result is **cultural diffusion**, or the spreading of culture.

Over time in North Africa, cultural diffusion has
45 happened through trade. North Africa's location made it a center of trade for people from Europe, Asia, and Africa. When the people of these regions traded goods, they also learned about one another's cultures. ✓

Conquest caused cultural diffusion and change too.
50 North Africa was home to the ancient Egyptians. They conquered other civilizations and, at times, were conquered by others. As power changed hands, more cultural diffusion took place.

More recently, North Africa has been influenced by
55 Western culture. Western culture is the cultures of Europe and North America. Some Muslims are concerned that their countries are becoming too Western. They are afraid that they will lose Muslim values and traditions. They want to preserve their traditions.

Review Questions

1. What are some of the different parts of culture?

_____

_____

2. How has Islam influenced the cultures of North Africa?

_____

_____

Key Term

cultural diffusion (KUL chur ul dih FYOO zhun) *n.* the spread of customs and ideas from one culture to another

Prepare to Read

Section 2
The Cultures of West Africa

Objectives

1. Learn about West Africa's ethnic diversity.
2. Find out about the importance of family ties in West African culture.
3. Examine the West African tradition of storytelling.

Target Reading Skill

Identify Contrasts Suppose that on a warm sunny day you stepped into an air-conditioned movie theater. The temperature and lighting inside the theater would be completely different from those outside. You would notice the contrast right away. It is a little more difficult to notice contrasts when you read. Sometimes two things are contrasted in the same sentence. Sometimes the contrast appears in different paragraphs or headings.

A chart is a good way to keep track of the contrasts. Use a chart like the one below to contrast languages in West Africa and in the United States.

West Africa	United States
• People speak four or five languages	• People speak one or two languages
•	•
•	•

Vocabulary Strategy

Finding Roots A root is a word with a few letters attached to its beginning or end to make another word. There are certain groups of letters that are attached to roots frequently. Usually, these letters make a syllable. A syllable is a group of letters that are spoken as a single sound. The chart below shows some common syllables and words in which they are used.

Common beginning syllables	Common ending syllables
un- (unsafe, unfriendly)	*-al* (traditional, musical)
re- (redo, redraw)	*-ed* (turned, walked)

When you come across a new word, look at it closely. See if it contains any common syllables. If you remove those syllables, is the word left behind a root that you recognize?

Section 2 Summary

Cultural Diversity of West Africa

West Africa is famous for its **cultural diversity**. Hundreds of ethnic groups with no common religion or language live there. West Africans speak hundreds of languages.

In order to communicate, most West Africans learn to speak more than one language. Some speak four or five languages. This helps to bring the many ethnic groups in a country together.

People in West Africa differ in other ways, too. They work at different kinds of jobs. They also live differently. For example, in the countryside, villages are surrounded by farmland. In the Sahara and the Sahel, many people herd livestock. Along the coast, most people fish. Some West Africans live in large cities and work in hospitals, hotels, or office buildings. ✓

West African Families

Kinship, or family ties, is very important to West Africans.

Levels of Kinship			
nuclear family: parents + children	extended family: parents + children + other relatives (such as grandparents, aunts, uncles, or cousins)	lineage: a group of families that share an ancestor, such as a great-great-grandparent	clan: a group of lineages

Often, the members of an extended family live, work, and make decisions together. They also take care of one another and help out their neighbors. ✓

Key Terms

cultural diversity (KUL chur ul duh VUR suh tee) *n.* a wide variety of cultures

kinship (KIN ship) *n.* a family relationship

nuclear family (NOO klee ur FAM uh lee) *n.* the part of a family that includes parents and children

extended family (ek STEN did FAM uh lee) *n.* the part of a family that includes parents, children, and other relatives

lineage (LIN ee ij) *n.* a group of families descended from a common ancestor

clan (klan) *n.* a group of lineages

✓ **Reading Check**

Give two examples of cultural diversity in West Africa.

1. _____

2. _____

Target Reading Skill

Contrast the nuclear family and the extended family. What is the difference?

_____

_____

_____

✓ **Reading Check**

What responsibilities do members of an extended family have toward one another?

_____

_____

_____

In the countryside, many West Africans identify the lineage and clan they are from. They do this in one of two ways. In some societies, a person's lineage is his or her mother's lineage. The person would inherit land or animals through the mother's lineage only. In other societies, a person's lineage is his or her father's lineage.

Family life is changing in West Africa. More and more people are moving from the countryside to urban areas, or cities. This is called urbanization. Many young men go to cities to find jobs. The women often stay in the countryside. They raise the children and farm. The men come home to visit their families and share the money they have earned.

Keeping Traditions Alive

Because cultures are changing, many West Africans think it is important to pass their history, values, and traditions on to young people. One way they do this is through storytelling. Traditional West African stories are spoken aloud rather than written down. The story-teller is called a griot (GREE oh). A griot uses storytelling as a way to pass traditions to the next generation. ✓

The traditions of West Africa have influenced other cultures, especially American culture. Many of the enslaved Africans that were brought to the United States came from West Africa. They brought with them their ideas, stories, dances, music, and customs. Two types of music—blues and jazz—have their roots in West African music.

Review Questions

1. Why do many West Africans speak more than one language?

_____

_____

_____

2. In what ways is storytelling important to West African culture?

_____

_____

_____

Vocabulary Strategy

The words listed below appear on this page. When you find each word, look for a common syllable attached to a root. Circle the syllable. Then underline the word left behind. Is it a root that you recognize?

urbanization

earned

traditional

✓ Reading Check

What does a griot do?

_____

_____

_____

Objectives

1. Find out how geography has affected the development of East African cultures.
2. Learn how and why ideas about land ownership are changing in East Africa.

Use Signal Words When drivers see a Detour sign, it is a signal to them that the route ahead will be different than usual. Similarly, when you read, you may find words or phrases that signal what is coming next.

All signal words point out relationships among ideas or events. Some signal words show contrasts. These are words such as *however, unlike, although, yet,* and *on the other hand.* They signal that what is coming will be different than what you are reading now. Other signal words show comparisons. These are words such as *like, as with, similarly,* and *just as.* They signal that what is coming will be similar to what you are reading now.

As you read, study each signal word or phrase. Decide whether it shows a comparison or a contrast. This will help you understand the connections in the text.

Vocabulary Strategy

Finding Roots You now know that syllables can be added at the beginning or end of a word to make a new word. The meaning of the new word is related to the original word but it is changed in some way.

In some cases, the spelling of the root changes slightly when a syllable is added. Often an *e* at the end of a root is removed when the syllable added is a *y.* For example, if we add the ending *–y* to the word *ease,* the new word is spelled *easy* (and not *easey!*). Similarly, if we add the ending *–ing* to the word *trade,* the new word is spelled *trading,* not *tradeing.*

Section 3 Summary

Geography and Cultural Diversity

East Africa has a lot of cultural diversity, much of it comes from dealing with other cultures. For example, East Africans have learned about other cultures through trade. East Africa lies along the west coast of the Indian Ocean. Across this ocean to the east live Arabs, Indians, and Asians. People from both sides of the Indian Ocean have used it for trade and travel for a very long time.

Nearly 2,000 years ago, Arab traders began to settle on the coast of East Africa. Over time, African and Arab ways of life blended in a new culture, **Swahili**. One of the strengths of the Swahili people is their ability to adjust to other cultures. At the same time, they try to keep their **heritage** alive and pass it down.

The Swahili live along East Africa's coast from Somalia to Tanzania. There are hundreds of other ethnic groups in East Africa as well. However, ethnic groups throughout the region use the Swahili language to communicate with one another. In Tanzania, children in elementary school are taught in Swahili. Later, they also learn English. By encouraging people to speak Swahili, East African nations help keep their people's heritage alive. Doing this also helps bring different peoples together.

Although most people in East Africa speak Swahili, many other languages are spoken there, too. A person may know three languages or more. About 1,000 languages are spoken in Sudan alone. Do you remember reading about the Bantu migrations? Many migrations have brought different groups and their languages to East Africa over time.

Key Terms

Swahili (swah HEE lee) *n.* an ethnic group in East Africa that resulted from the mixing of African and Arab ways more than 1,000 years ago; also a language

heritage (HEHR uh tij) *n.* the values, traditions, and customs handed down from one's ancestors

---

Vocabulary Strategy

The words below appear on this page. Each word contains a root that has changed from its usual spelling. Circle the words in the text. Then write the usual spelling of the root beside the word below.

cultural _____

encouraging _____

migrations _____

Target Reading Skill

What signal word in the bracketed paragraph signals a contrast between the use of Swahili and the other languages spoken in East Africa?

_____

_____

East Africans practice different religions. Islam was brought to the region by Arab traders. Christianity came to Ethiopia from North Africa. When Europeans arrived in East Africa, they spread Christianity even farther. Also, many people in East Africa practice traditional religions. ✓

Changing Ideas About Land

Before the 1800s, individual Africans did not buy or sell land. In fact, the idea of owning land did not exist. Instead, the right to farm land belonged to families; and they might farm different pieces of land over time.

Typically, members of an extended family farmed the land to grow food for the whole group. First, men cleared the land and broke the soil. Then, women planted seeds, tended fields, and brought in the crops while men herded farm animals or traded goods. ✓

European settlers arrived in the 1800s. They spread the idea of individuals owning land. In parts of East Africa, the British set up large plantations. When many African countries became independent, their governments sold different parts of these plantations to individual Africans.

Now, most of East Africa's land is owned. Much of what is not owned is not good for farming. Many people want to own land for farming. As a result, conflicts have developed over land.

The land where they grew up is very important to many Africans, but East Africa is becoming more urban. However, even people who spend most of their time in the city often expect to return to their villages later in life. Tanzania's former president, Julius Nyerere (JOOL yus nyuh REHR uh) did just that. After he retired in 1985, he moved back to his home village.

Review Questions

1. How has the Indian Ocean affected East African culture?

_____

_____

2. When did the idea of individuals owning land come to East Africa?

_____

_____

Prepare to Read

Section 4
The Cultures of Southern and Central Africa

Objectives

1. Learn about the cultural diversity of Southern Africa.
2. Examine different ways of life in Central Africa and learn about the diverse cultures of the region.

Target Reading Skill

Compare and Contrast When you compare, you look for the ways things are similar. When you contrast, you look for the ways things are different. Sometimes two things are alike in some ways, and different in other ways. A good way to keep track of both the similarities and the differences is to create a Venn diagram. You can use a Venn diagram like the one below to compare and contrast the cultures of Southern and Central Africa.

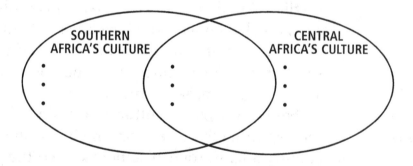

Vocabulary Strategy

Finding Roots You have already seen how the spelling of some words can change when syllables are added. In the last section, you saw how an *e* is dropped from some words before adding the suffix. To refresh your memory, look at the words in the box below.

-y, -ity		-ing	
ease ⟶ easy		*mine* ⟶ mining	
diverse ⟶ diversity		*settle* ⟶ settling	

In the same way, sometimes the *y* is dropped from the end of a word when adding a suffix. For example, look closely at the word *industrial*. Do you see that *industry* is the root word?

Diversity in Southern Africa

Vocabulary Strategy

The words below appear on this page. Each word contains a root that has changed from its usual spelling. Underline the roots in the words. Write the usual spelling of the word beside the words below.

diversity _____

mining _____

creating _____

industrialized _____

1 Like the rest of Africa, Southern Africa has a lot of cultural diversity. Most of the people are black Africans. They belong to a variety of ethnic groups. And, there are people of European descent. In fact, there are 5 more members of that group in Southern Africa than in other parts of Africa.

Europeans liked Southern Africa for a number of reasons. In the 1500s, the Portuguese came to Mozambique. They were able to take part in the slave trade. In 10 the 1600s, Dutch and British settlers moved to the southern tip of Africa. They grew wheat and herded cattle. Some of the Dutch also spread to the north, where they started a mining industry. They used Africans as laborers. The British also moved north.

15 Today, three main groups of people with European ancestry live in Southern Africa. One group is descended from the British settlers. These people speak English. Another group is Afrikaners (af rih KAHN urz). They are descended from the Dutch settlers. They speak 20 Afrikaans (af rih KAHNZ), which is related to Dutch. The third group is descended from the Portuguese settlers. These people speak Portuguese. ✓

✓ Reading Check

Name the three main groups of people with European ancestry who live in Southern Africa.

_____

_____

_____

Southern Africa's cultural diversity is also seen in the big differences between life in the cities and in the 25 countryside. European settlers started the process of creating big cities. The region now includes several cities of more than one million people.

South Africa is the richest, most urban, and most industrialized country in Africa. In the 1900s, its indus- 30 tries created a great need for laborers. Hundreds of thousands of **migrant workers** came from nearby countries to work in South African mines. They had to live together in **compounds** far from their families, clans, and ethnic groups. They worked long hours in danger- 35 ous conditions and did not get paid well.

Key Terms

migrant worker (MY grunt WUR kur) *n.* a laborer who travels away from where he or she lives to find work
compound (KAHM pownd) *n.* a fenced-in group of homes

Most of the workers who went to South Africa to find work were men. Women normally raised the children and farmed the land. But with the men gone for a year or two at a time, women had to make decisions for the household and the community. For most, this was a challenge. But it also helped women gain new rights and skills.

Life in Central Africa

As in the rest of Africa, Central Africa went through many cultural changes in the 1900s. But many people in the region still follow old traditions as well.

One reason for the cultural diversity in Central Africa is money. On the Atlantic coast, there are large oil reserves. Cities near the coast have gained the most wealth from the oil industry. Also, people who live near the coast mix more with outside cultures.

Living conditions get poorer as you go from the coast to the inland areas of Central Africa. Inland, villages are organized by kinship groups. Land is owned by clans. In areas with fewer people, individual families live and work on their own land.

Central Africa also has great ethnic diversity. The Democratic Republic of the Congo alone has about 200 ethnic groups.

The largest city in Congo is Kinshasa. Millions of people live in crowded, poor neighborhoods or cinderblock apartments in Kinshasa. They work in factories, offices, and hotels. Millions of others live in the countryside.

Central Africans also practice different religions. Some are Roman Catholic or Protestant. Others practice religions that blend Christian and traditional African beliefs. Still others are Muslim. Old, new, and mixtures of the two live on in all regions of Africa. ✓

Review Questions

1. Who began the process of building big cities in Southern Africa?

_____

_____

2. What industry has brought wealth to some of the countries on Central Africa's Atlantic coast?

_____

_____

Target Reading Skill

Read the bracketed paragraphs. What are the differences between Central Africa's coastal and inland areas?

_____

_____

_____

✓ Reading Check

What are some examples of religious differences in Central Africa?

_____

_____

1. Which of the following statements is true?
   A. Cultural diffusion only occurs on coasts.
   B. In general, Africa has little cultural diversity.
   C. Cultural changes often happen through trade and travel.
   D. Cultural diffusion and cultural diversity are the same thing.

2. How much of North Africa's population is Muslim?
   A. 5 percent
   B. 50 percent
   C. 80 percent
   D. 95 percent

3. One important way in which West African traditions are kept alive is through
   A. schools.
   B. books.
   C. storytelling.
   D. television.

4. The idea of individuals owning land was spread to East Africa by
   A. the Ethiopians.
   B. the Arabs.
   C. the Swahili.
   D. the Europeans.

5. A group of people with European ancestry that lives in Southern Africa is the
   A. Swahili.
   B. Afrikaners.
   C. Berbers.
   D. Tuareg.

Short Answer Question

What is culture?

_____

_____

_____

_____

CHAPTER 14

Prepare to Read

Section 1
Egypt: A Nation on the Nile

Objectives

1. Find out how Islam influences Egyptian culture.
2. Learn about daily life in Egypt.

Target Reading Skill

Recognize Causes and Effects A cause makes something happen. An effect is what happens. It is the result of the cause. Recognizing causes and effects can help you better understand situations.

As you read, select an event and ask yourself why it happened. The answer to that question is the cause. Then ask yourself what the result of the event was. The answer to that question is the effect.

For example, you will read that many people move to Cairo, Egypt, to find jobs, and so the city has become very crowded. You can think about that situation like this:

EVENT: *What is the event?* Many people move to Cairo.

CAUSE: *Why did the event happen?* People need jobs.

EFFECT: *What was the result of the event?* Cairo is very crowded.

Look for other causes and effects as you read.

Vocabulary Strategy

Recognizing Compound Words Compound words are made from two or more words. Each of the words by itself is a root. This makes it easy to recognize compound words. All you have to do as you read is look for words in which you recognize at least two roots. For example, you probably know the roots *note* and *book*. So if you see the word *notebook*, you know it is a compound word because it includes two roots. The same is true of *sailboat*, *pushpin*, and *henhouse*.

Section 1 Summary

Islam in Egypt

Egypt is in North Africa across the Red Sea from Saudi Arabia. Most people in Egypt are Muslims. But there are also Christians. Most of them are members of the Coptic Church. This is one of the oldest branches of Christianity in the world. It has been in Egypt for a few hundred years longer than Islam has.

The Quran says that Muslims must pray five times a day. Many Egyptians pray in mosques. As they pray, they face southeast so they are facing the holy city of Mecca. Mecca is in Saudi Arabia. Also, many Egyptian children attend religious classes in mosques. They learn to read the Quran and to memorize it. ✓

The Quran also teaches about something called **Sharia**. Sharia is the laws of Islam. Each day Muslims try to live in a way that obeys Sharia.

Most Muslims in Egypt believe that Egypt's laws should be based on the laws of Islam. The country's constitution now says Sharia is the main source of Egypt's laws. Still, some of Egypt's laws do not come from Sharia.

Daily Life in Egypt

In Egypt, about as many people live in cities as live in villages. People live very different lives depending on whether they live in a city or a village. But one thing they have in common is that they all depend on the Nile River to survive.

Most Egyptians live along the Nile River or in the Nile Delta region. With the help of the Aswan High Dam, the Nile allows farmers to irrigate their crops year-round. The river supplies water to people in the cities and the countryside.

✓ Reading Check

What city do Egyptian Muslims face when they pray each day?

_____

_____

_____

Target Reading Skill

Read the bracketed paragraphs. Most Egyptians live near the Nile River. What is the cause of this? What is the effect of it?

Cause: _____

_____

Effect: _____

_____

But there is a problem with Egypt's water supply. The dam keeps the Nile's rich silt from reaching farm-land downstream. Without the silt, the Nile Delta has been shrinking. Farmers have to use more fertilizer to grow crops. The fertilizers make Egypt's water supply less safe. The same is true of waste from the cities that gets into the water.

Nearly half of all Egyptians live in cities. Egypt's capital, **Cairo**, is also its largest city. It is home to more than 10 million Egyptians. Some parts of Cairo are more than 1,000 years old. Other parts are very modern. Most people live in air-conditioned apartments. But they still shop in the traditional **bazaars**.

Most people who live in Egypt's villages are farmers called **fellaheen**. Only a few fellaheen own the land they farm. The others rent land along the narrow riverbanks or work the fields of rich landowners. ☑

Many of the fellaheen live in small homes built of mud bricks or stones. The houses may have from one to three rooms and a courtyard. The family shares the courtyard with their animals. The homes have flat roofs. The fellaheen use them to dry fruits, dry laundry, or store food and firewood.

Review Questions

1. How does Islam affect daily life in Egypt?

_____

_____

_____

2. Name one thing that is similar about life in Egypt's cities and its villages.

_____

_____

_____

Vocabulary Strategy

As you read this page, circle at least four compound words.

✓ Reading Check

What land do the fellaheen farm?

_____

_____

_____

Key Terms

Cairo (KY roh) *n.* the capital of Egypt

bazaar (buh ZAHR) *n.* a traditional open-air market with shops or rows of stalls

fellaheen (fel uh HEEN) *n.* peasants or agricultural workers in Egypt and other Arab countries

Section 2 Algeria:
Varied Geography, Varied History

Objectives

1. Learn about the history and people of Algeria.
2. Find out about life in Algeria's different geographic regions.
3. Examine life in Algeria today.

Target Reading Skill

Use Signal Words Signal words point out the relationships among ideas or events. One type of relationship is cause and effect. As you read, you may come across words like *because, influence, as a result*, and *for that reason*. These are signal words that let you know a cause and effect relationship is being described. When you see them, study the words before and after them to find causes and effects.

In the following example, the signal words are *For that reason*. What comes before these words is the cause. What comes after them is the effect.

Algeria was a French colony. *For that reason*, many people in Algeria speak French today.

Vocabulary Strategy

Understanding Compound Words Compound words are like shortcuts. They make it easier to read or talk about things. Remember that compound words are made from two or more words. If you know the meanings of the words that make up the compound word, you can often figure out the meaning of the compound word itself.

For example, in the last section, you read the compound word *landowner*. The roots are *land* and *owner*. An owner is a person who owns something. Land is a thing. So a landowner is a person who owns land. The compound word is just a shorter way of saying so.

Section 2 Summary

Algeria's History and People

Over the years, many outside groups have ruled Algeria. The earliest known invaders were the Phoenicians (fuh NISH unz). The Phoenicians were sea traders from the region that is now Lebanon. They came to Algeria two to three thousand years ago and set up a trading post in Algeria. Today, Algeria's capital, Algiers (al JEERZ), sits where the trading post used to be.

In the A.D. 100s, the Romans invaded Algeria. The Berber farmers there paid taxes to the Romans. They also rented land from Roman nobles. Then, in the A.D. 600s, Arabs began to settle throughout North Africa. As a result, the Berber way of life began to change. For example, most Berbers accepted the religion of the Arabs, Islam. This helped bring peace to the region.

The port cities on Algeria's Mediterranean coast were controlled by different groups at different times. The groups included the Spanish, local pirates, and the Ottoman Turks. In 1830, the French captured Algiers and turned Algeria into a French colony. Algeria gained independence from France in 1962. ✓

Today, about 75 percent of Algeria's people are Arab. About 24 percent are Berber. The rest are mostly of European descent. The Arabs and Berbers are Muslim. But many Berbers have combined Islam with traditional religious beliefs.

The country's main languages are Arabic, several Berber languages, and French. Many Algerians speak more than one of these languages. The country has two official languages. They are Arabic and Tamazight (TAHM uh zyt), a Berber language.

Algeria's Geography

Algeria's coastal region is called the Tell. That is where most Algerians live. The country's best farmland is found in the Tell. Most of its cities are, too.

The cities include mosques for worship and **souqs** for shopping. The old parts of the cities are called

---

Key Term

souq (sook) *n.* an open-air marketplace in an Arab city

Use the words below to create compound words. You will find these words on this page.

farm + land = _____

country + side = _____

out + side = _____

Select one of the compound words you formed and write a definition for it on the lines below. Looking at the word's context may help you define it.

_____

_____

✓ Reading Check

How do people in Algeria's desert make a living?

_____

_____

_____

✓ Reading Check

Which language is used in Algerian schools today?

_____

_____

the casbah. The houses and stores there sit close together on narrow, winding streets. The new parts of the cities are modern, with wide streets and tall buildings made of steel and glass.

40 Most Berbers live in the countryside. Some Arabs live there too. But little of the land is good for farming. Still, about one third of Algerians are farmers. In the mountains, farmers build **terraces** for their crops. Terraces increase the amount of farmland. They also keep 45 the soil from washing away in the rain.

More than 80 percent of Algeria is desert. To live in the desert you need water. Most Algerians who live in the desert settle in oasis towns. They grow dates or citrus fruits. Nomads herd animals, such as camels, that 50 are suited to the desert climate. Some people in the desert work for companies that produce oil and natural gas. Those are Algeria's two main resources. ✓

Algeria Today

Some old Algerian customs and traditions are changing. For example, family is important. But people who 55 live in cities are having fewer children than before.

Education in Algeria today is better than it was during French rule. Children from ages 6 to 15 are required to go to school. They are taught in Arabic. New universities have been built and some people 60 study outside of the country. ✓

Review Questions

1. How is Algeria's history reflected by the languages spoken there today?

_____

_____

2. In which geographic area do most Algerians live?

_____

_____

Key Terms

casbah (KAHZ bah) *n.* an old, crowded section of a North African city

terrace (TEHR us) *n.* a flat platform of earth cut into the side of a slope, used for growing crops in steep places

1. In Egypt, the largest city is
   A. Cairo.
   B. Alexandria.
   C. Algiers.
   D. Tell.

2. What is Sharia?
   A. the laws of Egypt
   B. the laws of Islam
   C. the sacred book of Islam
   D. the name of Islam's founder

3. An Egyptian bazaar and an Algerian souq are both
   A. important food crops.
   B. open-air markets.
   C. places of worship.
   D. methods of terrace farming.

4. In 1962, Algeria gained independence from
   A. France.
   B. Spain.
   C. Britain.
   D. the Ottoman Turks.

5. Which type of vegetation covers 80 percent of Algeria?
   A. savanna
   B. rain forest
   C. coastal plains
   D. desert

Short Answer Question

How does the Aswan High Dam on the Nile River affect life in Egypt in both positive and negative ways?

_____

_____

_____

_____

Prepare to Read

Section 1
Nigeria: Land of Diverse Peoples

Objectives

1. Learn to identify Nigeria's three main ethnic groups.
2. Understand the major events in Nigeria's history.
3. Find out about the conflicts Nigeria faced on its path to democracy.

Target Reading Skill

Identify Main Ideas Good readers look for the main idea of what they read. The main idea is the most important point. All the other points work together to support the main idea. The other points are called supporting details.

The main idea of the paragraph below is underlined. You can see that the other sentences all support this idea.

<u>It has not been easy to make Nigeria's many ethnic groups feel they are one nation.</u> The groups live in different areas. They speak different languages. They practice different religions. Some have economic resources, some do not.

As you read, try to find the main idea of each paragraph.

Vocabulary Strategy

Using Prefixes and Roots A prefix is attached to the beginning of a word to make a new word. The prefix is made up of one or more syllables. The word the prefix is attached to is the root. Each prefix has its own meaning. The meaning of the new word combines the meanings of the prefix and the root.

Some common prefixes, their meanings, and some examples are listed below.

Prefix	Meaning	Example
de-	make the opposite of; remove from	defrost, derail
inter-	between or among	international
multi-	many	multipurpose
over-	above; beyond; excessive	overhead, overrate

Ethnic Groups of Nigeria

Nigeria is **multiethnic**. More than 250 ethnic groups live in the country. English is the official language. But the languages of Nigeria's major ethnic groups are the languages spoken most.

Nigeria's Ethnic Groups

Hausa-Fulani	Yoruba	Igbo	Other 250 + groups
• largest • live in the northwest	• second-largest • live in the southwest	• third-largest • live in the southeast	• live in center of country or scattered throughout

5　　In the early 1800s, the Fulani conquered the Hausa. They then ruled over the Hausa. But the Fulani did not force their own culture on the Hausa. Instead, many of the Fulani took on the Hausa's language and customs. Also, the Hausa and Fulani began to <u>intermarry</u>. Now
10　the two groups are known together as the **Hausa-Fulani**.

　　Most of the Hausa-Fulani live in the countryside. Some are cattle herders, while others are farmers or craftspeople. Trade has been an important part of their economy ever since they began building trading cities
15　in northern Nigeria hundreds of years ago.

　　For hundreds of years, the **Yoruba** have been the most urban of Nigeria's major ethnic groups. They began building cities around 1100. Each city was ruled by a king, and many people lived in the cities. ✓

20　　Today, many Yoruba also live outside cities. They are often farmers, traders, or craftspeople. Families live in compounds. Each compound includes several houses around a shared yard.

　　For much of their history, the **Igbo** have lived in
25　small farming villages. Each village is ruled democratically by a council of elders. Many Igbo have worked for Nigeria's city or national governments.

Key Terms

multiethnic (mul tee ETH nik) *adj.* having many ethnic groups living within a society

Hausa-Fulani (HOW suh foo LAH nee) *n.* Nigeria's largest ethnic group

Yoruba (YOH roo buh) *n.* Nigeria's second-largest ethnic group

Igbo (IG boh) *n.* Nigeria's third-largest ethnic group

Target Reading Skill

Which sentence states the main idea of the bracketed paragraph?

_____

_____

_____

Vocabulary Strategy

The word below appears on this page. It contains a prefix. Underline the prefix. Then use the chart on the previous page to write a definition of the word.

intermarry

_____

_____

✓ Reading Check

Which of Nigeria's ethnic groups is the most urban?

_____

_____

_____

Nigeria's History

For thousands of years, what is now Nigeria was ruled by many different African peoples. Then, in the late 1400s, Europeans began trading for slaves there. By 1914, Great Britain had taken control of Nigeria.

In 1960, Nigeria gained independence. Its capital was Lagos. The hundreds of ethnic groups in the region had always lived separately. The government wanted to help them all feel they were part of the same country. So, in 1991, the government moved the capital to Abuja (uh BOO juh) because it is in the middle of the country, near the three largest ethnic groups. Also, members of many ethnic groups live in Abuja. ✓

The Path to Democracy

It has not been easy to make Nigeria's many ethnic groups feel they are one nation. The groups live in different areas. They speak different languages. They practice different religions. Some have economic resources, some do not. Shortly after independence, tensions arose among the groups.

One source of tension is religion. Most of the Hausa-Fulani are Muslim. Some Yoruba are Muslim, and others are Christian. The Igbo are mainly Christian. Some members of all of Nigeria's ethnic groups practice traditional religions. At times, these religious differences cause conflict. ✓

Another source of tension is the country's oil. Almost all of the money Nigeria earns from exports is from oil. The government and the oil companies earn large profits. But the people who live near where the oil comes from do not benefit.

Since gaining independence, many Nigerians have tried to create a democratic government. In 1999, Nigeria held elections for the first time in more than 15 years.

Review Questions

1. Name the three largest ethnic groups in Nigeria.

_____

_____

2. List two reasons why Abuja was chosen as Nigeria's capital.

_____

_____

✓ **Reading Check**

What city became Nigeria's new capital in 1991?

_____

✓ **Reading Check**

Which different religions do people in Nigeria practice?

_____

_____

_____

Prepare to Read

Section 2
Ghana: Leading Africa to Independence

Objectives

1. Learn about the years of British colonial rule in the area that is now called Ghana.
2. Find out about the beliefs that helped move Ghana toward independence.
3. Discover how Ghana changed after achieving independence.

Target Reading Skill

Identify Implied Main Ideas The main idea of a paragraph or section is its most important point. Sometimes the main idea is not stated directly. Instead, the details in a paragraph or section add up to the main idea. In those cases, we say the main idea is implied. It is up to you to put the details together to identify the main idea.

For example, on the next page read the section titled "The Colonial Years." You could state the implied main idea this way: "The British influenced life in the Gold Coast in many ways." Do you see how the details in the section support this idea?

Vocabulary Strategy

Using Roots and Suffixes A suffix is attached to the end of a word to make a new word. The suffix is made up of one or more syllables. The word the suffix is attached to is the root. Like a prefix, a suffix has its own meaning. So when a suffix is added to a root, the new word has a different meaning than the root by itself. The meaning of the new word combines the meaning of the suffix and the root.

Some common suffixes are listed below, along with their meanings and examples. Notice that some of the suffixes have more than one meaning. Learning to identify suffixes, and knowing what they mean, will help you understand what you read.

Suffix	Meaning	Example
-al	of or like	coastal
-dom	position of or land ruled by; condition of being	kingdom; wisdom
-ment	the act of; the condition of being	improvement; disappointment

Section 2 Summary

The Colonial Years

Until 1957, present-day Ghana was called the Gold Coast. After Europeans began trading gold and slaves there, members of the Akan (AH kahn) ethnic group formed a kingdom. This kingdom was called the Asante (uh SAHN tee) kingdom. It became rich from trade. The Asante tried to stop the European takeover of their kingdom. But in 1874, Great Britain turned the Gold Coast into a colony. It used chiefs to rule the colony.

The British wanted to control the colony's economy. They encouraged farmers to grow cacao. They used the cacao to make cocoa, which they exported to Britain. There it was used to make chocolate. The British also exported timber and gold. ☑

Because Gold Coast Africans were busy producing these goods, they stopped growing as many food crops. This led to a problem. The people could not grow enough food on their own. Instead, they had to import food.

Also, when cocoa was made from cacao, the British made a profit, not the people of the Gold Coast. And because the people spent time farming, they spent less time making traditional crafts. Gold Coast people had to buy factory-made goods from the British.

The British also made changes to Gold Coast culture. For example, they built schools and introduced people to Christianity. They brought new ideas and ways of doing things to traditional communities. Many people blended the new ways with older African ways.

Moving Toward Independence

During the 1900s, African colonies began to demand independence. **Kwame Nkrumah**, from the Gold Coast, thought that Africans should rule themselves. The Akan, for example, had ruled much of the Gold Coast. Their elders had always chosen their rulers from members of the royal family. If the leader did not rule

Key Term

Kwame Nkrumah (KWAH mee un KROO muh) *n.* founder of Ghana's independence movement and Ghana's first president

fairly, the elders had the right to choose another.
35 Nkrumah traveled throughout the Gold Coast, convincing people to demand freedom. ✓

Independence Achieved

In 1957, Great Britain agreed to grant **sovereignty** to the people of the Gold Coast. The new government renamed the country Ghana after an ancient African
40 <u>kingdom</u>. Nkrumah became president. In all of Africa, only South Africa had already become independent of European rule. Ghana was second. Its success inspired many other Africans to push for <u>freedom</u>.

In 1966, however, Nkrumah was overthrown by a
45 military **coup d'état**. Why? Nkrumah had had great plans for Ghana. He had borrowed money to make them happen. He spent millions of dollars building a conference center and a superhighway. He also made an <u>agreement</u> with the United States to build a dam that
50 would provide electricity and irrigation for rural areas. But when world prices of cocoa fell, Ghana could not repay its loans. Many people blamed Nkrumah for the country's problems. ✓

In 1981, Jerry Rawlings seized power. He tried to
55 reform Ghana's politics and economy. He stressed the importance of hard work, and Ghana's economy grew. In 2000, Ghanaians democratically elected John Kufuor as president. He has continued to make improvements in Ghana.

Review Questions

1. How did the Gold Coast's economy change after the British began encouraging farmers to grow cacao?

_____

_____

2. Why did Nkrumah think the Gold Coast should become independent?

_____

_____

Key Terms

sovereignty (SAHV run tee) *n.* political control
coup d'état (koo day TAH) *n.* the sudden overthrow of a government by force

Vocabulary Strategy

The words below appear in this section. Each word contains a suffix. Underline the suffix. Then use the chart at the beginning of this section to write a definition of the word.

kingdom _____

freedom _____

agreement _____

✓ **Reading Check**

How did Nkrumah lose his position as president?

_____

_____

_____

Objectives

1. Discover how Mali's environment affects its economy.
2. Find out how desert can spread across the land.
3. Learn about the importance of preserving Mali's environment.

Target Reading Skill

Identify Supporting Details The main idea of a paragraph or section is supported by details. Details give more information about the main idea. They may give additional facts, reasons, or examples. Identifying the supporting details will help you understand the main idea completely.

Read the section entitled: "Mali's Environment." You could say the main idea is that Mali's environment affects the ways its people live. Now reread the section with this main idea in mind. Try to find at least three details that support this main idea.

Vocabulary Strategy

Using Roots and Suffixes You learned about suffixes in the previous section. There are many more suffixes than can fit in one chart!

Some more common suffixes are listed below, along with their meanings and examples of words that use them. Notice that some of the suffixes have more than one meaning. Also, one of them has two forms. Learning to identify suffixes and knowing what they mean will help you understand what you read.

Suffix	Meaning	Example
-ed	forms the past tense of many verbs	walked, wanted
-ent, -ant	that has, shows, or does; a person or thing that has, shows or does	insistent, flight attendant
-er	more; a person that does	greater, player
-est	most	greatest
-ing	the act of; the product of	talking, painting

Section 3 Summary

Mali's Environment

Mali is a very dry country. The Sahara covers about one third of the land. The Sahel lies between the Sahara and the savanna. The savanna is the one area in Mali that gets plenty of rain. Most Malians live in the Sahel or the savanna.

People have <u>lived</u> in the Sahel for thousands of years. Malians in the Sahel herd animals and grow food crops to feed their families. Many earn extra money by <u>growing</u> cash crops as well. Rains may fall in the Sahel from May to October. This is an ideal time for farming. During the rest of the year, people use water from sources such as rivers to farm. ☑

In the past, the Sahel's location between the Sahara and the savanna helped its economy succeed. From the 1300s through the 1500s, the city of Tombouctou was a wealthy center of trade. However, once European ships began trading along Africa's coast, trade through the Sahel decreased. It was faster and easier to ship goods by sea than by camel.

The Desert Spreads

Mali has little industry. Most people make their living by trading, farming, or herding. But these types of work are being threatened by **desertification**. In the countries of the Sahel, the desert is spreading south. Even the <u>wetter</u> lands are at risk of becoming desert. ☑

One possible cause of desertification in Mali is overgrazing. When animals graze, they often eat the roots of plants. The roots normally hold the soil in place. When the roots are gone, the wind blows the soil into the air, leaving less soil in the ground. The dust covers everything.

Key Term

desertification (dih zurt uh fih KAY shun) *n.* the process by which fertile land becomes too dry or damaged to support life

---

Vocabulary Strategy

The words below appear in this section. Each word contains a suffix. Underline the suffix. Then use the chart on the previous page to write a definition of the word.

lived _____

growing _____

wetter _____

✓ Reading Check

Which months are the best for farming in the Sahel?

_____

_____

_____

◎ Target Reading Skill

The main idea under the heading "The Desert Spreads" is that desertification is threatening the ways people in Mali make a living. Which details tell about this problem?

1. _____

_____

2. _____

_____

✓ Reading Check

What does desertification do to fertile land?

_____

_____

_____

Another possible cause of desertification in Mali is drought, or a long period with little rain. Droughts can turn land into desert. Over the last 30 years, the Sahel has received much less rain than it did before. Some
35 scientists think that a few years of good rainfall could stop desertification.

Preserving the Environment

People around the world are concerned about the future of the Sahel. The United Nations has formed a committee to help stop desertification.

40 Many of the people who live in the Sahel are nomads. The Tuareg are nomads who are finding it harder to live in the Sahel because of desertification. In addition, there were major droughts in the 1970s and 1980s. The Tuareg did not have enough water or food.
45 As a result, some of them settled on farms or moved to cities. Others built camps outside Tombouctou. ☑

Mali's economy is also affected because desertification makes it harder for farmers to grow cash crops. Mali's government has been trying to find solutions to
50 the problems caused by desertification. To help the economy, the government has been encouraging businesses to develop in Mali. It has also been working with the United Nations to teach people better ways to use land. There are hopes that irrigation and new ways of
55 farming will help.

Review Questions

1. Name two sources of water that make farming in the Sahel possible.

_____

_____

2. What are two possible causes of desertification in Mali?

_____

_____

> **Key Term**
> **overgrazing** (oh vur GRAYZ ing) *n.* allowing too much grazing by large herds of animals

✓ **Reading Check**

Why did many Tuareg settle on farms, move to cities, or build camps?

_____

_____

_____

1. Which of the following is NOT a Nigerian ethnic group?
   A. the Akan
   B. the Igbo
   C. the Yoruba
   D. the Hausa-Fulani

2. Which of the following was Nigeria's first capital after independence?
   A. Kano
   B. Abuja
   C. Lagos
   D. Tombouctou

3. What happened as a result of the export of goods such as cacao from the Gold Coast?
   A. Gold Coast Africans had to import food.
   B. Most of the profits went to Britain.
   C. People spent more time farming and less time making traditional crafts.
   D. all of the above

4. How does Mali's savanna differ from the Sahel and the Sahara?
   A. It gets less rain.
   B. It has a more northern location.
   C. It gets more rain.
   D. It is inhabited by fewer people.

5. Why is trade no longer practiced on a large scale in Tombouctou?
   A. because desertification has destroyed the city
   B. because the city has been taken over by the Tuareg, who do not engage in trade
   C. because modern highways have replaced camel caravans
   D. because transporting goods by ship is faster and easier than sending them by camel

Short Answer Question

What reasons did people in Ghana have for wanting independence?

_____

_____

_____

_____

Prepare to Read

Section 1
Ethiopia: Religious Roots

Objectives

1. Learn about the two major religions practiced in Ethiopia.
2. Understand the contrasts in the daily lives of rural and urban Ethiopians.

Target Reading Skill

Use Context Clues While you read, you may come across a word you do not know. Like a detective, you can look at clues in the surroundings to solve your case—that is, to figure out your word's meaning. In text, the words and sentences surrounding a word are called the word's context. Context clues may be definitions, explanations, or examples. Finding clues in the context will help you understand the word's meaning.

Vocabulary Strategy

Recognizing Signal Words Signal words are words or phrases that let you know something about what is coming next. There are many different types of signal words. The types include words that signal time, direction, place, how things compare, and how things are related.

For example, sometimes the way things are related is shown with cause or effect. When you see signal words such as *because, on account of*, and *since*, you will know that a cause is being described. When you see signal words such as *as a result, so, then*, and *therefore*, you will know that an effect is being described. Being able to recognize signal words will help you better understand what you are reading.

Major Religions of Ethiopia

Christianity had come to Ethiopia through trade along the Red Sea. It was brought by missionaries from Egypt and was in Ethiopia by the year A.D. 350. In A.D. 451, Egyptian Christians split from the rest of the Christian Church. They formed the Coptic Christian Church. This form of Christianity took hold in Ethiopia as well. ☑

Ethiopian Christians did not have much contact with Christians in other parts of the world. Ethiopia's mountains made it hard for people who lived in the country's interior to travel elsewhere. However, some people did travel overland or along the Red Sea. But Christians were not allowed to use these routes after Muslim Arabs arrived in the region in the A.D. 600s.

These Muslim Arabs did not try to take over Ethiopia. But they did settle in nearby areas and build cities along the Red Sea. Eventually, Muslim Arabs controlled all trade in North Africa, and some Ethiopians became Muslim.

In time, Muslim Arabs took over Ethiopia's coastal regions. Ethiopia's Christians then moved farther inland. As a result, the Christian parts of Ethiopia were surrounded by Muslim areas, and Christians there had very little contact with Christians living elsewhere. The Ethiopian Christian Church developed into a unique form of Christianity. It had its own traditions and its own language, **Geez** (gee EZ). Christian monks living in **monasteries** wrote down much of Ethiopia's history, using the Geez language.

Key Terms

Geez (gee EZ) *n.* an ancient Ethiopian language that was once used to write literature but is no longer spoken

monastery (MAHN uh stehr ee) *n.* a place where people, especially men known as monks, live a religious life

---

✓ **Reading Check**

How did Christianity first come to Ethiopia?

_____

_____

_____

Vocabulary Strategy

In the bracketed paragraph, a signal word or phrase is used to show cause and effect. Find the signal word or phrase and circle it. Then write the cause and effect below.

Cause: _____

Effect: _____

What do you think *reigned* means? If you do not know, consider the word's context. You know that Lalibela reigned for a few decades. You also know that he was the ruler of Roha. Write a definition in your own words on the lines below.

_____

_____

_____

The churches of the town of Lalibela (lah lee BAY lah) are also a unique part of Ethiopian Christianity. Origi-
35 nally called Roha, Lalibela was the capital of Ethiopia for about 300 years. It was renamed in honor of its most famous ruler, Lalibela. He reigned during the late 1100s and early 1200s. Under his rule, eleven churches were built. They were cut out of solid rock and built below the ground. Many people travel to Lalibela to visit these
40 churches, unique to this region.

During most of Ethiopia's history, Christians and Muslims have lived near each other peacefully. There have been times, however, when they fought wars because of religious differences. Today, about 35 per-
45 cent of Ethiopians are Christians. About 45 percent are Muslims. Most other Ethiopians practice traditional African religions. A small number are Jewish.

Contrasts in Daily Life

Only about 16 percent of Ethiopians live in cities. The rest live in the countryside. There, public services, such as
50 electricity and running water, are hard to find. For exam- ple, no one in the village of Gerba Sefer has electricity, and more people own donkeys than cars. People in nearby areas make a living by farming, herding cattle, or fishing. Some families are woodworkers or beekeepers. ☑

55 Addis Ababa is the capital of Ethiopia. It is in the center of the country. Life there is very different than in the countryside. People have many conveniences. They have running water, electricity, modern hospitals, a university, and a museum. They also can visit palaces
60 built by ancient emperors. Addis Ababa is a center of business and trade. Its population includes ethnic groups such as the Amhara, Tigrey, Galla, and Gurage.

Review Questions

1. Which religion came to Ethiopia first, Christianity or Islam?

   _____

   _____

2. What conveniences do people have in Addis Ababa but not in the countryside?

   _____

   _____

Prepare to Read

Section 2
Tanzania: Determined to Succeed

Objectives

1. Find out about early reforms that the government of Tanzania made after independence.
2. Learn about continued social, economic, and political progress and reforms that have been made in Tanzania.

Target Reading Skill

Use Context Clues When you come across a word you do not know, you can use context clues to figure out its meaning. One type of context clue is a definition. For example, your textbook often gives the definitions of new words or hard words. You might find the definition in the sentence in which the word is used or in another sentence nearby.

In this book, whenever you see a word or phrase highlighted in **blue**, you will find its definition at the bottom of the page. As you read, look for words that are accompanied by definitions or explanations.

Vocabulary Strategy

Recognizing Signal Words Signal words are words or phrases that should get your attention while you read. They clue you in to connections that are being made in the text.

There are different types of signal words. One type of signal word shows a relationship among ideas called sequence. Sequence is the order in which events occur. Understanding the order of events helps you understand how the events are related to one another. Some signal words that show sequence are *first, next, then, finally, before, earlier,* and *later.*

Early Reforms After Independence

Tanzania is on the Indian Ocean. Because of its location, it became an important center of trade. During the last 1,200 years, the area was ruled at different times by the Arabs, the Germans, and the British. The British named the mainland area Tanganyika (tan guh NYEE kuh). This area became independent in 1961. In 1964, it joined with the island state of Zanzibar to form Tanzania.

When Tanzania became independent, most of its people were poor. Few could read or write. The first president, Julius Nyerere, saw that Tanzania faced many challenges. He wanted to avoid tension among the country's 120 ethnic groups. Therefore he put some unusual policies in place. One had to do with language. Although different languages are spoken in East African homes, many people speak Swahili. Swahili is what is called a **lingua franca**. To help bring Tanzanians together, Nyerere made Swahili the national language. ☑

Nyerere also set up a new political system. He did not want each ethnic group to have its own political party. Instead, he created a <u>one-party system</u>. There were still several candidates to vote for, but they were all members of one party. Critics complained that this could lead to corruption in the government.

Next, Nyerere turned to the economy. He told Tanzanians that only hard work could end poverty. He also said that Tanzania should not depend on other nations for economic support.

Nyerere then started a program of *ujamaa* (oo jah MAH). The word is Swahili for "togetherness." Nyerere wanted farmers to live in villages where they could work together and share resources. He thought this would help them produce more crops. He also thought it would make it easier for the government to provide services such as education.

Key Term

lingua franca (LING gwuh FRANG kuh) *n.* a language used for communication among people who speak different first languages

---

✓ Reading Check

What language is the lingua franca of Tanzania?

_____

_____

Target Reading Skill

If you do not know what a one-party system is, look at the context. The phrase is followed by an explanation. Use this explanation to write a sentence describing a one-party system in your own words.

_____

_____

_____

Vocabulary Strategy

In the bracketed paragraphs, circle the signal words that indicate sequence. What events are being sequenced?

_____

_____

_____

Progress and Continued Reform

Nyerere retired from being president in 1985. By then, Tanzania had changed greatly. It had a national language and very little ethnic conflict. Education had improved and more people could read and write.

But Tanzania was still poor. The economy was suffering because the ujamaa program had failed. Many farm families had refused to move to the new villages. Instead of growing more crops, they had grown less.

The new government that followed Nyerere ended the ujamaa program. It tried to get farmers to use new methods to produce more cash crops and asked foreign countries for more help as well.

The government also decided to try **privatization**. Because of privatization, private companies run Tanzania's telephone and airline industries. Now, the economy is improving faster than others in Africa.

Because of all the economic changes, Tanzania's government also changed the one-party system to a multiparty system. In 1992, new political parties began to form. In October of 1995, Tanzania held its first elections under the **multiparty system**. ☑

In the 1995 and 2000 elections, Nyerere's party won the most votes and stayed in power. Not everyone liked that. Also, another party suggested that Zanzibar should no longer be part of Tanzania. These sorts of disagreements have created tensions in Tanzanian politics.

Review Questions

1. Why did Nyerere establish a one-party system?

_____

_____

2. What changes had taken place in Tanzania by 1985?

_____

_____

✓ Reading Check

What political change occurred in 1992?

_____

_____

_____

Key Terms

privatization (pry vuh tih ZAY shun) *n.* the sale of government-owned industries to private companies

multiparty system (MUL tee PAHR tee SIS tum) *n.* a political system in which two or more parties compete in elections

Objectives

1. Learn about the peoples of Kenya.
2. Discover what life is like in rural Kenya.
3. Find out what life is like in urban Kenya.

Target Reading Skill

Interpret Nonliteral Meanings Have you ever read something and then thought it could not possibly mean exactly what it said? What you read may have been nonliteral language. Nonliteral language and literal language are two different ways of saying things. When you use literal language, you say exactly what you mean. Your meaning is perfectly clear. When you use nonliteral language, you use images or comparisons to get an idea across. Someone else might need to interpret your meaning—that is, figure out what your images or comparisons really mean. Below are two different ways of describing a tough day at school.

"Taking two tests in one day was exhausting!"

"Taking two test in one day was a nightmare!"

The first statement uses literal language. The second one uses nonliteral language. Taking two tests in one day was not really a nightmare—it actually happened. But comparing it to a nightmare really gets across the way you felt about it.

Vocabulary Strategy

Recognizing Signal Words As you have learned, signal words are words or phrases that prepare you to make connections in the text you are reading. There are many types. One type of signal word prepares you to see that things or ideas contrast. That is, they alert you to a difference between the things or ideas. When you see signal words like *but, however, not, on the other hand, even though, yet,* and *despite,* you will know that a contrast is being described.

Section 3 Summary

Peoples of Kenya

Kenya's highest mountain is Mount Kenya. It lies just south of the Equator. To the southwest of Mount Kenya are highlands. Plenty of rain falls in the highlands, and the land is good for farming. Most Kenyans are farmers. Many of them live in the highlands in shambas. A shamba is a small farm owned and run by a Kenyan family. Other Kenyans live along the coast. There, the climate is warmer and the land is also good for farming.

Some Kenyans have European, Asian, or Arab backgrounds. Most come from families that have always lived in Africa. More than 40 ethnic groups live in Kenya. Each group is unique in some way. But they also share common culture. For example, some groups speak the same language. And most Kenyans are either Christian or Muslim. ✓

Most Kenyans also share family values. Many members of extended families are very close. Cousins are often considered like brothers or sisters.

Kenya's largest ethnic group is the **Kikuyu**. Many of them live in shambas in the highlands near Mount Kenya. Kikuyu homes are round buildings with mud walls and thatched roofs. The Kikuyu grow food and cash crops such as coffee and sisal, a fiber used to make rope. The **Maasai** are another ethnic group in Kenya. They are **seminomadic**.

Life in Rural Kenya

The majority of Kenya's farmers are women. They grow fruits and vegetables and herd animals. Kenyan men also farm, but they usually raise cash crops such as coffee and tea.

Life in Kenya is changing. As the country's population grows, many men are moving to the cities to find

✓ **Reading Check**

How many ethnic groups live in Kenya?

_____

_____

Vocabulary Strategy

In the bracketed paragraph, a signal word is used to show contrast. Find the signal word and circle it. What is being contrasted here?

_____

_____

Key Terms

Kikuyu (kee KOO yoo) *n.* the largest ethnic group in Kenya
Maasai (mah SY) *n.* a seminomadic ethnic group in Kenya
seminomadic (seh mee noh MAD ik) *adj.* combining nomadic wandering and farming in settlements

The word *harambee* means "let's pull together" in Swahili. Did Kenyatta really want people to pull on something? Or was he using the word nonliterally? How could you describe *harambee* in literal language?

_____

_____

work. Most women and children stay in the countryside. It is expensive for them to move. And many women find it easier to support their families by farming.

Kenya gained independence from the British in 1963. The first president was Jomo Kenyatta (JOH moh ken YAH tuh). He began a social policy he called **harambee**. Kenyatta encouraged harambee in politics, farming, education, and other areas.

Harambee has been successful in Kenya. A good example of it is the rise of women's self-help groups in the countryside. All over Kenya, women have gotten involved to solve problems the communities face. ✓

Life in Urban Kenya

Kenya's capital is Nairobi (ny ROH bee). It is one of the biggest cities in East Africa. It is also East Africa's most important center of industry and manufacturing, and where much of East Africa's banking and trade takes place.

Many Kenyans move to Nairobi looking for work. Its population grew from one million in 1985 to more than two million in 2000.

Men who move to the city are often homesick. And the women in the villages are left with lots of work. Harambee helps people get though those experiences. Many of the men are working to earn money to buy land in the countryside. Men in Nairobi who are from the same ethnic group often welcome one another, share rooms, and help one another. ✓

Review Questions

1. In what way do most Kenyans make their living?

_____

_____

2. Why do most Kenyan women stay in rural villages rather than move to the city?

_____

_____

> **Key Term**
> **harambee** (hah RAHM bay) *n.* a social policy started by Jomo Kenyatta and meaning "let's pull together" in Swahili

Chapter 16 Assessment

1. The branch of Christianity that spread from Egypt to Ethiopia was known as
   A. Coptic Christianity.
   B. Roman Catholicism.
   C. Eastern Orthodox Christianity.
   D. none of the above

2. The official language of Tanzania is
   A. Tanzanian.
   B. Lingua Franca.
   C. Swahili.
   D. Arabic.

3. Which of the following was true of Tanzania's ujamaa program?
   A. The program's goal was to increase manufacturing.
   B. The program's goal was for farmers to farm their own land.
   C. The program was very successful.
   D. The program's goal was to produce more crops.

4. Which is the word for family farm in Kenya?
   A. Maasai
   B. shamba
   C. harambee
   D. Kikuyu

5. Which of the following is an example of harambee?
   A. raising cash crops
   B. staying close to extended families
   C. women's self-help groups
   D. moving from the countryside to the city

Short Answer Question

Why did Julius Nyerere establish a lingua franca for Tanzania?

_____

_____

_____

_____

Prepare to Read

Section 1 Democratic Republic of the Congo: A Wealth of Possibilities

Objectives

1. Discover the physical geography and important natural resources of the Democratic Republic of the Congo.
2. Learn about the country's economic and political challenges since independence.
3. Find out how different groups and leaders have reshaped the nation.

Target Reading Skill

Understand Sequence A sequence is the order in which a group of events occurs. Understanding the sequence of events can help you understand the events themselves. You can track sequence of events by listing them in the order in which they happened.

As you read this section, list the sequence of events that occurred after Congo gained independence. You may want to list events in a chart like the one below.

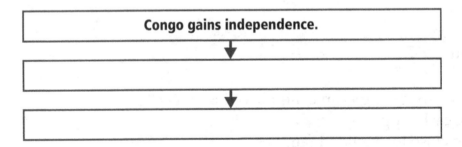

Vocabulary Strategy

Recognizing Word Origins In many English words, you will also find a word of Greek origin. If you know the meaning of the Greek word, it will help you figure out the meaning of the entire word. For example, in this section, you will read the phrase *hydroelectric plants. Hydro* is a Greek word that means "water." Knowing that, you can guess that the definition of *hydroelectric* involves water and electricity. As you read, you will find out that electricity is created with water at a hydroelectric plant.

Section 1 Summary

Physical Geography and Resources

The Democratic Republic of the Congo is Africa's third-largest country. It is the same size as the United States east of the Mississippi River. It has four major geographic regions: Congo basin, northern uplands, eastern highlands, and southern uplands. For the most part, Congolese (kahng guh LEEZ) live in all the regions except the Congo basin.

Most Congolese are farmers. But mining produces most of the country's wealth. Congo is one of the world's top producers of diamonds and copper. It also has other valuable minerals such as gold. Congo has the resources to develop many hydroelectric plants, which use swiftly flowing river water to create electricity. ☑

Natural resources have played an important role in Congo's history. For example, early kingdoms became powerful because they had fertile soil, plenty of rain, and iron tools that improved farming. Also, when the Portuguese arrived in the 1480s, they came to find gold.

400 years later, during the scramble for Africa, the Belgians took control of Congo. They forced Africans to harvest wild rubber for no pay. Belgium grew wealthy off this resource while Africans suffered and died.

Economic and Political Challenges

In 1960, Congo won its independence from Belgium. But its first years of freedom were difficult. Belgium had done little to prepare Congolese to rule their own country. Various groups fought one another for power.

The foreign companies that controlled Congo's mines were afraid that businesses would not do as well while the country faced problems. In 1965, these companies helped Joseph Mobutu (muh BOO too) take power. They hoped he would help calm the situation.

Mobutu tried to restore order by setting up an **authoritarian government**. He also tried to cut any

Key Term

authoritarian government (uh thawr uh TEHR ee un GUV urn munt) *n.* a nondemocratic form of government in which a single leader or a small group of leaders has all the power

You have probably seen the word geography many times. *Geo* is a Greek word that means "earth." *Graphy* is a Greek word that means "writing." Write a definition of geography based on the meanings of the Greek words.

_____

_____

_____

✓ Reading Check

Which industry produces most of Congo's wealth?

_____

_____

_____

Target Reading Skill

What important events led up to Mobutu's establishing an authoritarian government? List them in the order in which they occurred.

1. _____

2. _____

connection with the days of being a colony. He gave the country an African name, Zaire (zah IHR). And Mobutu **nationalized** the foreign-owned companies. ✓

Mobutu also borrowed money from foreign countries for projects to improve Zaire's economy. But most of his attempts to help the economy failed.

In the mid-1970s, the world price of copper fell sharply. Soon, Zaire's economy collapsed. Mobutu tried to help the situation by cutting the amount of money the government spent. But the cutbacks were hard on Zaire's poorest people. When people tried to challenge Mobutu's policies, he had them imprisoned or killed.

Reshaping the Nation

Mobutu ruled harshly throughout the 1980s. Zaire's economy became weaker and weaker. People asked for change both from inside and outside the country.

In 1996, a rebellion against Mobutu's government began. Mobutu fled to Morocco. The new government renamed the country the Democratic Republic of the Congo. A new leader, Laurent Kabila (law RAHN kuh BEEL ah), became president. But soon a new civil war broke out. Several nearby countries became involved. It was the first war in Africa since independence to involve several African nations. ✓

In 1999, the heads of the countries involved met to write a peace agreement. But neither side fulfilled it. By the end of 2002, many of the disagreements over the terms of peace were settled. But small conflicts have continued.

Review Questions

1. What are some of Congo's natural resources?

_____

_____

2. What changes did Joseph Mobutu make in Congo?

_____

_____

Key Term

nationalize (NASH uh nuh lyz) *v.* to transfer ownership of something to a nation's government

Prepare to Read

Section 2
South Africa: Struggle for Equality

Objectives

1. Understand how white rule in South Africa began.
2. Learn about the system of apartheid.
3. Find out how South Africans built a new nation after apartheid.

Target Reading Skill

Recognize Words That Signal Sequence Signal words are words or phrases that alert you to connections in the text. Words that signal sequence let you know the order in which events occurred.

You probably use sequence signal words all the time. For example, if you are telling a friend about your vacation, you might say, *"First we ... , and then ... , but before that ... ."* Common words that signal sequence include *first, then, before, when, during this time, after,* and *in (followed by a date).* As you read, recognizing sequence signal words will help you track the order of events.

Vocabulary Strategy

Recognizing Word Origins Many English words have Latin origins. Sometimes, the word in English is spelled differently than the Latin word. Being able to recognize the Latin parts of English words will help you learn their meanings.

In this section, you will read the word *Congress.* You may think that the word means a group of people who are elected to make laws. The word is often used that way in the United States. But it comes from the Latin words *com-,* which means "together," and *gradi,* which means "to walk." It can be used to describe any group of people that come together for some purpose.

Now think about other English words that use the Latin word *com-,* such as *community* and *communicate.*

Can you see how "together," is part of their definitions?

Target Reading Skill

As you read the section titled "Beginning of White Rule," take note of the words in the paragraphs that signal sequence. Circle them when you see them.

✓ Reading Check

When did the first white Europeans settle in what is now South Africa?

_____

_____

_____

Vocabulary Strategy

The word *government* comes from the Latin word *gubernare* ("to guide [a ship]") and the suffix *-ment* ("way of"). Based on the meaning of the Latin words, what do you think government means?

_____

_____

_____

Beginning of White Rule

1   In 1652, the Dutch became the first white Europeans to settle what is now South Africa. The settlers called themselves Boers (bohrz) which is the Dutch word for farmers. Their descendants called themselves Afrikan-
5   ers. They spoke a language called Afrikaans that is similar to Dutch. ✓

The Afrikaners founded their own states. But after diamonds and gold were discovered, the British wanted control. The British and Afrikaners fought from
10   1899 to 1902. The British won and took over the Afri-kaner states. In 1910, the British named all the land they controlled in this region the Union of South Africa.

The white-led <u>government</u> passed laws to keep land and wealth in white hands. Blacks were allowed to live
15   and own land in only 8 percent of the country. They could work in white areas, but they were paid little. Black and white workers were not allowed to work together. The whites were given the best jobs.

System of Apartheid

The British granted independence to South Africa in
20   1931. In 1948, an Afrikaner political party took control of the country. It was called the National Party. The new leaders called the system of treating whites and nonwhites differently **apartheid**, which is Afrikaans for "apartness." Laws made it legal to **discriminate** on the
25   basis of race.

South Africans were separated into four groups— blacks, whites, coloreds, and Asians. Coloreds were people of mixed race. Blacks made up 75 percent of the population. They had almost no rights.
30   Black South Africans were forced to move to the worst land in the country. Blacks became very poor.

Key Terms

apartheid (uh PAHR tayt) *n.* the legal system of South Africa in which the rights of nonwhites were greatly restricted

discriminate (dih SKRIM ih nayt) *v.* to treat people differently, and often unfairly, based on race, religion, or sex

---

They had had no citizenship rights in their own home-land. Nonwhites attended poor schools. They were barred from white restaurants, schools, and hospitals.

Many South Africans protested against apartheid. Over the decades, thousands of people were killed or imprisoned. The government banned peaceful protests. But people would not stop fighting for freedom. ☑

In the 1970s, other countries joined the movement against apartheid. Many nations stopped trading with South Africa. In 1990, South Africa began to respond. Led by President F. W. de Klerk, the government ended the apartheid laws.

Building a New Nation

Since the 1950s, **Nelson Mandela** had been a leader of a political party called the African National Congress (ANC). The ANC had long fought for all South Africans to be able to vote. In 1962, Mandela was sent to prison for life for fighting apartheid. In 1990, he was freed. He then became president of the ANC. In 1994, he became South Africa's president in the first election in which all South Africans could vote. ☑

There are still differences in how South Africans live. Blacks and whites usually live in different neighborhoods. Whites control most of the biggest businesses. However, new opportunities have been created for blacks. And tensions have eased.

In 1999, another ANC leader, Thabo Mbeki (TAH boh em BEK ee) became president. He has continued to build democracy in South Africa.

Review Questions

1. Why did the British want the Afrikaner states?

_____

_____

2. How did apartheid finally end?

_____

_____

Key Term

Nelson Mandela (NEL sun man DEL uh) *n.* black leader and South Africa's first president after apartheid ended

---

✓ Reading Check

What happened to South Africans who protested against apartheid?

_____

_____

_____

✓ Reading Check

What happened for the first time in South Africa's 1994 election?

_____

_____

_____

1. Which natural resource did NOT play a role in Congo's history?
   A. diamonds
   B. silver
   C. gold
   D. rubber

2. Why did foreign companies help Joseph Mobutu take power in Congo?
   A. They wanted him to nationalize their companies.
   B. They wanted to keep him busy so that he would leave them alone.
   C. They were afraid the country's problems would hurt business.
   D. They thought he would turn Congo back over to the Belgians.

3. Which of the following statements about Congo's rebellion and civil war is NOT true?
   A. The fighting caused Mobutu to flee the country.
   B. The fighting was a response to Mobutu's harsh rule.
   C. Congo's neighbors became involved in the war.
   D. The rebels were led by Joseph Mobutu.

4. What group gave the name apartheid to the system of treating South Africans differently based on race?
   A. the British
   B. the Boers
   C. the ANC
   D. the Afrikaners

5. When did apartheid end?
   A. 1910
   B. 1931
   C. 1948
   D. 1990

Short Answer Question

Why do you think South Africans chose someone who was black as their first president after apartheid?

_____

_____

_____

_____

Asia and the Pacific

Objectives

1. Learn about the landforms and water bodies found in East Asia.
2. Find out where most of the people in East Asia live.

Target Reading Skill

Set a Purpose for Reading Reading a textbook is different from reading a novel or the newspaper. To read to learn effectively, you must preview and set a purpose for your reading.

Before you read this section, take a moment to preview it. Look at the title "Land and Water" and the objectives. Now flip through the next two pages. Read each heading. Headings tell you about the section's contents. They tell you what to expect to learn in the section. As you preview, use this information to give yourself a reason to read the section.

Are you curious about anything in the section, such as what a country with more than a billion people is like? Read to satisfy that curiosity—that's your purpose for reading.

Vocabulary Strategy

Recognizing Compound Words When you come across a new word, you may be able to figure out what it means if you break it down into parts. For example, if you do not know what the word *landform* means, you can break it down into its parts: *land* and *form*. A landform is a form, shape, or structure made from the land. Many words in English are made by combining two or more words. These words are called *compound words*.

Here are some common compound words that are made up of two words:

anybody	earthquake	farmland
highland	homeland	mainland
countryside	mountaintop	northeast

Section 1 Summary

Landforms and Water Bodies

One nation takes up most of East Asia's land. It is China. Mountains, highlands, and **plateaus** make up much of China's landscape. The other countries of East Asia also have mountains. But only China and Mongolia have wide plains and plateaus. The other countries—Japan, Taiwan, North Korea, and South Korea—have narrow plains. These plains lie mainly along coasts and rivers.

About 50 million years ago, the movement of the continents caused the land surface of Asia to fold and bend upwards. This process created the Himalayas and the Plateau of Tibet. The Himalayas are the highest mountain range in the world. They include Mount Everest, the highest mountain in the world. The Himalayas run along the border of China and Nepal. North of these mountains lies the Plateau of Tibet, a huge highland area.

Natural forces also shaped the islands of Japan. Earthquakes forced some parts of the country to rise and others to sink. Lava and ash from volcanos formed new mountains. Japan's Mount Fuji is a volcano, but it has not erupted since 1707. Volcanoes and earthquakes still change the shape of the land in parts of East Asia.

More people live in China than in any other country. How many? Over one billion people live there!

Two thirds of China's land is mountains and deserts. A desert is a dry place with few plants. The Gobi is a desert in China. It lies farther north than any other desert on Earth.

China's most important rivers are the Chang and the Huang. They begin in Tibet and flow east. The Chang River is deep enough for cargo ships. The Huang River runs through the North China Plain. The plain is very **fertile**. More than 100 million people live in this fertile area.

Japan is an **archipelago** in the western Pacific Ocean. It has four main islands. Most of Japan's people live along the coast. Nearly 80 percent of the country has mountains. ☑

40 The largest of Japan's islands is Honshu (hahn shoo). It also has the most people. Most of Japan's major cities are located there. Japan's capital city, Tokyo, is on Honshu.

Korea is a peninsula. That means it is surrounded on 45 three sides by ocean. Korea is located between China and Japan. Since 1953, Korea has been divided into two countries. They are North Korea and South Korea.

Population in East Asia

East Asia has almost 1.5 billion people. They are spread unevenly across the land. Few people live in the 50 deserts, plateaus, and mountains. Most live on the plains and near the coasts because it is easier to grow food in those areas.

Places where many people live have a very high **population density**. The North China Plain is one 55 example. It has a very high population density because it is level and has fertile soil. ☑

In East Asia, cities, farms, and industries are crowded onto the level land. Almost half the people of Japan live on less than 3 percent of the land. In China, 60 most of the people live in the eastern half of the country. That is where the plains and coastal areas are.

✓ Reading Check

Why does the North China Plain have such a high population density?

_____

_____

_____

Review Questions

1. What are the major landforms of East Asia?

_____

_____

2. In what areas do most people in East Asia live? Why?

_____

_____

Key Terms

archipelago (ahr kuh PEL uh goh) *n.* a group of islands
population density (pahp yuh LAY shun DEN suh tee) *n.* the average number of people living in a square mile or square kilometer

Objectives

1. Examine the major climate regions in East Asia.
2. Discover how climate affects people and vegetation in East Asia.

Target Reading Skill

Predict Making predictions about what you will learn from your text helps you set a purpose for reading. It also helps you remember what you have read. Before you begin reading, preview the section. Look at the section title and objectives above. Then look at the headings. Then based on your preview, predict what the section will tell you.

What do you think this section will tell you about the climate and vegetation of East Asia? List two facts that you expect to learn.

Prediction 1: _____

Prediction 2: _____

As you read, check your predictions. Were they right? If they were not very accurate, you may need to pay closer attention when you preview the section.

Vocabulary Strategy

Recognizing Roots Often, a few letters are added to the beginning or end of a word to make another word. For example, the letters *re-* may be attached to the beginning of a word. Or the letters *-ing* may be attached to the end of a word. When you add letters to a word, that word is called a root. A root is a word used to make other words. The word *play* is the root of the word *replay*. The word *carry* is the root of the word *carrying*. Adding letters to the root changes its meaning.

When you come across a new word, look at it closely. See if it contains a root word that you already know. If it does, then you're not far from understanding the word's meaning.

East Asia's Climate Regions

There are five major climate regions in East Asia. They are semiarid, arid, humid subtropical, humid continental, and highland.

Much of eastern China has a **humid subtropical climate**. This means that the winters are cool, the summers are hot, and there is plenty of rain. The northeast is a **humid continental** area. There, summers are warm and winters are cold. In South Korea and Japan, summers are a bit cooler and winters a bit warmer than in other places at the same latitude. This is because these two countries are almost entirely surrounded by water.

The northern part of China is very dry. It has **arid** and **semiarid** climate regions. Temperatures there can be very hot or very cold. To the south, the Plateau of Tibet has a **highland** climate. It is cool and dry.

Monsoons are important to East Asia's climates. In summer, winds from the Pacific Ocean blow northwest toward Asia. They bring rainfall. It starts in June as a drizzle. In July, the rain gets heavier, and the winds cause hot, humid weather.

In winter, the winds change direction. They come from the northern part of Asia. They are icy cold and very dry. In parts of China, the winds cause dust storms that last for days. After they blow across ocean waters, they bring rain or snow to inland areas.

East Asia has hurricanes that are called **typhoons**. Whirling typhoon winds blow at high speeds of 74 miles an hour or more. The winds and heavy rains they bring can cause major damage. For example, in 1922, a typhoon that struck China caused about 60,000 deaths. ✓

Key Terms

monsoon (mahn SOON) *n.* a wind that changes direction with the change of season

typhoon (ty FOON) *n.* a hurricane or tropical storm that develops over the Pacific Ocean, with winds that reach speeds greater than 74 miles per hour

---

Target Reading Skill

Based on what you have read so far, are your predictions on target? If not, change your predictions now.

New Predictions: _____

_____

_____

✓ Reading Check

How are typhoons different from monsoons?

_____

_____

_____

The Influences of Climate

Climate affects what plants grow in East Asia. It also affects what crops people can raise on farms.

Much of East Asia's plant life is strong. It can stand the changes in temperature and rainfall that come with the change of seasons. For example, bamboo grows <u>quickly</u> during the wet season in <u>southern</u> China and Japan. But it can also survive dry spells. Even in China's deserts, plants will spring up quickly if it rains. **Deciduous** trees change with the seasons. Their leaves turn gold, orange, and red in the fall and then drop off.

Climate also affects life in East Asia. The region around the Huang River in China is a good example. The Chinese word *Huang* means "yellow." The river is named for the <u>brownish</u>-yellow soil called loess that is blown by the desert winds. The river carries the loess and leaves it on the North China Plain. This huge plain is one of the best <u>farming</u> areas in China.

The Huang River also floods. Dams help control the waters. But during monsoons, the river still sometimes overflows.

Climate also affects the diet of East Asians. Rice grows best in warm weather, so people in southern China grow and eat rice. In the <u>cooler</u> north, wheat grows better. People in the north eat more things made from wheat, such as noodles. ✓

Review Questions

1. What are the five major climate regions in East Asia?

_____

_____

_____

2. How do monsoons affect climates in East Asia?

_____

_____

_____

Key Term

deciduous (dee SIJ oo us) *adj.* describing plants that drop their leaves in the fall

Vocabulary Strategy

Each of the underlined words in the paragraphs to the left contains another word that is a root. Circle the roots you find in these words. The root of the first word, *quickly*, is *quick*.

Mark the Text

✓ Reading Check

How does climate affect the diet of East Asians?

_____

_____

_____

Prepare to Read

Section 3
Natural Resources and Land Use

Objectives

1. Learn about East Asia's major natural resources.
2. Find out how the people of East Asia use land to produce food.

Target Reading Skill

Ask Questions Looking for the answers to specific questions as you read can help you understand and remember important ideas. Before you read this section, preview the section title, objectives, and headings to see what the section is about. What do you think are the most important ideas in the section? How can you tell?

After you preview the section, write two questions that will help you understand or remember important ideas or facts in the section. You might turn the headings into questions, such as:

- What are East Asia's natural resources?
- What are the mineral resources of the two Koreas?

Vocabulary Strategy

Using Word Parts Sometimes when you come across a new word, you can figure out what it means if you break it into parts. For example, look closely at the word *aquaculture*. You can break it into *aqua* and *culture*.

Think of other words you know that begin with *aqua*. Perhaps you have gone to an aquatic center to swim. You may know that an aquarium is a tank filled with water and used to keep fish in. Both *aquatic* and *aquarium* are words that have something to do with water.

Next, think of other words you know that end with *culture*. You probably know that *agriculture* refers to growing crops and raising farm animals.

Now, put what you know about the parts together. *Aquaculture* means "growing things in water."

Section 3 Summary

Natural resources are things found in nature that are useful to people. They include fertile land, minerals, water, and forests.

East Asia's Natural Resources

East Asia has many natural resources. The ones used for energy include coal, oil, and water for hydroelectric power. Other resources are raw materials that are used to make manufactured goods. Water and fertile land are important resources for growing food.

Some East Asian countries have more natural resources than others. For example, North Korea, a **developing country**, has coal and iron. South Korea, a **developed country**, has manufacturing. But it lacks coal and iron.

Mineral Resources of East Asia	
Country	**Resources**
North Korea	**Has:** coal, iron
South Korea	**Imports:** iron, oil, chemicals
Japan	**Imports:** coal, natural gas, oil, iron, tin, copper
China	**Has:** coal, copper, tin, iron, oil

Both Koreas would benefit if they shared resources. But they are unfriendly to each other and do not share. So South Korea imports the materials it needs to make the manufactured goods it sells to other nations. It is one of East Asia's richest economies.

Japan is also a modern industrial society. It produces many manufactured goods even though it has to import huge amounts of minerals. In contrast, China has many mineral resources. It has one of the largest coal supplies in the world. ✓

Key Terms

developing country (dih VEL up ing KUN tree) *n.* a country where industry is not strong and there is little modern technology

developed country (dih VEL upt KUN tree) *n.* a country with many industries and a well-developed economy

---

Target Reading Skill

Turn the underlined sentence into a question. Read the paragraph and then write an answer to your question.

Question:_____

_____

Answer: _____

_____

✓ Reading Check

Based on what you have read, is Japan a developed country or a developing country?

_____

_____

East Asia's rivers can be used to produce hydroelectricity. That is electricity made by using the power of flowing water. Hydroelectric power is important to industry. But building dams and power plants is expensive. China is building a dam across the Chang River to produce more hydroelectric power. The Three Gorges Dam will also control flooding.

East Asia's waters are an important source of food. During the 1980s and 1990s, <u>overfishing</u> and pollution caused fish supplies to drop. That made aquaculture more important. Aquaculture is the farming of fish, shellfish, and seaweed. China is the leading aquaculture producer in East Asia.

Using the Land to Produce Food

To feed the large population, East Asians need to farm every bit of land. With so many mountains and plateaus, only a small percentage of the land is level farmland.

In China, Japan, and parts of Korea, farmers cut **terraces** into steep hillsides. That gives them space to grow crops. Where climate and soil allow it, farmers use **double-cropping**. In China, farmers often plant one type of crop between the rows of another crop. In some parts of southern China, they can grow three crops in a year. In southern Japan, rice seedlings are replanted in a larger field after wheat has been harvested from it. ☑

Review Questions

1. Name three natural resources in East Asia that can be used to produce energy.

   _____

   _____

2. How are both land and water used to produce food?

   _____

   _____

   _____

Key Terms

terrace (TEHR us) *n.* a flat area in a hillside
double-cropping (DUB ul KRAHP ing) *v.* growing two or more crops on the same land, in the same season, and at the same time

Vocabulary Strategy

If you do not know what the word *overfishing* means, try breaking it into parts. In this case, over means "too much," as in *overeating* or *overgrown*. *Fishing* means "catching fish." What do you think overfishing is?

_____

_____

✓ Reading Check

How do both terrace farming and double-cropping increase food supplies?

_____

_____

_____

Chapter 18 Assessment

1. Which country takes up most of East Asia's land?
   A. Japan
   B. Mongolia
   C. China
   D. South Korea

2. Most of the people in Japan live
   A. along the coast.
   B. in mountainous areas.
   C. on Japan's wide plains.
   D. on plateaus.

3. How does the Huang River affect the North China Plain?
   A. It brings rain and snow.
   B. Its dams produce hydroelectricity.
   C. It carries soil to the area.
   D. It is used for cargo ships.

4. In East Asia, monsoons do NOT bring
   A. winds over 74 miles per hour.
   B. dust storms in the winter.
   C. summer rains.
   D. rain and snow to inland regions.

5. The mineral resources of East Asia are
   A. spread evenly among the countries.
   B. not spread evenly among the countries.
   C. located only in Japan.
   D. shared by North and South Korea.

Short Answer Question

How do Japan and South Korea make up for their lack of mineral resources?

_____

_____

_____

_____

Prepare to Read

Section 1
South Asia: Physical Geography

Objectives

1. Learn about the landforms of South Asia.
2. Discover the most important factor that affects climate in South Asia.
3. Examine how people use the land and resources of South Asia.

Target Reading Skill

Reread or Read Ahead Have you ever replayed a scene from a video or DVD so you could figure out what was going on? Rereading a passage is like doing that. Sometimes you may not understand a sentence or a paragraph the first time you read it. When this happens, go back and read it again. You may need to read it two or more times.

Reading ahead can also help you understand something you are not sure of in the text. If you don't understand a word or passage, keep reading. The word or idea may be explained later. For example, you may be unsure of what it means when the Himalayas are called a barrier. If you keep reading, you will find an example of the Himalayas blocking cold air from the north.

Vocabulary Strategy

Using Context Clues Words work together to explain meaning. The meaning of a word may depend on the words around it, or context. The context gives you clues to a word's meaning.

Try this example. Say that you do not know the meaning of the word *subcontinent* in the following sentence:

The Indian subcontinent was once attached to the eastern coast of Africa.

You could ask yourself: "What information does the sentence give me about the word?" Answer: "I know that a continent is a very large landmass. The sentence says the subcontinent was attached to Africa. A subcontinent could be a landmass that is smaller than a continent." In fact, a subcontinent is a large landmass that is a major part of a continent.

Section 1 Summary

The Indian **subcontinent** was once attached to eastern Africa. Then, 200 million years ago, it broke away and slowly slid toward Asia. About 40 million years ago, it collided with Asia. Northern India and southern Asia crumpled where they met. This formed the Himalayas, which include the world's highest mountains.

Major Landforms of South Asia

South Asia is shaped like a triangle. The narrow tip extends into the ocean. The largest nation in South Asia is India. Pakistan (PAK ih stan) and Afghanistan (af GAN ih stan) are west of India. The Himalayas form India's northern border with Nepal (nu PAWL) and Bhutan (BOO tahn). To the east is Bangladesh (BAHNG luh DESH). The island nations of Sri Lanka (sree LAHNG kuh) and the Maldives (MAL dyvz) are off the southern tip of India.

The Himalayas form a barrier between South Asia and the rest of Asia. They stretch about 1,550 miles (2,500 kilometers) from east to west. Mount Everest, the world's tallest mountain, is in the Himalayas.

Two major rivers in South Asia start high in the Himalayas. They are the Ganges and the Indus. The Ganges flows across northern India. It empties into the Bay of Bengal. The Indus flows west into Pakistan. Many people live in the plains around both rivers.

Along the Indus and Ganges rivers are huge **alluvial** plains. The rivers carry water and minerals needed for farming. The rich fertile soil makes this area good for farming. Many people live and farm here. Remember that South Asia is shaped like a triangle? At the southern point and going up both sides are two mountain ranges. They are the Western Ghats (gawts) and the Eastern Ghats. Between these mountain ranges is the Deccan Plateau. *Deccan* means "south" in Sanskrit. That will help you remember where it is located. ✓

Key Terms

subcontinent (SUB kahn tih nunt) *n.* a large landmass that is a major part of a continent
alluvial (uh LOO vee ul) *adj.* made of soil deposited by rivers

Target Reading Skill

Read ahead through the bracketed paragraph to see why the Ganges and Indus rivers are important to the people of South Asia. List one fact you discovered by reading ahead.

_____

_____

✓ Reading Check

Where is the Deccan Plateau located?

_____

_____

The Climates of South Asia

35 Monsoons are important to South Asia's climate. The summer monsoons blow over the Arabian Sea and the Indian Ocean and pick up moisture. When the air passes over the hot land of western India, it rises and loses its moisture in the form of rain.

40 The rains cool the coastal lands somewhat. Then the next air mass travels farther inland before losing its moisture. In this way, the monsoon rains work their way inland until they reach the Himalayas.

During the winter, the monsoons blow from the chilly northeast. 45 <u>They move dry, frigid air toward South Asia</u>. But the Himalayas block the cold air. This means the countries of South Asia enjoy dry, mild winters. ✔

Land Use in South Asia

About 70 percent of South Asians live in rural areas. Most of these people are crowded into fertile river valleys. 50 They grow whatever crops they can. ✔

Some countries grow **cash crops**. These include tea, cotton, coffee, and sugar cane. They can bring in a great deal of money. But when prices fall or when crops fail, farmers may not earn enough money.

55 India has many mineral resources. Iron ore and coal are plentiful. But India has only a small amount of oil, so it uses hydroelectricity and nuclear power.

South Asia is one of the most densely populated regions in the world. Most of the people live where 60 there is plenty of rainfall. This includes coastal areas, northeastern India, and the country of Bangladesh.

Review Questions

1. Which landform is a natural barrier between South Asia and the rest of Asia?

   _____

   _____

2. List some cash crops raised in South Asia.

   _____

   _____

> **Key Term**
>
> **cash crop** (kash krahp) *n.* a crop that is raised or gathered to be sold for money on the local or world market

Vocabulary Strategy

What does the word *frigid* mean in the underlined sentence? Circle the clues in the surrounding words, phrases, or sentences that help you learn what *frigid* means. Define *frigid*.

_____

✓ Reading Check

Describe one way the summer monsoons differ from the winter monsoons.

_____

_____

✓ Reading Check

In what type of areas do most South Asians live?

_____

_____

Prepare to Read

Section 2
Southwest Asia: Physical Geography

Objectives

1. Learn about the major landforms of Southwest Asia.
2. Find out what the two most important resources in Southwest Asia are.
3. Examine how people use the land in Southwest Asia.

Target Reading Skill

Paraphrase Paraphrasing is putting what you read into your own words. It is another skill that can help you understand and remember what you read.

Look at the first two paragraphs under the heading "A Dry Region Bordered by Water." They could be paraphrased like this:

Southwest Asia is mostly desert. The world's largest desert covered entirely in sand is in Southwest Asia. Because there is very little rain, water is very valuable.

As you read, paraphrase the first paragraph or two after each heading.

Vocabulary Strategy

Using Context to Determine Meaning If you don't understand a word, sometimes you can pick up clues to its meaning from the words, phrases, and sentences around it. The underlined words in the paragraph below give clues to the meaning of the word *oasis*.

Travelers passing through the desert are happy when they find an **oasis**. Sometimes, the <u>water from an oasis</u> can support a community of people. It <u>can be pumped from under ground</u> to irrigate crops and water livestock.

An oasis is a place in a desert region where fresh water is available from under ground. Do you see how the context clues help make that clear?

Section 2 Summary

A Dry Region Bordered by Water

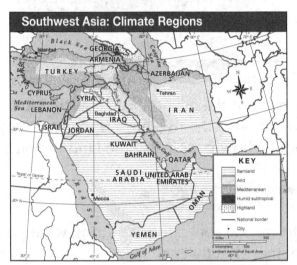

Southwest Asia: Climate Regions

KEY
Semiarid
Arid
Mediterranean
Humid subtropical
Highland
— National border
• City

1 Most of Southwest Asia is desert. Less than 10 inches (25 centimeters) of rain fall a year. The Rub' al-Kahli is the world's largest all-sand desert. Ten years can go by between rainfalls. Not all deserts are covered with
5 sand. Some include pebbles, gravel, and boulders.

Water is very valuable in Southwest Asia. Travelers in the desert are happy to find an **oasis**. An oasis in the desert can support a community. Farmers can grow crops. Nomadic shepherds can raise livestock.

10 There are some fertile areas in the region. The Tigris (TY gris) and Euphrates (yoo FRAYT eez) rivers begin in the mountains of Turkey and flow south through Iraq. When these rivers flood, they leave rich soil along their banks. In ancient times, one of the world's first civiliza-
15 tions grew up in this fertile area. The region was known as Mesopotamia. ✓

Southwest Asia is surrounded by water. Most of the region is hot and dry. <u>But some parts of Southwest Asia have a Mediterranean climate</u>. They have hot, dry
20 summers but mild, rainy winters. The coasts of the Mediterranean, Black, and Caspian seas have a Mediterranean climate. So do the mountain areas.

> **Key Term**
> **oasis** (oh AY sis) *n.* an area in a desert region where fresh water is usually available from an underground spring or well

✓ Reading Check

Where do the Tigris and Euphrates rivers begin?

_____

_____

Vocabulary Strategy

Look at the word *Mediterranean* in the underlined sentence. You may not have seen the word used this way before. But there are clues to what it means. Circle the words or phrases that help you learn its meaning in this context. Then write a definition of the term below.

_____

_____

_____

Southwest Asia's Major Natural Resources

The two most important natural resources in Southwest Asia are **petroleum** and water. Petroleum, also called oil, is a **nonrenewable resource.**

We get gasoline and other fuels from petroleum. It is the natural resource that brings the most money into Southwest Asia. Since much of the region has a dry climate, water is the resource that people need most.

30 Southwest Asia is the largest oil-producing region in the world. Money from selling oil has improved the **standard of living** in many Southwest Asian countries. They have enough money to import goods and workers from other countries. The countries with little or no oil 35 tend to have a lower standard of living. ✓

Most countries in the region must use irrigation to grow crops. People may use water from rivers or pump water from far underground.

Using the Land in Southwest Asia

Land in Southwest Asia is used for agriculture, 40 nomadic herding, and producing oil. Most farmland is in the northern part of the region. The Mediterranean climate along the coasts lets people grow many crops.

For centuries, Bedouins (BED oo inz) have lived in Southwest Asia's deserts. They are Arabic-speaking 45 nomadic herders. They move over a large area of land in search of grass and water for their animals. ✓

Review Questions

1. How do rivers and seas affect Southwest Asia?

_____

_____

2. Describe the different ways in which water and petroleum are important to Southwest Asia.

_____

_____

Key Terms

petroleum (puh TROH lee um) *n.* an oily liquid used as fuel
nonrenewable resource (nahn rih NOO uh bul REE sawrs) *n.* a natural resource that cannot be quickly replaced once it is used
standard of living (STAN durd uv LIV ing) *n.* a measurement of a person's or a group's education, housing, health, and nutrition

🎯 **Target Reading Skill**

Use your own words to paraphrase the bracketed paragraph. Be sure to explain what a nonrenewable resource is in your own terms. *Hint:* paraphrase the definition in the Key Terms box below.

_____

_____

✓ **Reading Check**

How has oil improved life in some countries of Southwest Asia?

_____

_____

_____

✓ **Reading Check**

Who are the Bedouins?

_____

_____

_____

Prepare to Read

Section 3
Central Asia: Physical Geography

Objectives

1. Learn about the main physical features of Central Asia.
2. Discover which natural resources are important in Central Asia.
3. Find out how people use the land in Central Asia.

Target Reading Skill

Summarize When you summarize, you state the main points you have read. You leave out the less important details. A summary is shorter than the original text. When you summarize, keep the main ideas or facts in the correct order.

Look at the following sentence: "The Kara Kum desert covers much of the land in Turkmenistan, and the Kyzyl Kum desert covers much of neighboring Uzbekistan." It could be summarized like this: "Much of Turkmenistan and Uzbekistan is desert."

As you read about, pause to summarize the main ideas.

Vocabulary Strategy

Using Context to Clarify Meaning When you come across a word that you do not know, you can look for clues in the words and sentences just before and after the word. These clues are called context clues. They can include examples, explanations, or definitions. Also, you may already know something about the topic that gives you a clue. As you read, use the graphic organizer to help you.

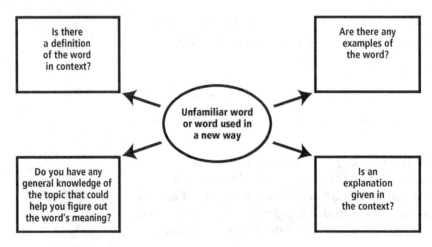

Section 3 Summary

Here are the countries of Central Asia. Kazakhstan (kah zahk STAHN) is the largest and northernmost country in Central Asia. To its south are Uzbekistan (ooz BEK ih stan), Kyrgyzstan (kihr gih STAN), Turkmenistan (turk MEN ih stan), and Tajikistan (tah jik ih STAN). Afghanistan forms the southern border of Central Asia. All of these countries except Afghanistan were once part of the Soviet Union.

Central Asia's Main Physical Features

Central Asia's main physical features are highlands, deserts, and **steppes**. The mountains are in the southeastern part of the region. The Tian Shan and the Pamir mountain ranges cover much of Kyrgyzstan and Tajikistan.

The land to the west of these mountain ranges is lower and flatter. The Kara Kum desert covers much of Turkmenistan. The Kyzyl Kum desert covers much of Uzbekistan. And the Kirghiz Steppe is located in nearby Kazakhstan.

Most of Central Asia has a dry climate. The interior is <u>arid</u>, or extremely dry. Around this dry region is a wide band of semiarid land, which gets a little more rain. ✓

There are two important bodies of water in this dry land. One is the Caspian Sea, which is really a salt lake. It is the largest lake in the world. It has some of the world's largest oil reserves.

The Aral Sea is located in the interior of Central Asia. It is also a salt lake. It was once the fourth-largest inland lake in the world. It has grown smaller since the 1960s because some of the lake has dried up. At that time, the former Soviet Union began using water from rivers that flow into the Aral to irrigate crops. This caused the lake to dry up.

Target Reading Skill

Summarize the bracketed paragraphs. Try to use 25 words or fewer.

_____

_____

_____

_____

✓ Reading Check

What type of climate does most of Central Asia have?

_____

_____

_____

Vocabulary Strategy

Suppose you don't know what the underlined word *arid* means. Look at the context of the word for clues. Use the graphic organizer on the previous page to help you figure out what it means. Write a brief definition of *arid* below.

_____

_____

Key Term

steppe (step) *n.* large, mostly level, treeless plains that are covered in grasses

Natural Resources in Central Asia

Petroleum is a major natural resource in Central Asia. Another is natural gas. Kazakhstan, Uzbekistan, and Turkmenistan have large oil and gas reserves. Turkmenistan has the fifth-largest reserve of natural gas in the world. ☑

Central Asia has other valuable minerals as well. Kazakhstan has large deposits of coal. It exports much of its coal to former Soviet republics. The region also has major deposits of gold, copper, iron, lead, and uranium.

Land Use in Central Asia

Most of the land in Central Asia is used for agriculture. Raising livestock and farming are both important. People in Central Asia have raised sheep, horses, goats, and camels for thousands of years. Cotton is a major crop.

Farming in Central Asia depends on irrigation. In the 1960s, the Soviet Union wanted to increase cotton production. Canals were built to carry water from two rivers to irrigate the cotton fields. Between 1960 and 1980, cotton production more than tripled.

This irrigation project took water from two rivers that flow into the Aral Sea. As a result, the Aral Sea began drying up. The land around the Aral Sea is also damaged. Huge amounts of pesticides were used on the cotton crops. These chemicals, which kill insects and weeds, have polluted the soil. The destruction of the Aral Sea is one of the world's worst environmental disasters. ☑

Review Questions

1. What are Central Asia's three main physical features?

   _____

   _____

   _____

2. What were the effects of irrigation on the Aral Sea?

   _____

   _____

   _____

What are two major natural resources in Central Asia?

1. _____

2. _____

How have pesticides damaged the land in Central Asia?

_____

_____

_____

Chapter 19 Assessment

1. The Indus and Ganges rivers make the plains of northern India good for
   A. mining.
   B. farming.
   C. aquaculture.
   D. hydroelectricity.

2. South Asian countries have climates with warm, dry winters because
   A. they are located along the Equator.
   B. they are located in a desert region.
   C. the Himalayas block cold air blown in by the winter monsoons.
   D. the Eastern Ghats block cold air blown in by the winter monsoons.

3. Most of Southwest Asia is
   A. irrigated by monsoons.
   B. covered by the Himalayas.
   C. covered by deserts.
   D. used for terrace farming.

4. Which brings the most money into Southwest Asia?
   A. water
   B. petroleum
   C. gold
   D. farm products

5. Farming in Central Asia depends on
   A. irrigation.
   B. monsoons.
   C. imported workers.
   D. traditional methods.

Short Answer Question

Why do you think one of the world's first civilizations grew up in Mesopotamia rather than elsewhere in Southwest Asia?

_____

_____

_____

_____

Prepare to Read

Section 1
Southeast Asia: Physical Geography

Objectives

1. Learn about the major landforms of Southeast Asia.
2. Find out about the kinds of climate and vegetation in Southeast Asia.
3. Examine how people use the land and resources of Southeast Asia.

Target Reading Skill

Identify Main Ideas Have you ever asked someone, "What's your point?" With that question, you were asking for the main idea. Good readers look for the main ideas of what they read. To help you find the main idea of a paragraph, read it through once. Then ask yourself what the paragraph is about. Do all the sentences focus on the same subject? If so, you've found the main idea. Sometimes the main idea is stated directly in the first sentence or two.

The main idea of the paragraph below is underlined:

Southeast Asia is divided into mainland and island areas. The mainland is a peninsula. It juts out from the main part of Asia. The islands run east and west between the Indian and Pacific oceans.

Vocabulary Strategy

Using Context to Clarify Meaning When you come across new words in your text, they are often defined for you in context. Context is the nearby words and sentences. Sometimes the definition appears in a separate sentence. Sometimes there is a brief definition in the same sentence. Often, the word *or* is used to introduce the definition. Look at the following examples.

subsistence farming, or *farming that provides only enough food for a family*

commercial farming, or *raising crops and livestock for sale*

They grow rice in paddies. A paddy is a *level field that is flooded to grow rice.*

The underlined words are defined in context. In these examples, brief definitions appear in italics. When you come across a new word in your text, look both before and after the word for the definition of the word.

Section 1 Summary

The Land of Southeast Asia

Southeast Asia is divided into mainland and island areas. The mainland is a peninsula. It juts out from the main part of Asia. The islands run east and west between the Indian and Pacific oceans.

The nations on the mainland are Cambodia, Laos (LAH ohs), Malaysia (muh LAY zhuh), Myanmar (MYUN mahr), Thailand (TY land), and Vietnam. Malaysia is part of both mainland Southeast Asia and island Southeast Asia.

There are five major nations in island Southeast Asia. They are Singapore, Malaysia, Brunei (broo NY), Indonesia, and the Philippines. The largest of them is Indonesia. ☑

The islands are part of the Ring of Fire. It is a region of volcanoes and earthquakes that surrounds the Pacific Ocean. Some of the islands are the tops of underwater volcanoes.

Climate and Vegetation

Most of island Southeast Asia has a tropical wet climate with hot temperatures all year round. There is no dry season. Along the coast of mainland Southeast Asia, much of the land also has a tropical wet climate. But inland areas have a tropical wet and dry climate or a humid subtropical climate.

Monsoons are important to Southeast Asia. There are two summer monsoons. One blows from the southwest, off the Indian Ocean. It hits the west coast. The other blows from the southeast, off the Pacific Ocean. It hits the southeast coast. Also, a winter monsoon blows from the northeast, off the Pacific Ocean. It hits the Philippines and Indonesia. (In the parts of Indonesia in the Southern Hemisphere, this is a summer monsoon.)

The monsoons bring heavy rains that often cause flooding. All of this moisture supports tropical rain forests. The rain forests of Southeast Asia are green and thick with plants. ☑

Unfortunately, tropical climates also have typhoons. These are strong storms with high winds and heavy rain. They often cause property damage and loss of life.

✓ Reading Check

Name the largest nation in island Southeast Asia.

_____

_____

Target Reading Skill

In the bracketed paragraph, underline the sentence that states the main idea.

✓ Reading Check

What are the results of Southeast Asia's monsoons?

_____

_____

_____

Using the Land and Resources of Southeast Asia

Some people in Southeast Asia practice **subsistence farming**. They grow just enough food for their families. Others work on large plantations. This is one type of **commercial farming**. Cash crops grown there include coffee, tea, and rubber.

Rice has long been the main crop in Southeast Asia. It needs a hot climate and plenty of water. In fact, rice grows best when it is planted in water. In Southeast Asia, farmers use the **paddy** system to grow rice. Indonesia and Thailand are among the top rice producers in the world. Rice is also a main food for the local people.

Tropical rain forests cover large parts of the region. Many kinds of plants grow in them. They are a source of lumber, medicines, and chemicals. Unfortunately, huge areas have been cut down to provide lumber and create farmland. One result has been mudslides. Southeast Asia is trying to balance the need for economic growth with the need for rain forests. ✓

Bamboo is another forest resource. This grass has a woody stem and grows quickly. It is used to make houses, irrigation pipes, ropes, and bridges. Several Southeast Asian countries sell bamboo to other countries.

There are large amounts of oil and natural gas in the area. The countries of Southeast Asia use natural gas to make electricity. They do not need to buy oil from other countries.

Review Questions

1. Describe the climate of island Southeast Asia.

_____

_____

2. Why does rice grow well in Southeast Asia?

_____

_____

Key Terms

subsistence farming (sub SIS tuns FAHR ming) *n.* farming that provides only enough food for a family or for a village

commercial farming (kuh MUR shul FAHR ming) *n.* raising crops and livestock for sale on the local or world market

paddy (PAD ee) *n.* a level field that is flooded to grow rice

Prepare to Read

Section 2
Australia and New Zealand: Physical Geography

Objectives

1. Find out why Australia and New Zealand have unique physical environments.
2. Learn about Australia's physical geography.
3. Explore New Zealand's physical geography.

Target Reading Skill

Identify Supporting Details The main idea of a paragraph or section is its most important point. The main idea is supported by details. Details give more information about the main idea. They tell you *what, where, why, how much*, or *how many*.

The main idea of the paragraphs under the heading "Unique Physical Environments" is given below.

Australia and New Zealand have plants and animals like nowhere else because they are located far from other continents.

When you read, notice how the details in these paragraphs tell you more about the features that are special to Australia and New Zealand, and how and why they happened.

Vocabulary Strategy

Using Context to Clarify Meaning When you come across a word that you do not know, you may not need to look it up in a dictionary. Continue to read to the end of the paragraph. See if you can figure out what the word means from its context, or the words and sentences near the unfamiliar word. Context clues can include examples and explanations. In this example, the context clues to one meaning of the underlined word are in italics.

Marsupials include *kangaroos, koalas*, and *opossum*.

How do the examples help you understand the word *marsupials*?

Unique Physical Environments

¹ Australia and New Zealand lie between the Pacific and Indian oceans. They are both in the Southern Hemisphere (south of the Equator). So their seasons are the opposite of those in the United States. ✓

⁵ New Zealand and Australia are very far from other continents. Many of their plants and animals are <u>unique</u>. They are found nowhere else on Earth. For example, kiwi and yellow-eyed penguins live only in New Zealand. And kangaroos and koalas live only in Australia. These last two animals are **marsupials**. In Australia, almost all mammals are marsupials. This is not true anywhere else in the world.

The animals of Australia and New Zealand are unique, or one of a kind, because of their isolation. The ¹⁵ movement of **tectonic plates**—parts of the Earth's crust—caused their isolation. Australia, New Zealand, and the Pacific islands are on a tectonic plate that was once part of Africa. Hundreds of millions of years ago, this plate broke away from Africa. It moved slowly—an ²⁰ inch or two a year—toward Asia.

Over the centuries, small changes have occurred naturally in the animals and plants of Australia and the islands. For example, many birds have lost the ability to fly. Because they are so far from other landmasses, these animals have not spread to other regions.

Australia's Physical Geography

Australia is Earth's smallest continent. It is about the size of the United States without Alaska and Hawaii.

Winds blowing across the Pacific Ocean bring rain and a mild and pleasant climate to the east coast. Most ³⁰ Australians live in cities along Australia's east and southeast coasts. Rivers flow through fertile farmland in the southeast part of the country. ✓

Key Terms

marsupial (mahr SOO pea ul) *n.* an animal, such as a kangaroo, that carries its young in a body pouch

tectonic plate (tek TAHN ik playt) *n.* a huge slab of rock that moves very slowly over a softer layer beneath the surface of Earth's crust

---

✓ Reading Check

In which hemisphere are Australia and New Zealand located?

_____

_____

Vocabulary Strategy

From context clues, write a definition of the word *unique* . Circle words or phrases in the text that helped you write your definition.

_____

_____

_____

◎ Target Reading Skill

Which detail in the bracketed paragraph supports the main idea—that the plants and animals of Australia and New Zealand are not like those elsewhere?

_____

_____

_____

✓ Reading Check

Why are Australia's east and southeast coasts good places to live?

_____

_____

_____

New Zealand's Physical Geography

New Zealand is much smaller than Australia. It is made up of two major islands, North Island and South Island. Both islands have forests, lakes, and mountains. The islands were formed by volcanoes.

New Zealand's climate is cooler than Australia's because it is farther from the Equator. Also, no place in New Zealand is very far from the ocean. As a result, the country has a mild climate and plenty of rainfall.

There is a volcanic plateau in the middle of North Island. It includes three active volcanoes. North of the volcanoes, **geysers** shoot hot water into the air. New Zealanders use this energy to produce electricity. New Zealand's capital, Wellington, is located on North Island. So is its largest city, Auckland.

South Island has a high mountain range called the Southern Alps. Glaciers cover the mountains. There are also lakes and **fiords**. To the southeast is the flat, fertile Canterbury Plain. Most of New Zealand's crops are grown here. Ranchers also raise sheep and cattle. ☑

✓ **Reading Check**

Why is the Canterbury Plain important to New Zealand?

_____

_____

_____

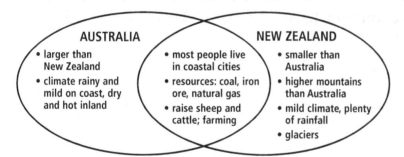

AUSTRALIA
- larger than New Zealand
- climate rainy and mild on coast, dry and hot inland

- most people live in coastal cities
- resources: coal, iron ore, natural gas
- raise sheep and cattle; farming

NEW ZEALAND
- smaller than Australia
- higher mountains than Australia
- mild climate, plenty of rainfall
- glaciers

Review Questions

1. Describe the way that Australia and New Zealand became isolated from other continents.

_____

_____

2. How were the islands of New Zealand formed?

_____

_____

Key Terms

geyser (GY zur) *n.* a hot spring that shoots a jet of water and steam into the air

fiord (fyawrd) *n.* a long, narrow stretch of the sea bordered by steep slopes that were created by glaciers

Prepare to Read

Section 3
The Pacific Islands: Physical Geography

Objectives

1. Examine features of high islands and low islands.
2. Learn about the three main island groups.
3. Find out what kind of climate and vegetation the islands have.
4. Discover how land is used in the Pacific islands.

Target Reading Skill

Identify Main Ideas How can you find the main idea of a section or paragraph if it is not stated directly? Sometimes as a reader you have to work a little harder to find out what the main idea is. Sometimes it is up to you to put all the details together and come up with the main idea.

Let's say you just finished reading the paragraphs under the heading "Melanesia, Micronesia, and Polynesia" and you noted that the main idea was not stated. Use the section title, headings, and a chart like the one below to find the main idea.

Melanesia, Micronesia, and Polynesia Details: 1. 2. 3.
Main Idea:

Vocabulary Strategy

Using Context to Clarify Meaning When you come across a word that you do not know, you may not need to look it up in the dictionary. In this workbook, key terms appear in **blue**. The definitions are in a box at the bottom of the page. Looking at the definition breaks up your reading. Before you do that, continue to read to the end of the paragraph. See if you can figure out what the word means from its context. Clues can include examples and explanations. Then look at the definition on the bottom of the page to see how accurate you were. Finally, reread the paragraph to make sure you understood what you read.

Section 3 Summary

The Pacific Ocean covers nearly one third of Earth's surface. It is dotted with thousands of islands. They include the second-largest island in the world, New Guinea. They also include the world's smallest island nation, Nauru (NAH oo roo). It is just 8 square miles (21 square kilometers).

The Pacific islands are divided into three main groups—Melanesia (mel uh NEE zhuh), Micronesia (my kruh NEE zhuh), and Polynesia (pahl uh NEE zhuh). Each of these groups covers a particular area.

High Islands and Low Islands

Pacific islands are also divided into high islands and low islands. **High islands** are mountainous. They have been formed by volcanoes. Their fertile soil is made up of volcanic ash. Because of their larger size and because people can grow crops there, high islands can support more people than low islands can. ✓

Low islands are made up of **coral** reefs or **atolls**. Far fewer people live there. This is partly because low islands are very small. Also, they have poor, sandy soil and little fresh water. It is hard to raise crops on them. Most people on low islands survive by fishing.

Melanesia, Micronesia, and Polynesia

The island group with the most people is Melanesia. It is north and east of Australia. Most of its large islands are high islands. New Guinea, Fiji, and the Solomon Islands are part of Melanesia.

Micronesia is mostly low islands. It covers an area of the Pacific the size of the continental United States. Most of the islands are north of the Equator and very small. The largest is Guam.

Key Terms

high island (hy EYE lund) *n.* an island formed from the mountainous top of an ancient volcano

low island (loh EYE lund) *n.* an island formed from coral reefs or atolls

coral (KAWR ul) *n.* a rocklike material made up of the skeletons of tiny sea creatures

atoll (A tawl) *n.* a small coral island in the shape of a ring

---

Target Reading Skill

In one sentence, state the main idea of the bracketed paragraphs.

_____

_____

_____

Vocabulary Strategy

Before you read the definition *high island* in the box below, try to use context to understand the word. Circle any words or phrases that give you clues.

✓ Reading Check

On which type of island do most Pacific island people live? Why?

_____

_____

_____

Polynesia is the largest island group in the Pacific. It includes the state of Hawaii. Polynesia has many high islands, including Tahiti and Samoa. Their high volcanic mountains are covered by dense rain forests. Along the shores are sandy beaches with palm trees. Tonga is one of Polynesia's few low islands. ✓

Climate and Vegetation of the Pacific Islands

The Pacific islands are in the tropics. Temperatures are hot all year. But ocean winds keep the temperatures from getting too high.

Some Pacific islands have wet and dry seasons. However, most of them get heavy rainfall all year long. Some low islands get only scattered rainfall.

The rich vegetation of the high islands is a result of their high temperatures, plentiful rainfall, and fertile soil. Hills are covered by tropical rain forests. Savanna grasses grow in the lowlands. However, low islands have little vegetation. Their poor soil supports only palm trees, grasses, and small shrubs. ✓

Natural Resources and Land Use

The Pacific island region has few natural resources. The most important one is the coconut palm. It provides food, clothing, and shelter. Another important resource is fish.

Some Pacific island countries grow cash crops. For example, Fiji produces sugar cane. Another important cash crop in the region is copra. It is dried coconut. It is used in margarine, cooking oils, soaps, and cosmetics. ✓

The Pacific islands' most valuable resource may be their natural beauty. Tourism is an important source of income in the region.

Review Questions

1. Name the three Pacific island groups.

_____

_____

2. Tell the difference between high islands and low islands in the Pacific.

_____

_____

_____

✓ Reading Check

Which island group is Hawaii part of?

_____

_____

✓ Reading Check

Why do low islands have little vegetation?

_____

_____

_____

✓ Reading Check

Give two examples of cash crops grown in the Pacific islands.

_____

_____

_____

Chapter 20 Assessment

1. Thailand, Cambodia, and Vietnam are part of
   A. island Southeast Asia.
   B. Polynesia.
   C. Micronesia.
   D. mainland Southeast Asia.

2. The region of volcanoes and earthquakes surrounding the Pacific Ocean is called
   A. coral atolls.
   B. high islands.
   C. Malaysia.
   D. the Ring of Fire.

3. Where do most Australians live?
   A. along the west and northern coasts
   B. along the east and southeast coasts
   C. along the west and southern coasts
   D. in the center of the country

4. New Zealanders use the energy from _____ to produce electricity.
   A. volcanoes
   B. coral
   C. earthquakes
   D. geysers

5. Pacific island natural resources include
   A. margarine, cooking oil, and soap.
   B. paddies, monsoons, and typhoons.
   C. coconut palm, fish, and their natural beauty.
   D. oil, natural gas, and water.

Short Answer Question

Why would a subsistence farmer in Southeast Asia raise rice instead of rubber?

_____

_____

_____

_____

Objectives

1. Learn about civilizations of East Asia.
2. Learn how Chinese culture influenced the rest of East Asia.
3. Find out how East Asia was affected by Western nations.

Target Reading Skill

Use Context Clues What can you do when you see a word used in an unfamiliar way? You could look the word up in a dictionary. But often you can get a good idea of what the word means from its context. A word's context is the words and sentences around it.

Let's use the word *emperor* as an example. The context may give clues about the word, as in the first example below. Or it may give the word's definition, as in the second example. Read the examples.

Ancient China had an emperor. This man was the ruler of the empire, which is similar to being the president of a country.

Ancient China was ruled by an emperor—a male ruler of an empire.

Did you figure out that an emperor is a male ruler of an empire?

Vocabulary Strategy

Recognizing Signal Words Have you ever noticed road signs that say "Rest Stop 10 Miles Ahead" or "Last Gas for Next 30 Miles"? Road signs prepare you for what is coming next. In the same way, when you read text, signal words prepare you for what is coming next.

Some signal words show time. They let you know the order in which events take place.

Some examples of signal words or phrases that show time are given in the box below.

then	when	around 1650
in 1808	later	earlier
as early as 200 B.C.	in time	

Civilizations of East Asia

Important Parts of a Civilization	
cities	social classes
a central government, which rules the entire area	workers who are good at particular jobs

1　　The Chinese civilization has existed longer than any other civilization. For centuries, China kept to itself. The proud leaders called China the Middle Kingdom. To them, China was the center of the universe.

5　　The ancient Chinese invented paper, gunpowder, silk weaving, the magnetic compass, the printing press, and clockworks. They also built canals, dams, bridges, and irrigation systems. ✓

　　Starting in ancient times, China was governed by
10 **emperors**. Since that time, China has been ruled by eight major **dynasties**.

　　Another civilization arose in Korea. Korea's history is closely tied to China's. For example, settlers from China shared Chinese knowledge and customs with the
15 Koreans. Korea was also ruled by dynasties, but only three. The first one, called the Shilla dynasty, <u>unified</u> Korea as one country in A.D. 668.

　　An early civilization also developed in Japan. For much of Japan's history, **clans** fought each other for
20 land and power. Around A.D. 500, the Yamato (yah MAH toh) clan became powerful. Their leaders made themselves emperors, but they had little power. For more than 700 years, shoguns (SHOH gunz), or "emperor's generals," made Japan's laws. Warriors
25 called samurai (SAM uh ry) enforced the laws.

　　Japan did not deal with other countries from about 1640 to 1853. Its rulers believed that this would keep the country united.

✓ Reading Check

Name four inventions of the Chinese.

_____

_____

_____

_____

🎯 Target Reading Skill

Look for the underlined word *unified*. Circle the phrase in the sentence that provides a context clue for unified.

Key Terms

emperor (EM pur ur) *n.* a male ruler of an empire
dynasty (DY nus tee) *n.* a number of rulers in a row who are from the same family
clan (klan) *n.* a group of families who share the same ancestor

Vocabulary Strategy

As you read this page, look for the following signal words and phrases that indicate when something happened. Circle the signal words when you find them.

later
in 1899
around the same time
after World War II

✓ Reading Check

Give an example of something that spread from China to Korea and Japan through cultural diffusion.

_____

_____

The Spread of Cultures in East Asia

Many Chinese discoveries spread to Korea and Japan. This spreading of ideas is called **cultural diffusion**. Beliefs also spread. For example, the religion of Buddhism (BOOD iz um) had come to China from India. Later, it spread from China to Korea and Japan. ✓

Westerners in East Asia

During the 1800s, Europeans and Americans wanted to sell products in East Asia. In 1853, U.S. Commodore Matthew Perry sailed to Japan with four warships. He forced Japan to begin trading with the United States. In 1899, the United States announced that China, too, would be open for trade, and with all nations.

The Chinese blamed the emperor for the situation. In 1911, a revolution broke out in China. Instead of an empire, a republic was then set up.

Around the same time, Japan began wanting to control other Asian countries. Japan wanted their resources. In 1941, Japan caused the start of World War II in East Asia by attacking nearby countries. The United States and its allies defeated Japan in 1945. ✓

After World War II, civil war broke out in China between the Nationalists and the Communists. The Communists won in 1949. They turned China into a **communist** nation. Korea was split into two parts after World War II. In 1950, communist North Korea invaded South Korea. The United States sent troops to help South Korea. They fought for three years. But neither side won. Korea is still two countries today.

Review Questions

1. Who ruled East Asia's ancient civilization?

_____

_____

2. Why did Matthew Perry sail to Japan in 1853?

_____

_____

> **Key Terms**
>
> **cultural diffusion** (KUL chur ul dih FYOO zhun) *n.* the spreading of ideas or practices from one culture to other cultures
> **communist** (KAHM yoo nist) *adj.* having a government that controls the country's large industries, businesses, and land

Prepare to Read

Section 2 People and Cultures

Objectives

1. Examine some ways in which East Asia's past affects its modern-day culture.
2. Find out how the people of China are different from the people of the Koreas and Japan.

Target Reading Skill

Use Context Clues Sometimes as you read, you come across a word or phrase that does not make sense to you. Often when this happens, you can use context clues and your own general knowledge to figure out what the word means.

Sometimes you will find a context clue in the same sentence as the word or phrase you want to understand. Other times, you may need to keep reading to find a context clue. On the next page, you will find the sentence *Marriages are still arranged*. You may not understand what *arranged* means when used this way. But keep reading and you will find out:

In an arranged marriage, parents or other family members decide who will marry whom.

Vocabulary Strategy

Recognizing Signal Words Signal words are words or phrases that give you clues or directions when reading. Some signal words or phrases explain how what you just read connects to what you will read next. These words or phrases help signal causes or effects of events that you are reading about.

Words/phrases that signal causes:	Words/phrases that signal effects:
because	as a result
if	so
since	then
on account of	therefore

Target Reading Skill

Use the bracketed paragraph to help you define *private land ownership* . Circle the phrases that give you clues. Then write a definition below.

_____

_____

_____

Tradition and Change

In 1949, the Communists took power in China. They began making changes to China's traditions. For example, people used to own their own farms and land. The government replaced the old system of private land ownership with **communes**.

Many farmers were used to working in family groups in small fields. They refused to work in the communes. So the communes did not produce enough food for all the people. Food production finally increased when the government allowed some private land ownership.

Another change began in the 1970s. China's population was large. The Communists tried to slow its growth by keeping families small. Couples were supposed to marry later and have only one child.

The Communists also changed women's rights. They passed a law allowing a woman to own property, choose her husband, and get a divorce. But today, men still hold most of the power. Marriages are still arranged. In an arranged marriage, parents or other family members decide who will marry whom.

In East Asia today, tradition and change mix in many ways. In China, old traditions are strongest in the countryside. But they do exist in the cities. Tiny shops sit next to modern buildings. People may ride in cars or in three-wheeled taxis that are pedaled like a bike.

In both Koreas, daily life is influenced by traditions. The family is important. But families today are smaller than before. In the countryside, grandparents, parents, aunts, and uncles may live in one household. In cities, usually only parents and children live together. The role of women has also changed. In the past, Korean women had few opportunities. Today, women can work and vote.

Japan is the most modern East Asian country. There, people use many modern technologies. Nearly 80 percent of Japan's people live in cities. At the same time,

Key Term

commune (KAHM yoon) *n.* a community in which people own land as a group and where they live and work together

many people still follow traditional customs at home. For example, at home they may wear kimonos, or robes, and sit on mats at a low table to eat. ☑

East Asia's People

East Asia is a mix of old and new cultures. Within each country, though, people tend to share a single culture.

About 19 of every 20 Chinese people are from the Han **ethnic group**. The Han live mostly in eastern China. All Han use the same written language. But they speak different **dialects** from one region to another.

The other Chinese come from 55 different minority groups. These groups live mainly in western and southern China. In terms of ethnic groups, China has more diversity than most other countries. ☑

Korea has much less diversity. Historians believe that the ancient Korean language was brought by **nomads** from the north. Over time, these groups came to share the same traditions. The population became **homogeneous**. That means the people are all very alike. There are few minority groups in the Koreas today.

Japan is an island nation. And for many years, it did not deal with the rest of the world. For these reasons, it has one of the most homogeneous populations on Earth. Nearly all of Japan's people belong to the same ethnic group. Japan also makes it hard for anyone who is not Japanese to become a citizen.

Review Questions

1. What changes did the Communists make in China?

_____

_____

2. To which ethnic group do most Chinese belong?

_____

_____

Key Terms

ethnic group (ETH nik groop) *n.* a group of people who share such characteristics as language, religion, and ancestry

dialect (DY uh lekt) *n.* a variation of a language that is spoken in a particular region or area

nomad (NOH mad) *n.* a person who has no settled home but who moves from place to place

homogeneous (hoh moh JEE nee us) *adj.* identical or similar

✓ Reading Check

Which is the most modern country in East Asia?

_____

_____

_____

✓ Reading Check

How is the population of China different from the populations of most other countries?

_____

_____

_____

Vocabulary Strategy

In the bracketed paragraph, a signal word or phrase is used to show cause and effect. Find the signal word and circle it. Then write the cause and effect below.

Cause:_____

_____

Effect: _____

_____

1. Which civilization has existed longer than any other civilization?
   A. China
   B. North Korea
   C. South Korea
   D. Japan

2. Why did Japanese leaders want to avoid dealing with other countries?
   A. They did not want to buy goods from other lands.
   B. They did not have enough goods to sell to other countries.
   C. They believed that it would keep the country united.
   D. They did not want to learn foreign languages and customs.

3. Buddhism spread from China to the Koreas. This is an example of
   A. cultural migration.
   B. irrigation.
   C. cultural diffusion.
   D. Communist rule.

4. How did the rights of Chinese women change under communism?
   A. They lost many of their old rights.
   B. They were often forced to marry husbands they did not choose.
   C. They were no longer allowed to get a divorce.
   D. They were allowed to own property.

5. Which country in East Asia has the greatest number of ethnic groups?
   A. North Korea
   B. South Korea
   C. China
   D. Japan

Short Answer Question

What are the important parts of a civilization?

_____

_____

_____

_____

Prepare to Read

Section 1
South Asia: Cultures and History

Objectives

1. Find out which religions became part of South Asian cultures.
2. Understand which empires shaped the history of South Asia.
3. Learn about the present-day religions and languages of South Asian cultures.

Target Reading Skill

Analyze Word Parts Often, when you come across an unfamiliar word, you can break the word into parts. This can help you recognize and pronounce it. You may find roots, prefixes, or suffixes.

A root is the base, or main part, of the word. It is the part of the word that has meaning by itself. A prefix goes in front of the root and changes the word's meaning.

For example, the description of South Asia you are going to read is a *nonfiction* text. The prefix *non-* means "not." *Fiction* describes stories that are imagined or make-believe. So the word *nonfiction* refers to text that tells about something that really happened (is not make-believe).

In this section, you will read the word *nonviolent*. Now that you know the meaning of the prefix *non-*, you can break *nonviolent* into a root and a prefix to figure out the word's meaning.

Vocabulary Strategy

Using Word Origins Many English words come from other languages. When you learn about the origins of words, you also learn about history. For example, you will read in this section that the British ruled India for many years. This is one way words from the Hindi language (spoken in India) entered the English language. You may be surprised to learn that *pajamas, shampoo, jungle,* and *bungalow* are all Hindi words.

Have you ever heard of a **cashmere** sweater? Cashmere is a very fine and expensive wool from goats that are raised in a region on the border of India and Pakistan. Read on to find out the name of this region. Think about how it relates to the word *cashmere*.

New Religions

The Indus Valley, in present-day South Asia, was home to an early civilization. The civilization thrived for centuries. But by 1500 B.C. it was coming to an end.

About the same time, newcomers arrived in the region. They brought a new culture with them. Their culture then combined with the ancient languages and beliefs of the Indus Valley people. As a result, a new culture was created. The people who practiced this mixed culture were called Aryans (AYR ee unz).

The Aryans ruled northern India for more than 1,000 years. They divided people into four classes. The classes were 1) priests and the educated; 2) rulers and warriors; 3) farmers, artisans, and merchants; and 4) laborers. This division was called the **caste** system.

The caste system became part of a new religion founded in India, Hinduism. It is one of the world's oldest religions. Hindus worship many gods and goddesses. Each one stands for different parts of a single spirit. Today, Hinduism is the main religion of India. ✓

Buddhism also developed in India. Buddhism is based on the idea that giving up selfish desires will free all people from pain. Buddhism spread to many parts of Asia. It spread to China, Tibet, Korea, and Japan. But it has almost died out in India.

From Empires to Nations

Look at the chart below to learn about three empires of ancient India.

Maurya Empire 321 B.C. to 185 B.C.	Gupta Empire A.D. 320 to A.D. 550	Mughal Empire 1556 to 1700s
• conquered many kingdoms • supported Buddhism • had laws for fair government	• strong central government • developed system of writing numerals • created temples and wall paintings	• introduced Islam • supported arts and literature

✓

> **Key Term**
>
> **caste** (kast) *n.* in the Hindu religion, a social group into which people are born and which they cannot change

In the late 1700s, much of the Indian subcontinent was ruled by the British. In 1858, India officially became a British **colony**.

In the early 1900s, the people of India wanted independence from Great Britain. An Indian leader named Mohandas K. Gandhi (GAHN dee) called for Indians to fight against British rule. But Gandhi wanted to fight in nonviolent ways. For example, he encouraged a **boycott** of British goods. Britain gave India its freedom in 1947.

Muslims in India were outnumbered by Hindus. They were afraid of losing their rights after independence. So they decided to fight for a separate state. Fighting led to a **partition** of the subcontinent into Pakistan and India in 1947. Most people in Pakistan were Muslims; most people in India were Hindus.

Since independence, Pakistan and India have fought for control of Kashmir (KASH mihr). Kashmir is an area on the border of India and Pakistan.

South Asian Cultures Today

History shapes South Asia's cultures. Hinduism and Islam are the major religions of South Asia today. About 80 percent of the people of India are Hindus. Hinduism is also the main religion of Nepal. Islam is the main religion of Pakistan and Bangladesh. ✓

Many languages are spoken in South Asia. India has 15 major languages. About 30 percent of Indians speak Hindi. English is also an official language there.

Review Questions

1. Which group of people developed the caste system?

_____

_____

2. What led to the partition of India in 1947?

_____

_____

Target Reading Skill

Look for the word *subcontinent* in the bracketed paragraph. The prefix *sub-* means a smaller or less important part. What is the difference between a subcontinent and a continent?

_____

_____

_____

Vocabulary Strategy

What is the name of the region that India and Pakistan have fought over since partition? (It is also known for a wool called cashmere.)

_____

_____

✓ Reading Check

In which two South Asian countries is Hinduism the main religion?

_____

_____

Prepare to Read

Section 2
Southwest Asia: Cultures and History

Objectives

1. Find out that one of the world's earliest civilizations grew in Southwest Asia.
2. Understand that three of the world's great religions began in Southwest Asia.
3. Examine the different ethnic groups and religions of Southwest Asia.
4. Learn about the conflict between Arabs and Israelis in Southwest Asia.

Target Reading Skill

Analyze Word Parts Remember that a root is the base of a word. It has meaning by itself. A suffix comes at the end of a root and changes its meaning. A suffix may change the root's part of speech. For example, adding a suffix may change a verb into a noun.

In this section, you will read the word *creation*. The suffix *-ion* added to the root makes the new word a noun. If you know what the word *create* means, you can figure out the meaning of *creation*.

Vocabulary Strategy

Using Word Origins Many English words come from ancient Greek. Many words of Greek origin combine more than one root. Often a Greek word is the root of many words in English.

In this section you will read the word *monotheism*. Break it down for a closer look.

Greek Origin of *monotheism*			
	prefix	**root**	**suffix**
Word Part	mono-	the	-ism
Greek Word	mono-	theo	-ismos
Meaning	one	god	belief in

Monotheism means "the belief in one god." Some other words that contain some of these Greek roots include *monogamy, monopoly, monotonous,* and *theology.* Can you think of any others?

Section 2 Summary

Mesopotamia

One of the world's earliest civilizations developed between the Tigris and Euphrates rivers. The region was called Mesopotamia, which means "between the rivers." It lies in present-day Iraq. ☑

The Mesopotamians developed a system of writing. They also had ideas about law that people use today. For example, they believed that all people must obey the same laws.

Birthplace of Three Religions

Three of the world's major religions began in Southwest Asia. They are Judaism, Christianity, and Islam.

Around 2000 B.C., Judaism was founded by Abraham. Abraham was a Mesopotamian who moved to Canaan, on the eastern shore of the Mediterranean Sea. Canaan later became known as Palestine. The Jews saw Palestine as their homeland.

Almost 2,000 years later, Jesus began preaching in Israel. Jesus was a Jew who traveled through Palestine. Christianity is based on the life and teachings of Jesus.

In about A.D. 600, the founder of Islam, Muhammad, began teaching in present-day Saudi Arabia. Today Islam is the largest religion in Southwest Asia. Five times a day, Muslims pray when called by a **muezzin**.

People who practice these three religions share a belief in **monotheism**. They worship the same God. He is known as Allah in Islam.

Major Religions Founded in Southwest Asia			
	Judaism	**Christianity**	**Islam**
Birthplace	Palestine	Palestine	Saudi Arabia
Founded in	2000 B.C.	A.D. 30	A.D. 600
Founded by	Abraham	Jesus	Muhammad
Belief System	monotheism	monotheism	monotheism
Sacred Text	Torah	Bible (includes the Torah)	Quran
Followers	Jews	Christians	Muslims

☑

Key Terms

muezzin (myoo EZ in) *n.* a person whose job is to call Muslims to pray
monotheism (MAHN oh thee iz um) *n.* a belief that there is only one god

---

✓ **Reading Check**

In what present-day country did Mesopotamia develop?

_____

_____

Vocabulary Strategy

Monotheism is the belief in one god. *Poly-* means "many." What do you think the word *polytheism* means?

_____

_____

✓ **Reading Check**

Why is Southwest Asia considered the birthplace of Judaism, Christianity, and Islam?

_____

_____

_____

Diverse Cultures in Southwest Asia

The people of Southwest Asia belong to a mix of ethnic groups. Arabic-speaking Arabs are the largest ethnic group in the region. Islam is the main religion. Non-Arab people live mainly in Israel, Turkey, and Iran. In
30   Israel, most people are Jewish. Most people in Turkey are Turkish, but some are Kurdish. About half the people in Iran are Persian. ☑

Southwest Asia: Recent History

Before and during World War II, Nazi Germany killed more than six million European Jews just because they
35   were Jewish. This is known as the **Holocaust**. Many Jews see Palestine as their homeland. But most were pushed out of the area in ancient times. Many Holocaust survivors migrated to Palestine. In 1948, Jews created a Jewish state, Israel.

40   Arabs who lived in Palestine saw it as their homeland, too. So several Arab nations invaded Israel. Israel drove away the Arab forces. Since 1948, Israel and its Arab neighbors have fought several wars.

Israel and the Palestinians have worked towards
45   peace. But conflict between the groups continues.

Another conflict in the area took place in Iraq. Iraq was defeated in the 1991 Persian Gulf war. But its leader, Saddam Hussein (suh DAHM hoo SAYN), refused to cooperate with the United Nations. In March 2003, U.S.
50   forces attacked Iraq. Three weeks later, Saddam fell from power. Iraq held democratic elections in 2005, but problems remain. ☑

Review Questions

1. Describe Mesopotamia's location.

_____

_____

2. Which ethnic groups live in Southwest Asia today?

_____

_____

Key Term

Holocaust (HAHL uh kawst) *n.* the systematic killing of more than six million European Jews and others by Nazi Germany before and during World War II

Prepare to Read

Section 3
Central Asia: Cultures and History

Objectives

1. Learn that many cultures and peoples influenced Central Asia in ancient times.
2. Discover how Central Asian nations became independent and why they are a focus of world interest.

Target Reading Skill

Recognize Word Origins The origin of a word is where the word comes from. The English language is full of words from other languages, such as Greek, Latin, and German. Some of these words are used in their original form. Often, they have changed over time. Sometimes, a foreign word or root is joined with English prefixes or suffixes. It then makes a new word.

In this section, you will read the word *government*. It contains the root word *govern*, which comes from the Latin word *gubernare*, meaning "to steer." In *government*, the suffix *-ment* means "act or process." Knowing a word's origin can help you better understand the word's meaning. Can you see how government is related to the process of "steering" a country?

Vocabulary Strategy

Using Word Origins In this section, you will read about five former Soviet republics in Central Asia. Before the breakup of the Soviet Union, they were Soviet Socialist Republics (which was usually abbreviated as SSR). They were called Kazakh SSR, Kirghiz (or Kyrgyz) SSR, Tajik SSR, Turkmen SSR, and Uzbek SSR. Each one was named for its main ethnic group.

When they became independent, they no longer wanted to be called Soviet Socialist Republics. They needed to find new names. To their south was Afghanistan. The suffix *-stan* comes from the Persian language. It means "place of" or "land." The former Soviet Socialist Republics of Central Asia took on this suffix and became Kazakhstan, Kyrgyzstan, Tajikistan, Turkmenistan, and Uzbekistan.

Meeting Place of Empires

Central Asia is located between East Asia and Europe. It was a crossroads for trade caravans and armies. Over time, dozens of ethnic groups settled there. Each group brought new ideas and ways of living.

More than 2,000 years ago, the Silk Road linked China and Europe. For hundreds of years it brought Central Asia into contact with East Asia, Southwest Asia, and Europe. Along with goods, the traders exchanged ideas and inventions. Cities grew up at oases along the route.

The Silk Road brought wealth. It also brought invaders. Many groups of conquerors fought to control Central Asia. Some ruled for hundreds of years. But each group was replaced by new invaders.

Each conqueror left a mark on the region. For example, around A.D. 700, a Muslim empire spread across Central Asia. Many people started to practice Islam. Today, most people in the region are Muslims.

By the late 1200s, people stopped using the Silk Road as a main trade route. They used sea routes instead. But this did not stop foreign powers from trying to take over the region.

In the 1800s, Russia took over parts of Central Asia. Russia built railroads, factories, and large farms in the region. Some Russians moved in and brought new ways of life. But the lives of most people stayed the same. They practiced Islam and lived as nomadic herders.

In 1922, Russian Communists formed the Soviet Union. They extended their control over much of Central Asia. They divided the region into five republics.

The Soviets forced people to stop living as nomads. Instead, people had to work on **collective farms**. The farms didn't always produce enough food. About one million Central Asians starved to death during the 1930s. ✓

✓ Reading Check

What was the result of collective farms that the Soviets in Central Asia set up?

_____

_____

_____

> **Key Term**
>
> **collective farm** (kuh LEK tiv farhm) *n.* in a Communist country, a large farm formed from many private farms collected into a single unit controlled by the government

The Soviets gave people few freedoms. They tried to do away with Muslim religion and culture.

In 1979, the Soviets invaded Afghanistan. Afghan forces fought the Soviets for years. The Soviets gave up and pulled out their troops in 1989. Then a group known as the Taliban took control of most of the country. In 2001, the United States invaded the country and defeated the Taliban. Since then, the Afghan people have held democratic elections.

After Independence

In 1991, the Soviet Union split up. The five Soviet republics in Central Asia became independent countries.

Each of the new countries named itself after its main ethnic group. The suffix -stan is a Persian word that means "place of" or "land." Kazakhstan means "place of the Kazakhs." The five countries, along with Afghanistan, are sometimes called "the Stans."

The new countries are different in many ways. The largest is Kazakhstan. It has important natural resources, such as oil and natural gas. The smallest is Tajikistan. It is in the mountains and is very poor. ✓

Since independence, the new countries have started governing themselves. Most are hurt by weak economies. Many people are jobless. There is not good health care or education, and both are hard to get.

But people are proud of their culture. They are teaching their children about their religion. And they are allowed to use their native languages in schools, books, and the news.

Review Questions

1. Where is Central Asia located?

_____

_____

_____

2. Describe one way that Soviet rule affected Central Asia.

_____

_____

_____

1. Which of the following events in South Asia happened last?
   A. The Maurya Empire was founded.
   B. The Aryans came to northern India.
   C. India became a colony in the British Empire.
   D. During the Gupta Empire, mathematicians came up with the system of writing numerals that we use today.

2. When India was divided in 1947, the Muslim state that was created was called
   A. Kashmir.
   B. Afghanistan.
   C. Pakistan.
   D. Bangladesh.

3. People who practice Judaism, Christianity, and Islam share a belief in
   A. the caste system.
   B. monotheism.
   C. many gods.
   D. Buddha.

4. The largest religion in Southwest Asia today is
   A. Hinduism.
   B. Buddhism.
   C. Judaism.
   D. Islam.

5. What was one result of the formation of the Soviet Union in 1922?
   A. The Soviets encouraged the growth of Islam in Central Asia.
   B. Central Asia was divided into five republics.
   C. Food production in Central Asia increased.
   D. More people in Central Asia lived as nomads.

Short Answer Question
What impact did the Silk Road have on Central Asia?

_____

_____

_____

_____

Section 1
Southeast Asia: Cultures and History

Objectives

1. Find out why Southeast Asia is a culturally diverse region.
2. Learn how colonial powers affected Southeast Asia.
3. Understand how years of conflict affected Vietnam, Cambodia, and Laos.

Target Reading Skill

Understand Sequence A sequence is the order in which a series of events takes place. A timeline is a useful tool for keeping track of sequence.

A timeline represents a period of years. The earliest date is marked on the left end of the timeline, and the latest date is marked on the right end. The timeline below represents the years from 1900 to 2000. Notice how an event has been included in the timeline.

As you read, list important events on a timeline to help you remember what you have learned.

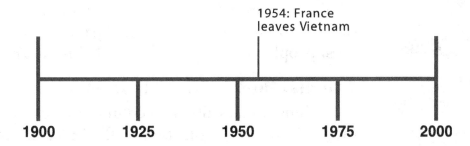

1954: France leaves Vietnam

1900   1925   1950   1975   2000

Vocabulary Strategy

Using Context Clues to Determine Meaning Many English words have more than one meaning. You can use context clues to figure out the meaning of a word. For example, in the sentences below, the word *back* is used in two different ways.

He wrote his answers on the **back** of the worksheet.

By using context clues, you can figure out that in this sentence, *back* means "reverse side."

She asked her friends to **back** her plan.

Context clues tell you that in this sentence, *back* means "support."

Section 1 Summary

The **Khmer Empire** was at its <u>height</u> from about A.D. 800 to 1434. It was one of many kingdoms in Southeast Asia.

A Region of Diversity

For a long time, Southeast Asia's mountains kept groups of people apart. As a result, each group had its own way of life. Eventually, Southeast Asia came into contact with its neighbors, India and China. They soon had a strong effect on the cultures of Southeast Asia.

Indian traders sailed across the Indian Ocean to Southeast Asia over 2,000 years ago. Indians brought the religions of Hinduism and Buddhism to the region. Later, Muslim traders from northern India brought Islam to Indonesia and the Philippines.

In 111 B.C., China conquered Vietnam. It ruled the country for more than 1,000 years. The Vietnamese adopted Chinese ways of farming and government.

Today, most people in Myanmar, Thailand, Laos, Vietnam, and Cambodia are Buddhist. Most people in Malaysia and Indonesia are Muslim, and some are Hindu. Singapore has a mix of religions. European missionaries brought Christianity to the region in the 1500s. Most people in the Philippines are Christian. ✓

Colonial Rule in Southeast Asia

Europeans traders also arrived in the 1500s. At first, they built trading posts. But, by the 1800s, European nations controlled most of Southeast Asia. Thailand was the only country in Southeast Asia that was not under colonial rule by 1914. ✓

Spain ruled the Philippines for about 350 years. In 1898, the United States won the Spanish-American War, taking control of the Philippines.

The colonial rulers in Southeast Asia built roads, bridges, ports, and railroads. This helped the economies of the colonies. People and goods could move around more. The colonial rulers also built schools.

Vocabulary Strategy

The word *height* has several meanings. You may already know one of its meanings. What is its meaning in this context? You may want to consult a dictionary.

_____

_____

_____

✓ Reading Check

List four religions practiced in Southeast Asia.

1. _____

2. _____

3. _____

4. _____

✓ Reading Check

Which country in Southeast Asia was not under colonial rule by 1914?

Country: _____

Key Term

Khmer Empire (kuh MEHR EM pyr) *n.* an empire that included much of present-day Cambodia, Thailand, Malaysia, and part of Laos

By the early 1900s, **nationalists** in Southeast Asia were working to gain independence for their countries. During World War II, the Japanese invaded Southeast Asia and forced the European powers out. After the war, Southeast Asian countries did gain independence.

Vietnam, Cambodia, and Laos

Laos, Cambodia, and Vietnam were French colonies before World War II. Together, they were known as French Indochina. After the war, France tried to regain control of them. Nationalist forces in Vietnam fought against the French. In 1954, the French gave up and left.

In 1954, Vietnam was divided in two. North Vietnam was Communist. South Vietnam was non-Communist. Leaders in North Vietnam wanted one country under Communist rule. They invaded South Vietnam. South Vietnam fought back with help from the United States.

After years of fighting, the United States withdrew its forces. In 1975, North Vietnam took over South Vietnam. The reunited country was Communist. ✓

Cambodia and Laos became independent from France in 1953. As in Vietnam, Communists and non-Communists struggled for power.

In 1975, Cambodia's Communist party, the **Khmer Rouge**, took over the government of Cambodia. The Khmer Rouge had brutal policies. It killed more than a million Cambodians. Cambodia held elections in 1998 that put a new government in place. The new government worked to make Cambodia safe and free.

Target Reading Skill

Read the bracketed paragraph. When did Vietnam split into two countries?

_____

✓ Reading Check

Which country did the United States support with troops during the Vietnam War?

_____

_____

Review Questions

1. Which two Asian countries neighbor Southeast Asia?

_____

_____

2. Which colonies did French Indochina include?

_____

_____

Key Terms

nationalist (NASH uh nul ist) *n.* a person who is devoted to the interests of his or her country

Khmer Rouge (kuh MEHR roozh) *n.* the Cambodian Communist party

Prepare to Read

Section 2
The Pacific Region: Cultures and History

Objectives

1. Find out how people settled Australia and New Zealand.
2. Learn which groups shaped the cultures of Australia and New Zealand.
3. Understand how Pacific island nations have been affected by other cultures.

Target Reading Skill

Recognize Signal Words Signal words are words or phrases that prepare you for what is coming next. They are like the directions in a recipe for baking a cake. When baking, you need to know when to add the ingredients, how long to mix or bake, and when to ask an adult to take something out of the oven.

When you read, look for words such as *first, before, later, next,* and *recently.* They signal the order in which events took place.

Vocabulary Strategy

Using Context to Clarify Meaning Sometimes you may read a word you recognize, but you aren't sure about its meaning. Many words have more than one meaning. What a word means depends on its context. Look for clues in the surrounding words or sentences. For example, the word *standard* has many meanings. You will find out which meaning the author had in mind by looking at the context.

Some examples of *standard* are listed below.

Word	Definitions	Examples
standard	a flag or banner	The winners raised their standard in the air.
	something used as a basis for comparison	The government set standards for clean air.
	something used as a base or support	The flag was attached to a standard.
	a piece of music that remains popular through the years	She has released a CD of old standards.

Section 2 Summary

Settlement

The first people in New Zealand were the **Maori**. They had traveled from Asia to Polynesia. Then, about 1,000 years ago, the Maori sailed to New Zealand.

The first settlers in Australia were the **Aborigines**. Many scientists think that the Aborigines traveled from Asia to Australia more than 40,000 years ago. For thousands of years, they moved from place to place, hunting and gathering food. People lived in small family groups. They had strong religious beliefs about nature and the land.

In 1788, the British founded the first colony in Australia. It was a **penal colony**. Other colonists soon settled there. Then, in 1851, gold was found. The population soared. In 1901, Australia gained its independence. ✓

The British settled New Zealand at about the same time as Australia. The colony had good harbors and fertile soil. It attracted many British settlers. It gained independence in 1947.

The Cultures of Australia and New Zealand

Most Australians and New Zealanders are descendants of British settlers. They share British culture and customs. Most have a high standard of living. ✓

Since the arrival of Europeans, the Aborigines have suffered hardships. Settlers forced them off their lands. Thousands died of European diseases. Others were forced to work on sheep and cattle **stations**. Even their children were taken from them to grow up with non-Aborigines. Today, Aborigines make up less than 1 percent of the population.

Key Terms

Maori (MAH oh ree) *n.* a native of New Zealand whose ancestors first traveled from Asia to Polynesia, and later to New Zealand
Aborigine (ab uh RIJ uh nee) *n.* a member of the earliest people of Australia, who probably came from Asia
penal colony (PEEN ul KAHL uh nee) *n.* a place where people convicted of crimes are sent
station (STAY shun) *n.* in Australia, a large ranch for raising livestock

🎯 **Target Reading Skill**

In the paragraph at the left, circle the words that signal when and how the Maori came to New Zealand.

✓ **Reading Check**

What happened after gold was found in Australia?

_____

_____

_____

Vocabulary Strategy

In the bracketed paragraph, how is the word *standard* used? Copy the correct definition from the chart at the beginning of this section.

_____

_____

✓ **Reading Check**

Why do most Australians and New Zealanders share British culture and customs?

_____

_____

30 Non-British people also settled in Australia. Many came during the gold rush, including the Chinese. Almost 3 percent of Australia's population is Chinese.

When New Zealand became a British colony, Britain promised to protect Maori land. But settlers broke that 35 promise. For many years, the Maori and the settlers fought. The settlers won. The Maori were forced to adopt English ways. Now, the Maori can practice their culture. About 15 percent of New Zealand's people are Maori. Their culture is important to New Zealand life.

40 After World War II, many Europeans migrated to New Zealand. People from Polynesia have also settled there. New Zealand's largest city, Auckland, has more Polynesians than any other city in the world.

The Cultures of the Pacific Islands

Scientists believe the first people to live on the Pacific 45 islands were settlers from Southeast Asia. They came to the Pacific islands more than 30,000 years ago. First, they settled on the island of New Guinea.

The island groups were too far apart for people to stay in touch. Each group developed its own language, 50 customs, and religious beliefs. But they did have much in common. They got their food from the ocean. They also used the ocean for travel and trade.

In the 1800s, Western nations began to move into the Pacific islands. By 1900, the United States, Britain, 55 France, and Germany had claimed nearly every island.

After World War II, most of the islands gained independence. By then, traditional cultures had blended with other cultures. Most had democratic governments. Many Pacific islanders read and spoke 60 English. ✓

Review Questions

1. In what ways were the histories of the Aborigines and the Maori similar?

_____

_____

2. From where do scientists believe the first people to live in the Pacific islands came?

_____

_____

✓ **Reading Check**

What were Pacific island cultures like after World War II?

_____

_____

_____

Chapter 23 Assessment

1. Which two countries had a strong influence on Southeast Asian cultures?
   A. India and Britain
   B. China and India
   C. India and France
   D. China and Japan

2. What happened after the Khmer Rouge took over the government of Cambodia?
   A. Cambodia became a democratic country.
   B. People in Cambodia were able to live freely and peacefully.
   C. Cambodia finally gained independence from France.
   D. The government killed more than a million Cambodians.

3. The first colony in Australia was set up by
   A. Great Britain.
   B. the United States.
   C. India.
   D. France.

4. Besides the British settlers, many people from _____ came to Australia during the gold rush.
   A. Cambodia
   B. India
   C. China
   D. Laos

5. After World War II, most Pacific islands gained
   A. independence.
   B. their own colonies.
   C. additional land.
   D. membership in the European Union.

Short Answer Question

How did communism affect Southeast Asia starting in the 1950s?

_____

_____

_____

_____

Objectives

1. Find out how China controlled its economy from 1949 to 1980.
2. Learn about the growth of Taiwan since 1949.
3. Discover how China's government operated after the death of Mao Zedong.
4. Examine aspects of life in China today.

Target Reading Skill

Compare and Contrast When you compare, you look for the way two things are alike. When you contrast, you look at how two things are different. For example, in this section, you will notice that the "two Chinas"—China and Taiwan—are alike because the people of both countries are Chinese. On the other hand, each country has a different form of government and a different economic system.

Comparing and contrasting is another way to process information and understand what you read.

Vocabulary Strategy

Recognizing Word Usage The Chinese use a completely different writing system than the alphabet used in English. Their system uses symbols for words. In English, the alphabet uses symbols for sounds. For example, in Chinese characters, China's first Communist leader's name is 毛澤東. As you can see, you cannot read the name unless you can read Chinese characters. So that westerners can read Chinese names, there is also a system of spelling called Pinyin. Pinyin means "join together sounds." In Pinyin, the first Communist leader's name is Mao Zedong. The Chinese government uses Pinyin when it sends printed news releases to the Western world.

Section 1 Summary

China's Economy, 1949–1980

In 1949, the Chinese Communist party set up a new government. Mao Zedong (mow dzuh doong) was in charge. The government took over China's factories, businesses, and farmland. In 1958, Mao began a **radical** program. It was called the "Great Leap Forward." It was supposed to help farms and factories produce more goods. Unfortunately, many factories made low-quality or useless products. ☑

At the same time, poor weather destroyed crops. There was not enough food. Between 1959 and 1961, as many as 30 million people starved to death.

In 1966, Mao introduced another radical plan, the Cultural Revolution. He wanted to create a new society. Mao encouraged students to rebel and to join the **Red Guards**. Mao's Red Guards destroyed some of China's ancient buildings. They put artists and teachers in jail. When the Cultural Revolution ended in 1976, hundreds of thousands of people were dead.

Taiwan Since 1949

Taiwan is an island southeast of mainland China. The Nationalists had fought the Communists for control of China after World War II. The Communists won in 1949. The Nationalists fled to Taiwan and formed their own country, the Republic of China. Both Taiwan and China claimed the right to rule the other.

Nationalists used the **free enterprise system**. Taiwan's economy soon became one of Asia's strongest. New programs helped farms produce more crops, which helped Taiwan make more money. Businesses in Taiwan now sell many goods to other countries, which has also helped the economy grow. These goods include computer products and other electronics. ☑

✓ Reading Check

What was the purpose of China's Great Leap Forward?

_____

_____

_____

✓ Reading Check

What kind of economic system did the nationalists in Taiwan use?

_____

_____

_____

Key Terms

radical (RAD ih kul) *adj.* extreme

Red Guards (red gahrdz) *n.* groups of students who carried out Mao Zedong's policies during the Cultural Revolution

free enterprise system (free ENT ur pryz SIS tum) *n.* an economic system in which people can choose their own jobs, start private businesses, own property, and make a profit

Read the paragraphs under the heading "Changes in China." List three ways China was different after Mao Zedong died.

1. _____

2. _____

3. _____

How did China's government respond to demands for democracy in 1989?

_____

_____

_____

Changes in China

Many Western countries would not trade with China. At the same time, some of Mao's policies hurt the country. In the 1970s, the Communists began to see that
35 they needed to change their policies.

First, China began to fix relations with the West. In 1971, it joined the United Nations. In 1972, Richard Nixon was the first American president to visit China. The two nations began to trade.

Mao died in 1976. The new leader, Deng Xiaoping (dung show ping), started a program, The Four Modernizations, to improve farming, industry, science, and defense.

Deng allowed some foreign companies to own busi-
45 nesses. He allowed some Chinese citizens to run private businesses. By 2000, private businesses produced about 75 percent of China's **gross domestic product.**

In 1997, China took back control of Hong Kong, which had been a British colony since the late 1800s. It
50 was a major center for trade, banking, and shipping. ✓

China Today

China is now a major economic power. But the government has been criticized for the way it treats its people. People who want a democratic government are sometimes put in prison, wounded, or killed. In 1989, the
55 government killed and wounded thousands of people demanding democracy in Beijing's Tiananmen Square. ✓

In 2003, Hu Jintao became China's president. Hu may loosen government control over the economy.

Review Questions

1. Who took control of China in 1949?

_____

_____

2. Where is the Republic of China?

_____

_____

> **Key Term**
>
> **gross domestic product** (grohs duh MES tik PRAHD ukt) *n.* the total value of all goods and services produced in an economy

CHAPTER 24

Prepare to Read

Section 2
Japan: Tradition and Change

Objectives

1. Learn about the growth of Japan's economy.
2. Find out about successes and challenges in Japan's economy.
3. Examine aspects of life in Japan.

Target Reading Skill

Make Comparisons When you compare you look for the way two things are alike. It is often easier to understand new facts by comparing them with facts you already know. For example, which of the following facts is easier to understand?

> Japan has a total area of 145,841 square miles (377,727 square kilometers).

> Japan is slightly smaller than California.

Most people would choose the second fact. It can be hard to picture the actual size of a place you don't know. But when it is compared to a place you do know, such as California, you can probably picture it much better.

Vocabulary Strategy

Recognizing Word Usage There are two ways that people who use the English language shorten words to save time or space. One way is by using abbreviations. Another is by using brief forms. Brief forms are shortened forms of words.

Some common brief forms include *auto* (for *automobile*), *sub* (for *submarine*), *mike* (for *microphone*), and *phone* (for *telephone*).

Often, the brief form becomes much more common than the full form. For example, *fax* is used more often than its full form, *facsimile*. In fact, many people probably don't even realize that *fax* is a brief form!

In this chapter, you will read the word *stereo*. Did you know that it is a brief form for *stereophonic*? It can refer either to a small listening device or to a large sound system.

What other brief forms can you think of?

Section 2 Summary

Building a Developed Economy

In the early 1900s, the Japanese worked to build their industries. By the 1920s, Japan was an important manufacturing country.

World War II left Japan in ruins. The United States helped rebuild its industries. Also, the Japanese government helped rebuild by giving **subsidies** to industries. Companies built large factories and sold more goods.

High-technology industries are an important part of Japan's economy. Japan produces industrial robots, watches, and cameras. Japan builds and sells cars and produces huge amounts of steel, ships, televisions, bicycles, and compact discs (CDs).

Japanese companies also made existing products better. The videocassette recorder (VCR) was invented in the United States. But it cost too much to make there. A Japanese company bought the invention. Now Japan is a leading maker of VCRs.

Japanese companies also invented many new things, such as small electronic games you hold in your hand. Also, a Japanese company and European company together made the first CD. The Japanese also helped create the digital video disc (DVD). ✓

Successes and Challenges

In the 1980s, Japan had one of the largest and strongest economies in the world. Its economy depended on selling its products to America and Europe. But the Japanese did not buy many goods from America and Europe.

This situation hurt Japan's trade relationship with other countries. Then, in the early 1990s, there was a **recession** in Japan. The economy made less money. Some companies began to lay off workers. ✓

Key Terms

subsidy (SUB suh dee) *n.* money given by a government to assist a private company

recession (rih SESH un) *n.* a period during which an economy and the businesses that support it make less money

---

Vocabulary Strategy

What is the brief form for bicycle?

_____

_____

✓ Reading Check

Name two high-technology products made in Japan.

1. _____

_____

2. _____

_____

✓ Reading Check

How was Japan affected by the recession in the 1990s?

_____

_____

_____

Since 2004, Japan's economy has improved. Japan still has one of the largest economies in the world. Manufacturing is still important. But now, more people work in Japan's service industries than in manufacturing. Service industries include banking, communications, sales, hotels, and restaurants.

Life in Japan

Life in Japan today is a mix of traditional values and modern changes. One Japanese tradition is working together as a group. For example, companies form *keiretsu* (kay ret soo). Keiretsu is a group of companies that work toward one another's success. A keiretsu may include different kinds of companies—some that make goods, some that provide raw materials for the goods, and some that sell the goods.

The tradition of marriage is changing. Today, many Japanese are choosing not to marry or to get married later. As a result, the **birthrate** is low.

Before World War II, few women in Japan worked outside the home. Today, more women work than stay home. And half the people who work are women.

Today, Japan needs more workers. Because of the low birthrate, Japan does not have enough young workers. At the same time, the number of older people who can no longer work is growing. With a smaller **labor** force, or fewer workers available, companies must pay more to attract workers. This increases the cost of the goods and services they produce. ☑

Review Questions

1. Describe Japan's role in the high-technology industry.

_____

_____

2. Why does Japan not have enough workers?

_____

_____

🎯 Target Reading Skill

In the bracketed paragraphs, find one Japanese tradition that has remained the same and one tradition that has changed.

_____

_____

_____

✓ Reading Check

What happens when there are fewer workers available?

_____

_____

_____

Key Terms

birthrate (BURTH rayt) *n.* the number of live births each year per 1,000 people

labor (LAY bur) *n.* the work people do for which they are paid

1. Understand why North Korea has been slow to develop.
2. Find out how South Korea became an economic success.

Target Reading Skill

Identify Contrasts Suppose that on a warm sunny day, you stepped into an air-conditioned movie theater. The temperature and lighting inside the theater would be completely different from those outside. You would notice the contrast right away.

It is a little more difficult to notice contrasts when you read. But it is an important skill. Sometimes two things are contrasted in the same sentence. Sometimes the contrast is in different paragraphs, and sometimes it is under different headings. A chart is a good way to keep track of contrasts.

Use a chart like the one below to keep track of the differences between North Korea and South Korea.

North Korea	South Korea
• Low economic growth	• High economic growth
• Low industrial growth	• High industrial growth

Vocabulary Strategy

Recognizing Word Usage As you read, you will often see abbreviations used in place of full terms. Abbreviations save space and time. An abbreviation may be a shortened form of a word. For example, *Mr.* is an abbreviation for *Mister*. Many abbreviations are made up of initials, as in *NY* for *New York*.

You already know that *USA* is the abbreviation for *United States of America* and that *UN* is the abbreviation for *United Nations*. Other common abbreviations for country names include *UK* (*United Kingdom*) and *USSR* (*Union of Soviet Socialist Republics*).

In this section, you will see the abbreviation *DMZ*. Read the next page to find out what it stands for.

Section 3 Summary

The border between North Korea and South Korea is not like any other in the world. It runs through the **demilitarized zone**, or DMZ. The DMZ is about 2.5 miles (4 kilometers) wide and about 151 miles (248 kilometers) long. Weapons and defenses line both sides.

North Korea has an estimated one million troops at the border. South Korea has about 600,000 troops. Why does the DMZ exist? In 1953, a **truce** ended the Korean War. But no peace treaty was signed. Since then, the border dividing the two countries has been defended by military more heavily than any other border.

More than the DMZ divides the Koreas. There are many differences between the two countries.

North Korea: Economic Challenges

North Korea is a communist country, under a dictatorship. The government runs the economy. The country has shut itself off to much of the world. It has kept out new technology and ideas. But it has rich mineral resources. Until the end of World War II, it was Korea's industrial center.

Today North Korea makes poor goods in government-owned factories. The government has done little to **diversify** the economy. The economy is in bad shape.

Farming methods are also outdated in North Korea. Many farmers burn hillsides to get ready to plant crops. After a few years of this, rain washes the good soil away. Then fields can no longer be farmed. In 1995, North Korea faced **famine**. Officials estimated that 220,000 people starved to death between 1995 and 1998. For the first time, North Korea asked noncommunist countries for help. However, the government said in 2005 that it would stop accepting help from other countries. ✓

Key Terms

demilitarized zone (dee MIL uh tuh ryzd zohn) *n.* an area in which no weapons are allowed
truce (troos) *n.* an agreement to end fighting
diversify (duh VUR suh fy) *v.* to add variety to
famine (FAM in) *n.* a huge food shortage

How is North Korea's government different from South Korea's government?

_____

_____

_____

✓ **Reading Check**

Name three products made in South Korea.

1. _____

2. _____

3. _____

✓ **Reading Check**

What happened when North Korea announced it was developing nuclear weapons?

_____

_____

_____

South Korea: Economic Growth

In the mid-1950s, South Korea had few industries. Now it has a strong economy.

South Korea is a democracy. Its economy is based on free enterprise. After World War II, its factories made cloth and processed foods. Today, South Korea produces many different kinds of goods. These include ships, electronics, and silicon chips. South Korea also processes oil to make plastics, rubber, and other goods. ✓

South Korea's government has helped industry grow. And it has helped farmers. Some of its programs helped farmers produce more crops. Other programs helped improve housing, roads, and water supplies.

As successful as South Korea is, it does face some challenges. For example, it does not have many natural resources. It must bring in raw materials from other countries to keep industry running.

Years of Tension

The two Koreas have had a tense relationship since the end of the Korean War. There have been many clashes between their troops. In 2000, the leaders of the two countries agreed to work toward peace and cooperation.

But in 2002, North Korea announced that it had been developing nuclear weapons. The news hurt hopes for peace between the two countries. It caused great concern all over the world. Talks between North Korea and other countries led to a new agreement. However, it has not been carried out yet. ✓

Review Questions

1. Why is North Korea's economy less successful than South Korea's?

_____

_____

_____

2. How did the relationship between North Korea and South Korea improve in 2000?

_____

_____

_____

Chapter 24 Assessment

1. The goal of China's Great Leap Forward was to
   A. build backyard furnaces for making steel.
   B. take farmers away from farming the land.
   C. help farms and factories produce more goods.
   D. release businesses and farms from government control.

2. After 1976, Chinese leaders such as Deng Xiaoping began to change China's economy by
   A. tightening government control over industry.
   B. focusing on improvements in farming, industry, science, and defense.
   C. not allowing free enterprise.
   D. limiting political freedom.

3. Japan has
   A. communes.
   B. a high birthrate.
   C. a growing labor force.
   D. a successful economy.

4. How are the governments of China and North Korea similar?
   A. They are both ruled by kings.
   B. They both have communist governments.
   C. They both use the free enterprise system.
   D. They both have democratic governments.

5. Which is NOT true of South Korea?
   A. It is a democracy.
   B. Its economy is strong.
   C. The government has improved housing and roads.
   D. It has all the raw materials it needs for industry.

Short Answer Question

What was the purpose of the Cultural Revolution?

_____

_____

_____

_____

Prepare to Read

Section 1
India: In the Midst of Change

Objectives

1. Learn about key features of India's population.
2. Examine the state of India's economy.
3. Understand major challenges facing India.

Target Reading Skill

Identify Causes and Effects A cause makes something happen. An effect is what happens. It is the result of the cause. As you read, pause to ask yourself, "What happened or is going to happen?" The answer to that question is the effect. Then ask yourself, "Why is this happening?" The answer to that question is the cause. Practice using this example.

> India has more than one billion people. And its population is growing. By 2050, India is expected to have more people than any other country.

> Ask yourself, "What is going to happen?" The answer—India is going to have more people than any other country—is the effect. Now ask yourself, "Why is that going to happen?" The answer—because the population is growing—is the cause.

Vocabulary Strategy

Recognizing Roots A root is a base word that has meaning by itself. Many words have a few letters attached to the beginning or the end of a root to make another word. These added letters change the meaning of the base word. The table below shows examples of words that are made from attaching letters to different roots.

Attached Letters	Root	New Word
un-	clear	unclear
-ing	do	doing

When you come across a new word, see if it contains a root that you already know. You can use the root to help you figure out what the word means.

Section 1 Summary

Key Features of India's Population

Right now, China has more people than any other country in the world. India is second. India has more than one billion people. And its population is growing. By 2050, India is expected to have more people than any other country in the world.

About 72 percent of India's people live in the countryside, but nearly 300 million people live in cities. By 2030, more than 600 million will be living in cities. That's about the same as all the people who live in the United States, Mexico, South Korea, and Russia together. ☑

About one fourth of India's people live in poverty. That means that they make just enough money to buy the food they need to live and nothing else. Recently, though, the middle class has been growing. People in the middle class make enough money to buy goods and services that make their lives better. India's middle class may be one of the largest in the world.

A Growing Economy

India's economy is growing quickly. In the early 1990s, India's government made it easier for companies from other countries to do business in India. The middle class helps the economy, too. Middle class people buy many of the goods and services made in India. This keeps money in India and helps businesses grow. As the middle class grows, the number of poor people should shrink.

Growing industries also help India's economy. Computer software programming is a major industry that employs many highly educated and skilled workers. India also produces large quantities of other products, such as electrical appliances. And India produces more movies than any other country. ☑

India buys more than it sells. But it can produce all its own food. India sells **textiles**, gemstones, and jewelry. The United States is one of India's biggest customers.

Key Term

textiles (TEKS tylz) *n.* cloth made by weaving or by knitting

---

Vocabulary Strategy

The words listed below appear on this page. Each of these words contains another word that is its root. Underline the roots in the text as you read.

growing
government
programming
electrical

Did knowing the root help you figure out the meaning of the words?

✓ Reading Check

List two facts about India's population.

1. _____

   _____

2. _____

   _____

✓ Reading Check

Name two major industries in India.

1. _____

   _____

2. _____

   _____

Progress and Challenges

35 For many years, India and Pakistan have fought over Kashmir. Kashmir is an area of land on the northern borders of India and Pakistan. The two countries have tried to settle the disagreement over Kashmir. In 2004, the two countries agreed to a cease fire. Peace talks have also brought new hope to the region.

India's biggest challenge will be taking care of its growing population. Each year more people will need jobs, housing, health care, and education. They will also need food, water, and electricity.

45 Disease and **malnutrition** are problems for millions of Indians now. But these problems are slowly getting better. The government has taken steps to improve health care. It is paying for more doctors to work in rural areas. There are also programs to protect people 50 from certain diseases. ✔

As a result, people in India are living longer. The average **life expectancy** was 53 years in 1981. In 2003, it was 63 years. This is an important measure of how well a country is caring for its citizens.

55 Another way of measuring how well a country is doing is the **literacy rate**. In 1991, just over 50 percent of Indians could read and write. In 2001, the rate had gone up to 65 percent. As education improves, the literacy rate will keep going up.

Review Questions

1. How does the middle class help India's economy?

_____

_____

2. Why is life expectancy increasing in India?

_____

_____

Target Reading Skill

Look at the bracketed paragraph to find two effects a growing population can have on a country.

1. _____

_____

2. _____

_____

✓ Reading Check

How has India improved health care for its people?

_____

_____

_____

Key Terms

malnutrition (mal noo TRISH un) *n.* poor nutrition caused by a lack of food or an unbalanced diet
life expectancy (lyf ek SPEK tun see) *n.* the average number of years a person is expected to live
literacy rate (LIT ur uh see rayt) *n.* the percentage of a population age 15 and over that can read and write

Prepare to Read

Section 2
Pakistan: An Economy Based on Agriculture

Objectives

1. Find out that Pakistan's economy is based on agriculture.
2. Learn about Pakistan's industries.

Target Reading Skill

Understand Effects Remember that a cause makes something happen. The effect is what happens as a result of the cause. One cause can have more than one effect.

As you read this section, look for the effects of Pakistan's water supply on its economy. Write the effects in a chart like the one below.

CAUSE		EFFECTS
• Water is in short supply in Pakistan.	→	• Farmers use canals to carry water to their fields. •

Vocabulary Strategy

Recognizing Roots Remember that a root is the base of a word that has meaning by itself. When groups of letters are added to a root word, they make a new word with a different meaning. But the meaning is still related to the root. There are many groups of letters that can be attached to roots to make new words. The table below shows some common examples.

Attached Letters	Root	New Word
non-	stop	nonstop
-ern	west	western
-ly	large	largely

When you come across an unfamiliar word, look at it closely. See if you can use its root to help you figure out what the word means.

The words listed below appear on this page. Each of these words contains a group of letters that you have learned about attached to a root. Underline the root within each of these words.

melting
northern
mostly

How does the root help you figure out the meaning of these words?

✓ Reading Check

Why does most of Pakistan's farming take place in the Indus River basin?

_____

_____

_____

Target Reading Skill

In the bracketed paragraph, look for three effects of Pakistan's use of canals and ditches for irrigation.

Effect 1. _____

_____

Effect 2. _____

_____

Effect 3. _____

_____

Section 2 Summary

Pakistan does not get much rain. The country's water supply comes from three main sources: the Indus River, monsoon rains, and slow-melting glaciers. Pakistan needs to make good use of the little water it does get. To
5 do this, it has built the world's largest irrigation system.

In 2001, Pakistan was in the middle of a terrible **drought**. The government was worried about the lack of water. It even thought about melting part of the glaciers in northern Pakistan to get water. They decided against
10 it because they worried about hurting the environment.

An Agricultural Nation

Pakistan's economy is based mostly on agriculture, or farming. That is why water is so important.

Most of Pakistan's farming takes place in the Indus River basin. That is where the irrigation system is.
15 Farmers grow cotton, wheat, sugar cane, and rice. Pakistan is one of the top ten cotton producers in the world. It grows so much rice it can sell it to other countries. ✓

Wheat is the major food crop in Pakistan. The **Green**
20 **Revolution** has helped farmers there grow more wheat. The program helped by spreading modern farming methods and special kinds of grain. In 2000, Pakistan finally grew enough wheat to feed its people and still sell some to Afghanistan. One of Pakistan's major goals
25 is to become **self-sufficient** in wheat production.

Pakistan's farmers use thousands of canals and ditches to move water from the Indus River and its **tributaries** to their fields. This gives them a steady flow of water, even when there is no rainfall. As a result, more land can be farmed and more crops are produced.

Key Terms

drought (drowt) *n.* a long period of dry weather
Green Revolution (green rev uh LOO shun) *n.* a worldwide effort to increase food production in developing countries
self-sufficient (self suh FISH unt) *adj.* able to supply one's own needs without any outside assistance
tributary (TRIB yoo tehr ee) *n.* a river that flows into a larger river

Irrigation solves many problems, but it creates others. For example, river water has salt in it. When crops are watered with river water, the salt ends up in the soil. This salty soil makes plants grow more slowly. As a result, Pakistani scientists are now looking for ways to help wheat grow in salty soil.

Another water problem in Pakistan is flooding. Heavy monsoon rains are to blame. The government has built dams to catch these rains. The water is then let into irrigation canals when needed.

Industry in Pakistan

Dams help both farmers and industries. Dams use the power of rushing water to make electricity. This hydroelectricity runs factories. Most of Pakistan's industry is located on the Indus River near sources of hydroelectric power.

Pakistan's industrial growth began with agriculture, because that is what the people knew best. Industries used crops that Pakistanis had grown for a long time, such as cotton. Today, Pakistan's economy depends largely on the textile industry. Textiles are cloth products made by weaving or knitting. Pakistan's textile products include cotton yarn and clothing. More than 60 percent of what Pakistan sells to other countries is made by the textile industry. ✓

There are also other industries. The chemical industry makes a variety of products. There are also several steel mills. They allow Pakistan to make most of the steel it needs. Making steel is cheaper than buying it from other countries.

Millions of Pakistanis work in small workshops instead of large factories. They make field hockey sticks, furniture, knives, and saddles, as well as beautiful carpets that are famous all over the world.

Review Questions

1. Explain one bad result of irrigation in Pakistan.

_____

_____

2. How does Pakistan's textile industry help the country's economy?

_____

_____

✓ Reading Check

Give one example of an industry in Pakistan based on agriculture.

_____

_____

Prepare to Read

Section 3
Israel: Economics and Cultures

Objectives

1. Discover how Israel's economy has grown and changed over the years.
2. Learn about the different peoples living in Israel.

Target Reading Skill

Recognize Multiple Causes A cause makes something happen. An effect is what happens. Often, an effect can have more than one cause. For example, in this section, you will read about disagreements between the Israelis and the Palestinians. As you read this section, identify two causes for these disagreements.

Looking for more than one cause will help you fully understand why something happened. As you read this section, look for other things that have multiple causes.

Vocabulary Strategy

Using Roots and Suffixes A suffix is one or more syllables attached to the end of a word to make a new word. The word it is attached to is known as the root. When a suffix is added to a root, the new word has a new meaning.

Some common suffixes are listed below, along with their meanings and examples. Notice that some have more than one meaning. Learning to identify suffixes and their meanings will help you understand what you read.

Suffix	Meaning	Example
-ery	the practice of; the behavior or condition of	robbery, pottery, poverty
-ing	an action; result of an action	trying, drawing
-ism	act or practice of; teaching	terrorism, socialism
-less	without	treeless
-ly	in a certain manner; like	seriously, manly
-ness	state or quality	happiness

Israel's Economy

Israel has a harsh landscape. It is hot and dry. There is a shortage of fresh water. A lot of its land is not good for farming. Still, the people of Israel have created a country with a modern economy and lively culture.

Israelis have made farms in the desert. They use **irrigation** to grow fruits, vegetables, cotton, and other crops. The Sea of Galilee is a freshwater lake in northern Israel. The Israelis pump water from the lake through canals and pipelines. To create more farmland, Israelis drained Lake Hula and nearby swamps in the 1950s.

Another reason for the success of Israeli agriculture is cooperation. Most of Israel's farmers live in small villages called *moshavim*. They share equipment and information about new methods of farming. They also pool their crops so they can get better prices.

About one out of four Israelis works in manufacturing. Most Israeli industry is in high technology. Israel makes high quality electronic and scientific equipment.

Some <u>manufacturing</u> is done in special settlements called kibbutzim. People on a **kibbutz** eat together, work together, and share profits equally. Originally, most kibbutzim centered on farming. But modern farm machinery has reduced the need for farm workers. As a result, many kibbutzim have turned to manufacturing.

The most important part of Israel's economy is the service industry. One type of service industry is trade. Israel is on the Mediterranean Sea. Its main port is Haifa. Many of the products Israel buys and sells pass through Haifa. Israel has few natural resources. It must buy much of what it needs from other countries. ✓

Vocabulary Strategy

The suffix -*ing* has several meanings. Some of them are listed in the table on the previous page. Choose the correct meaning to write a definition of *manufacturing* .

_____

_____

_____

✓ Reading Check

What industry is the most important part of the Israeli economy?

_____

_____

Key Terms

irrigation (ihr uh GAY shun) *n.* the watering of crops using canals and other artificial waterways

kibbutz (kih BOOTS) *n.* a cooperative settlement

The People of Israel

There are about 6.5 million people in Israel. More than 90 percent of them live in cities.

About 80 percent of the people of Israel are Jews. But there are a lot of differences among them. When Israel was founded in 1948, most Jews who moved there were from Europe and North America. These people came from countries that were modern, and they helped make Israel a modern, developed country. Later, groups of Jews came from other Middle Eastern countries, from Ethiopia in Africa, and from Russia. ✓

About 16 percent of Israel's people practice Islam. Most Muslims living under Israeli control are Palestinian Arabs. Before 1948, the region was known as Palestine. Both Jews and Palestinian Arabs believe Palestine is their homeland. Israel won parts of Egypt, Jordan, and Syria through a chain of wars with its Arab neighbors. Arabs call these the "occupied territories." They include the **West Bank** and the Golan Heights. Israel gave control of the **Gaza Strip** to the Palestinians in 2005.

For years, there has been violence between the Palestinians and Israelis. People on both sides have tried to make peace, but the violence goes on. One reason is that many Palestinians who left their homes during the Arab-Israeli wars now want to return. But Israelis are against this. Another reason is that many Israelis want to stay in the homes that they built in the occupied territories. But Palestinians are against this.

Review Questions

1. How do Israeli farmers grow crops in a desert?

_____

_____

2. What percentage of Israel's population is Muslim?

_____

_____

Key Terms

West Bank (west bank) *n.* a disputed region on the western bank of the Jordan River

Gaza Strip (GAHZ uh strip) *n.* a disputed region on the Mediterranean coast

Prepare to Read

Section 4
Saudi Arabia: Oil and Islam

Objectives

1. Learn how oil has affected Saudi Arabia's development and economy.
2. Discover how Islam affects everyday life in Saudi Arabia.
3. Understand the main features of Saudi Arabia's government.

Target Reading Skill

Understand Effects Remember that a cause makes something happen. The effect is what happens as a result of the cause. Just as an effect can have more than one cause, a cause can have more than one effect. You can find the effect or effects by answering the question, "What happened?" If there are several answers to that question, the cause had more than one effect.

As you read this section, find two effects of oil wealth on the development of Saudi Arabia. Then find two effects of Islam being the main religion. Write your findings in a chart like the one below.

What happened because oil was discovered in Saudi Arabia?	What happens in everyday life in Saudi Arabia because of Islam?
• •	• •

Vocabulary Strategy

Finding Roots Syllables or groups of syllables are often added at the beginning or at the end of a word. This creates a new word.

Sometimes the root word changes a little bit before a syllable is added to the end. Often, the final *e* is dropped. For example, we can add the syllable *-y* to the end of the word *ease* to create a new word. It is spelled *easy* (and **not** *easey*!). But you can still recognize the root word. Another example: *dance + ing = dancing* (**not** *danceing*!).

For more than a thousand years, Muslims from all over the world have traveled to the city of Mecca, in Saudi Arabia. Traveling to Mecca is an important part of the Muslim religion. The journey has a name—the hajj. Muslims must make the hajj at least once in their lives.

Oil Wealth and Saudi Arabia

In 1900, Mecca was a very poor town. Saudi Arabia was one of the poorest countries in the world. Most of Saudi Arabia is covered by desert. Many of its people made a living by herding animals.

In the 1930s, oil was discovered in Southwest Asia. Oil is a valuable natural resource. One of the many products made from oil is gasoline, which is used to run cars. Finding oil changed everything. It made Saudi Arabia rich. Large cities grew and are still growing. When oil prices are high, buildings go up quickly. When oil prices are low, the building comes to a stop. This is because the economy is based on oil.

Saudi Arabia has the biggest oil economy in the world. It has about one fourth of the world's oil. ✓

Oil money has changed the lives of all Saudis. Beginning in the late 1960s, the government used money from the sale of oil to modernize the country. It built modern highways, airports, seaports, and a telephone system.

The Saudis also built thousands of schools. The country has eight big universities. In 1900, many Saudis could not read or write. Today, they become doctors, scientists, and teachers.

Everyday Life in Saudi Arabia

In Saudi Arabia, Islam is part of daily life. For example, before a new type of product, such as a cell phone, can be used, the nation's religious leaders study it. They decide whether it goes against Muslim values. If it does, Saudis cannot use it.

> **Key Term**
> **hajj** (haj) *n.* a pilgrimage or journey to Mecca undertaken by Muslims during the month of the hajj

Target Reading Skill

Read the paragraphs under the head "Oil Wealth and Saudi Arabia." Several effects occurred because oil was discovered. List three effects.

1. _____
   _____

2. _____
   _____

3. _____
   _____

✓ Reading Check

About how much of the world's oil is in Saudi Arabia?

_____

_____

In Saudi Arabia, there are department stores, hotels, and universities. But there are no movie theaters or night clubs. Most Saudis follow a branch of Islam that forbids these kinds of entertainment.

Alcohol and pork are illegal. Shops close five times a day when Muslims pray. Saudis do use some Western inventions. But they make sure that these inventions do not go against Islamic traditions.

Many laws and traditions deal with the role of women. Women are protected in some ways. They are not allowed to do certain things. For example, Saudi women must cover themselves with a full-length black cloak when they go out in public. They may not vote or drive a car. However, women can work at many jobs. They can own and run businesses.

Saudi women are also allowed to get an education. Today, there are more women than men studying in Saudi universities. But boys and girls go to different schools. At universities, women and men do not study together.

Most of the rules for daily life come from the **Quran**. The Quran is the holy book of Islam. Muslims view the Quran as a guide for living. ✓

The Government of Saudi Arabia

Islam guides more than daily life in Saudi Arabia. The country's government is based on the Quran. It is an absolute **monarchy** ruled under Islamic law. The king and the royal family make up most of the government. Political parties and elections are not allowed. ✓

Review Questions

1. On what natural resource is Saudi Arabia's economy based?

_____

_____

2. How do Muslims view the Quran?

_____

_____

Key Terms

Quran (koo RAHN) *n.* the holy book of Islam
monarchy (MAHN ur kee) *n.* a state or a nation in which power is held by a monarch—a king, a queen, or an emperor

Vocabulary Strategy

The words below appear in the paragraphs at left. Their roots were changed slightly when these words were made. Write the root of each word on the line after it. Then circle the words as you read them in your text.

education _____

daily _____

living _____

✓ Reading Check

Give two examples of how Islam is a part of daily life in Saudi Arabia.

1. _____

_____

2. _____

_____

✓ Reading Check

What kind of government does Saudi Arabia have?

_____

_____

Prepare to Read

Section 5
The Stans: A Diverse Region

Objectives

1. Examine the factors that have caused war and conflicts in the Stans.
2. Learn about the economies of the Stans.
3. Discover how environmental issues affect life in the Stans.

Target Reading Skill

Recognize Cause-and-Effect Signal Words As you read, watch for clues that show cause and effect. Often, a word will give you a signal that what is being described is either a cause or an effect. Words such as *affect*, *as a result*, and *from* signal a cause or effect.

In the following example, *because* signals a cause:

Because the Taliban refused to hand bin Laden over to the United States, American troops invaded Afghanistan in October 2001.

The cause is the Taliban refusing to hand bin Laden to the United States. The effect is American troops invading Afghanistan. As you read, look for words that signal other causes and effects.

Vocabulary Strategy

Using Roots and Suffixes A suffix is one or more syllables attached to the end of a word to make a new word. The word it is attached to is known as the root. When a suffix is added to a root, the new word has a new meaning.

Some common suffixes are listed below, along with their meanings and examples. Notice that some have more than one meaning. Learning to identify suffixes, and knowing what they mean, will help you understand what you read.

Suffix	Meaning	Example
-al	of or like	coastal
-dom	position or domain of; condition of being	kingdom; wisdom
-ic	like or having to do with	angelic
-ist	person who does; believer in	socialist
-ly	in a certain manner; like	seriously; manly

Section 5 Summary

Afghanistan, Kazakhstan, Uzbekistan, Tajikistan, Turk-menistan, and Kyrgyzstan make up the Stans.

Warfare and Unrest in Afghanistan

Afghanistan has been troubled by unrest for many years. The Soviet Union invaded it in 1979. Many people fled to Pakistan. There they lived in **refugee** camps. The Soviet troops withdrew in 1989.

In 1996, a group called the Taliban gained power in Afghanistan. They followed a very strict form of Islam. They made everyone in the country follow their rules. Anyone who violated these rules was killed or harshly punished. Girls were not allowed to attend school.

Osama bin Laden was a Saudi Arabian living in Afghanistan who supported the Taliban. Bin Laden led a terrorist group called al-Qaeda. He was the main suspect in the terrorist attacks of September 11, 2001. Because the Taliban did not hand bin Laden over to the United States, American troops invaded Afghanistan in October 2001. The Americans quickly overthrew the Taliban, and the Afghan people now have a democratic government. ✓

Conflicts in Other Central Asian Countries

Other countries in Central Asia have also had conflicts. Central Asia is a mix of ethnic groups and cultures. For many years, strong Soviet rule kept tensions under control. When Soviet rule ended, conflicts erupted.

Kazakhs and Russians have disagreed in Kazakh-stan. Civil war raged in Tajikistan through much of the 1990s. It left the country in ruins. Extreme Muslims in Uzbekistan tried to overthrow the government.

Some governments in the region took away political freedoms and violated human rights. Several countries have turned toward **dictatorship**. Some Western countries have started to help the Stans. They have given money to help the countries build democracies. ✓

Key Terms

refugee (ref yoo JEE) *n.* a person who flees war or other disasters
dictatorship (DIK tay tur ship) *n.* a form of government in which power is held by a leader who has absolute authority

---

Vocabulary Strategy

The word below appears on this page. It contains a suffix. Underline the suffix. Then write the definition of the suffix on the lines provided.

freedom

_____

_____

Add the meaning of the suffix to the meaning of the root word. What does *freedom* mean?

_____

_____

_____

✓ Reading Check

What happened in Afghanistan after the terrorist attacks on September 11, 2001?

_____

_____

✓ Reading Check

What have some Western countries done to help the countries of Central Asia?

_____

_____

_____

Economic Conditions in Central Asia

The Stans are mainly poor countries. Farming is the backbone of their economies. However, other industries are growing.

During the Soviet era, large cotton farms produced huge amounts of cotton for export. Cotton farming is still important. But more grains, fruits, and vegetables are being grown, and more livestock is being raised. ✓

Central Asian cities are growing. Many people live in apartments and work in offices or factories. Many of the factories are old and don't work well. Some are being updated.

Several of the Stans are rich in oil, natural gas, and other minerals. Foreign companies would like to export these resources. However, one problem is that these countries are **landlocked**. Pipelines are planned to carry oil and gas out of the region.

Environmental Issues

The Soviet Union hurt the environment of Central Asia. For years, it did nuclear tests in northern Kazakhstan. Because of these tests, the region has terrible radiation pollution. Radiation has hurt the people who live nearby. The pollution will take years to clean up.

Another major problem is the drying of the Aral Sea. For years, the Soviets took water from rivers that feed the sea. As a result, it is now drying up. ✓

However, large parts of Central Asia are still untouched. They are a key resource for the region.

Review Questions

1. What is the main economic activity in the Stans?

_____

_____

2. How has nuclear testing affected Kazakhstan?

_____

_____

Key Term

landlocked (LAND lahkt) *adj.* having no direct access to the sea

Chapter 25 Assessment

1. For many years, India and Pakistan have fought over an area called
   A. Kashmir.
   B. the Stans.
   C. Taliban.
   D. Haifa.

2. Pakistan's economy is based mostly on
   A. farming.
   B. the textile industry.
   C. carpets.
   D. hydroelectricity.

3. The most important part of the Israeli economy is
   A. agriculture.
   B. manufacturing.
   C. service industries.
   D. tourism.

4. Muslims from around the world must travel to Mecca in Saudi Arabia
   A. to buy cheap gasoline.
   B. to get a good education.
   C. to vote in Saudi Arabian elections.
   D. to complete the religious trip known as the hajj.

5. Several countries of Central Asia have turned toward
   A. absolute monarchies.
   B. democracies.
   C. dictatorships.
   D. constitutional monarchies.

Short Answer Question

Why has there been continued conflict between Israelis and Palestinians?

_____

_____

_____

_____

Prepare to Read

Section 1
Vietnam: A Nation Rebuilds

Objectives

1. Find out how Vietnam was divided by conflicts and war.
2. Learn how Vietnam has rebuilt its economy.

Target Reading Skill

Identify Main Ideas It is hard to remember every detail that you read. Good readers are able to find the main ideas of the text they are reading. The main idea is the most important point of a section of text. It summarizes all the other points, or details.

To find the main idea of a paragraph, read it through once. Then ask yourself what the paragraph is about. Do all the sentences center on the same point? If so, you've found the main idea. Sometimes, it is stated in the first sentence or two.

The main idea of the paragraph below is underlined:

<u>In the early 1970s, the fighting spread.</u> North Vietnam was sending supplies to its troops through the nearby nations of Laos and Cambodia. The United States bombed this supply route and then invaded Cambodia. The South Vietnamese attacked Laos.

As you read this section, look for the main idea of each paragraph.

Vocabulary Strategy

Recognizing Signal Words Signal words are words or phrases that prepare you for what is coming next.

There are different kinds of signal words. Often signal words tell you the order in which events happen. These are sequence signal words. Some sequence signal words are shown below. Use these words to help you keep track of events as you read.

first	next	then
finally	before	earlier
later	from May to July	in 1959

Section 1 Summary

Decades of Conflict and War

Vietnam went through a long period of conflict. From 1946 to 1954, the Vietnamese fought together to defeat France. Then Vietnam was divided into two nations. Communists ruled North Vietnam. The United States supported the non-communist government of South Vietnam. Elections were promised to unite Vietnam under one government.

Instead there was a **civil war**. The elections were not held because the United States and the leaders of South Vietnam feared that the Communists might win. This worried the leaders of the United States because they believed in the **domino theory**. This theory said that if the Communists won in Vietnam nearby nations would become Communist, too.

In 1959, the Communists started a war to take over the South. Their leader, Ho Chi Minh (hoh chee min), wanted all of Vietnam to be one Communist nation. At first, the United States sent military advisors to help South Vietnam. Later, hundreds of thousands of American troops arrived to fight the Communist troops, called the Viet Cong. By 1968, there were more than 500,000 American troops in Vietnam. ✓

In the early 1970s, the fighting spread. North Vietnam was sending supplies to its troops through the nearby nations of Laos and Cambodia. The United States bombed this supply route and then invaded Cambodia. The South Vietnamese attacked Laos.

Thousands of American soldiers were being hurt or killed in Vietnam. Many Americans wanted the war to end. In 1973, the United States pulled its troops out of Vietnam. More than 3 million Americans had served in the Vietnam War.

Key Terms

civil war (SIV ul wawr) *n.* a war between political parties or regions within the same country

domino theory (DAHM uh noh THEE uh ree) *n.* a belief that if one country fell to communism, neighboring nations would also fall, like a row of dominoes

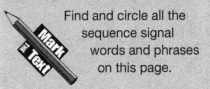

Vocabulary Strategy

Find and circle all the sequence signal words and phrases on this page.

✓ Reading Check

Why did North Vietnam launch a war against South Vietnam?

_____

_____

_____

After the Vietnam War

North Vietnam conquered South Vietnam in 1975. The country was then reunited. It had a Communist govern-
35 ment. Vietnam had been badly hurt by the war. More than a million people had been killed or wounded. And Vietnam needed to rebuild homes, farms, and factories destroyed in the war.

However, the Vietnamese economy was not grow-
40 ing. Vietnam had to make some changes. Vietnam is still a Communist country today. But now the govern-
ment lets some people run their own businesses. That means it uses the free enterprise system. This has improved the lives of many Vietnamese.

45 Vietnam's biggest success has been in rebuilding its cities. Hanoi, in the north, is the capital. The wealthiest city is Ho Chi Minh City. It used to be called Saigon, when it was the capital of South Vietnam. Today, it is a center of trade. ✓

50 Some Vietnamese who live in the cities have more money than other Vietnamese. They can afford many of the same things Americans enjoy. Many of them run businesses that help Vietnam's economy.

Vietnam's economy grew quickly during most of the 1990s. People from other countries began to invest their money in Vietnam's businesses. Farming doubled. Vietnam no longer had to buy its food from other countries. Instead, it became one of the countries that sells a very large amount of rice to other nations.

Review Questions

1. Describe the roles that the United States played in the Vietnam War.

_____

_____

_____

2. In what ways has Vietnam had success in rebuilding its economy?

_____

_____

_____

✓ **Reading Check**

Which city in Vietnam is the wealthiest and also the nation's center of trade?

_____

_____

Target Reading Skill

Which sentence in the bracketed paragraph states the main idea of the paragraph?

_____

_____

Prepare to Read

Section 2
Australia: A Pacific Rim Country

Objectives

1. Learn about the major economic activities in Australia.
2. Find out how Aboriginal people in Australia are working to improve their lives.

Target Reading Skill

Identify Supporting Details The main idea of a paragraph or section is its most important point. The main idea is supported by details. Details give more information about the main idea. They may explain the main idea. They may give additional facts or examples. They tell you *what, where, why, how much,* and *how many.*

The main idea of the section titled "Aborigines: Improving Lives" is stated in this sentence: "Aboriginal leaders have worked to make the lives of their people better." As you read, notice how the details tell you more about the life of the Aborigines and how things are changing for them.

Vocabulary Strategy

Recognizing Signal Words Signal words are words or phrases that give you clues. They help you understand what you read. They prepare you for what is coming next.

There are different kinds of signal words. Signal words may be used to show relationships, such as contrast. Contrast shows the differences between things or ideas.

Some signal words that show contrast are listed below. Use these words to help you understand what you are reading in this section.

but	however
not	on the other hand
even though	yet
despite	

Economic Activities

1   Australia used to be a colony of Great Britain. Since Australia became independent, its population has become very diverse. That means that people from many different nations and backgrounds have come to
5   make Australia their home.

Today, Australia has close ties with other nations of the Pacific Rim. The Pacific Rim countries border the Pacific Ocean. They include Japan, South Korea, China, and Taiwan. The United States is another major Pacific Rim nation. It is one of Australia's main trading partners. Australia's economy depends on trade with Pacific Rim countries.

Australia sends products to many countries in Asia. Large cargo ships carry Australian cattle, wool, and
15 meat to markets in other countries. They also carry Australian minerals to Japan.

Only 7 percent of Australia's land is good for farming. Most of this land is in southeastern Australia and along the east coast. The country's few rivers are in
20 those areas. Farmers use the rivers to irrigate their crops. Australia's most important crop is wheat. Australia is one of the world's leading wheat growers.

Ranching is also important to Australia's economy. Sheep and cattle provide meat for sale to other coun-
25 tries. Australia is the world's leading wool producer. Most cattle and sheep are raised on large ranches called **stations**. Some of the largest stations are in the **outback**. Few people live in this hot, dry region. ☑

In the outback, there is little grass for the animals to
30 eat. That is why stations are so large. There is one outback station that covers nearly 12,000 square miles (31,080 square kilometers)—that is larger than the state of Maryland! In the outback, ranchers use **artesian wells** to supply water for their cattle.

Target Reading Skill

What details in the bracketed paragraph explain the meaning of the "Pacific Rim"?

_____

_____

_____

✓ Reading Check

How does ranching help Australia's economy?

_____

_____

_____

Key Terms

outback (OWT bak) *n.* the dry land consisting of plains and plateaus that makes up much of central and western Australia
artesian well (ahr TEE zhun wel) *n.* a well in which water flows under natural pressure without pumping

Aborigines: Improving Lives

Aboriginal people were the earliest people of Australia. Today, they are working hard to save their culture. They are also taking a bigger part in Australia's economy. For example, Aboriginal people now own their own companies.

Aboriginal leaders have worked to make the lives of their people better. Their schools now teach Aboriginal languages. Aborigines mark important events with songs and dances. These songs and dances have been passed down from parents to children for hundreds of years. Artists are also helping bring attention to Aboriginal culture. They create traditional rock paintings and tree bark paintings.

Aboriginal leaders have helped their people in another important way. They helped the government of Australia understand that it had to make changes. The government has begun to give Aboriginal land back to Aborigines. The government has built schools and hospitals on their land. It has also begun to protect some of the places that are important in Aboriginal religion.

Aborigines have more rights now. But their main goal is to get back the lands that used to belong to their people. The courts have helped them to achieve this goal. However, many ranchers and farmers now live on those lands. They do not want to give the land back. It may take many years to work out the solution to this problem. ☑

Review Questions

1. Why do few people make their home in Australia's outback?

_____

_____

_____

2. Give two examples showing how Aboriginal leaders have worked to improve the lives of their people.

_____

_____

_____

Vocabulary Strategy

In the last paragraph, two signal words are used to show contrast. Find the signal words and circle them.

✓ Reading Check

What is a main goal for Aboriginal people in Australia today?

_____

_____

_____

1. What did the United States fear might happen if it did not help South Vietnam fight against North Vietnam?
   A. The French would take control.
   B. North Vietnam would attack China.
   C. Communists would take over South Vietnam.
   D. The United States would lose control of North Vietnam.

2. Today, Vietnam is
   A. divided into two nations.
   B. a Communist nation that allows some free enterprise.
   C. one of the richest countries in Asia.
   D. still unable to rebuild its cities.

3. Some of Australia's trading partners in the Pacific Rim include China, Taiwan,
   A. India, and France.
   B. Italy, and the United States.
   C. Britain, and New Zealand.
   D. Japan, and the United States.

4. Where are some of Australia's largest ranches, or stations, located?
   A. in the southeast part of the country
   B. along the east coast
   C. on the west coast
   D. in the outback

5. How are Aborigines working to improve the lives of their people?
   A. Their schools now teach Aboriginal languages.
   B. They play a bigger part in Australia's economy.
   C. Their artists help bring attention to their culture.
   D. all of the above

Short Answer Question

How has Vietnam changed since the end of the Vietnam War?

_____

_____

_____

_____